The Lost Wave

The Lost Wave

Women and Democracy in Postwar Italy

MOLLY TAMBOR

OXFORD
UNIVERSITY PRESS

OXFORD
UNIVERSITY PRESS

Oxford University Press is a department of the University of Oxford.
It furthers the University's objective of excellence in research, scholarship,
and education by publishing worldwide.

Oxford New York
Auckland Cape Town Dar es Salaam Hong Kong Karachi
Kuala Lumpur Madrid Melbourne Mexico City Nairobi
New Delhi Shanghai Taipei Toronto

With offices in
Argentina Austria Brazil Chile Czech Republic France Greece
Guatemala Hungary Italy Japan Poland Portugal Singapore
South Korea Switzerland Thailand Turkey Ukraine Vietnam

Published in the United States of America by
Oxford University Press
198 Madison Avenue, New York, NY 10016

Material from Chapter 4 has been adapted from Molly Tambor, "Prostitutes and Politicians:
The Women's Rights Movement in the Legge Merlin Debates," in *Women in Italy, 1945–1960: An
Interdisciplinary Study*, edited by Penelope Morris, 2006, Palgrave Macmillan, reproduced with
permission of Palgrave Macmillan. The full published version of this publication is available from
http://www.palgraveconnect.com/pc/doifinder/10.1057/9780230601437.

Library of Congress Cataloging-in-Publication Data

Tambor, Molly.
The lost wave : women and democracy in postwar Italy / Molly Tambor.
pages cm
Includes bibliographical references and index.
ISBN 978–0–19–937823–4 (alk. paper)
1. Women—Political activity—Italy—History. 2. Feminism—Italy—History.
3. Women and democracy—Italy—History. 4. Women politicians—Italy—History.
5. Italy—Politics and government. I. Title.
HQ1236.5.I8T36 2014
320.082—dc23
2013047263

1 3 5 7 9 8 6 4 2
Printed in the United States of America
on acid-free paper

CONTENTS

ACKNOWLEDGMENTS

In New York, thanks to the librarians and staff of Long Island University Post, Barnard College, Columbia University, and the New York Public Library. In Rome, the librarians and archivists at the Biblioteca di Storia Moderna e Contemporanea, the American Academy in Rome, the Unione Donne Italiane, the Centro Italiano Femminile, the Casa Internazionale delle Donne (especially Mila Corvino), the Istituto Gramsci, and the Camera dei Deputati allowed me access to the sources I needed and brought me materials I didn't even know I was looking for until they showed me. In addition the staff at the Biblioteca Italiana delle Donne in Bologna, the Centro Documentazione Donna in Modena, and the members of the local chapters of UDI in Modena and Bologna offered precious help and even a lift when I got a bit lost outside of Modena one spring day. I received generous support for research from the German Marshall Fund, the American Academy in Rome, the National Endowment for the Humanities, and my own home institution of LIU Post.

Colleagues in Italy, America, and the United Kingdom offered insight, hospitality, and support: Vanessa Roghi, Perry Willson, Marco Mariano, Silvio Pons, Silvia Salvateci, David W. Ellwood, Sandro Bellassai, Linda Kerber, Patrizia Gabrielli, Mary Gibson, Maria Grazia Giammarinaro, Maria Teresa Antonia Morelli, Dominique Reill, Deborah Valenze, Jeanie Attie, and Sara Gronim. Thanks to Penny Morris and Arne Westad for important early opportunities to publish my ideas. Special thanks to my former advisor and staunch advocate Victoria de Grazia. Thanks also to my students at Post, Barnard, and Cooper Union, who remind me that teaching and scholarship inform each other, and always reveal aspects of readings I wouldn't have seen on my own.

Several people read portions of the manuscript and improved it immensely, though all shortcomings of course remain my own. John Davis read the entire manuscript and offered excellent revisions. Nadia Zonis was extremely generous with her time and journalistic expertise and tried to restrain my wordiest run-ons. Speaking of running, the amazing Julie Crawford logged innumerable miles around Central Park with me but never lacked breath to offer valuable critical reading and clarity on the big ideas and arguments. My gratitude to the members of the Columbia History department's graduate reading group, the Barnard Junior Faculty Writing Group, and the Columbia University Seminar on Modern Italian Studies for offering working structure and valuable feedback.

Susan Ferber has been a wonderful editor and has brought this project forward through several crucial moments. Thanks to her and the rest of Oxford University Press.

My gratitude and admiration to the women who shared long conversations, private materials, and personal memories: Luciana Viviani, Maria Cocco, Tullia Carretoni, Marisa Ombra, and Giglia Tedesco. Without them the book truly could not exist. I only wish I could have been in time to meet Lina Merlin, Teresa Noce, and the other protagonists of this season of activism.

My family has supported this project for more years than I care to admit. My love and thanks to all of them, in California, Massachusetts, New York, South Carolina, and Washington, D.C. Special mention to Theo and Mason Moore, who were intrepid adventurers with me in Italy and through the wilds of academia. This book is dedicated to my mother, Joyce Karel, who has always been my most important reader, teacher, and model of how to be a woman.

ABBREVIATIONS

AC: *Azione Cattolica,* Catholic Action

ACLI: *Associazione cattolica di lavoratori italiani,* Catholic Association of Italian Workers (the labor union organized to compete with the Left's unions)

CGIL: *Confederazione Generale Italiano di Lavoro,* the biggest national labor union

CIDD: *Centro Italiano di Difesa della Donna,* Italian Center for Women's Defense (founded in 1950, an organization to support the Merlin Law through aid to ex-prostitutes)

CIF: *Centro Italiano Femminile,* Italian Women's Center (a federation of Catholic women's associations)

CLN: *Comitati di Liberazione Nazionale,* National Liberation Committees (the governing coalition of Resistance groups); the CLNAI (AI stands for *Alta Italia*) were the committees in northern Italy when the country was split by the Nazi occupation during World War II

CSIL: *Confederazione Italiana Sindacati Lavoratori,* Catholic trade union created in 1948 after union split

DC: *Democrazia Cristiana,* Christian Democrat Party

FIOT: *Federazione Italiana di Operai Tessili,* Italian Textile Workers' Union

GDD: *Gruppi di difesa della donna,* Women's Defense Groups (multi-party Resistance organization for women)

GF: *Gioventù femminile,* Female Youth (one of many specialized sections of Catholic Action)

MSI: *Movimento Sociale Italiano,* Italian Social Movement, right-wing party with many ex- and neo-Fascist members

P d'A: *Partito d'Azione,* Action Party

PCI: *Partito Comunista Italiano,* Italian Communist Party

PLI: *Partito Liberale Italiano,* Italian Liberal Party

PNM: *Partito Nazionale Monarchico,* National Monarchical Party

PRI: *Partito Repubblicano Italiano,* Italian Republican Party

PSI: *Partito Socialista Italiano,* Italian Socialist Party

UDI: *Unione donne italiane,* Union of Italian Women (a Leftist women's association, counterpart to CIF, technically autonomous but in fact Communist-led in 1940s and 1950s)

UIL: *Unione Italiana del Lavoro,* social-democratic union founded in 1950 after union split

The Lost Wave

Introduction

Women, the Bulwark of Democracy

Around four o'clock on the afternoon of Monday, October 1, 1945, a visitor to Rome passing the Palazzo Venezia could note that the light symbolically left burning in Mussolini's office throughout his two-decade regime was now quite dark. Instead, only steps away along the Via del Corso, the members of the *Consulta* (Consultative Assembly) were coming to order with a great bustle and brightness, beginning only the sixth day of democratic self-government in Italy in more than twenty years. The *Consulta* had the task of acting as Italy's legislature until a new constitution could be written and formal elections held. As its 447 members took their seats in Palazzo Montecitorio, the light might have seemed to shine especially brilliantly on just five faces in that sea of hundreds as the speaker announced, "Counselor Angela Maria Guidi Cingolani has requested to speak. You have the floor." One of those five faces, the only female ones in the chamber, now held everyone's attention. Guidi Cingolani rose and became the first woman ever to speak in an Italian legislative session.

In response to the loud and prolonged applause greeting her, she began: "Colleagues, I hear in your applause a salute for the first woman to speak in this chamber. Not a personal applause for me, but as a representative of all Italian women who now, for the first time, participate in the political life of our country." As she spoke, she outlined the long story of women's battle for rights, but concluded that perhaps it was best that women should begin their contribution at this "tragic" moment Italy had to overcome. Women had learned to conquer pain and suffering through long experience and were now "proud to stand in the front lines of the struggle to resurrect" Italy. She went on, "Don't be afraid that women's contribution will be a return to a matriarchy, if such a thing ever existed. We know better than to aspire to that; but even if we did, we certainly couldn't do any worse than you men have done!"[1] There was laughter, and more applause. But something very serious had just occurred. With this inaugural sentiment Guidi Cingolani ushered in the Lost Wave; a movement for women's equality that justified itself by the entire society's need to be redeemed and protected from the threats men had unleashed in the form of war, totalitarianism, and anti-democratic agitation. In a moment when Italian aggression and nationalism were discredited as Fascist and even the non-Fascist political classes seemed weak, less than manly, and unable to govern, these women activists pushing for a new presence and equality of women in the public sphere paradoxically appeared more serious, patriotic, and committed to democratic antifascism than their political forbears. Above all they appeared to promote the proper reconstruction of the gender roles that constituted not only the return to normality of individual families, but the family of the nation and of the new model of interdependent Western nations.

What were the origins of this wave of women's activism? In the 1920s and 1930s many Europeans seemed to want nothing more than a strong patriarch. In the grip of the trauma caused by the Great War, the precarious economy and chronic mass unemployment of the Depression, and the inefficient and ineffective politics of new Parliaments in the nations drawn onto the map by the Treaty of Versailles, Europeans felt lost and uncertain. For Italians, it was all too easy to be seduced by Benito Mussolini's claim that democracy had become a deserted temple and that the future would be won by Fascism. Italians, he argued, needed a decisive man to take charge, a virile and charismatic leader who could restore stability, prosperity, and not least, the proper hierarchy between men and women in a world turned upside down. Mussolini was a master of the photo opportunity in which, shirtless and glistening with manly sweat, he reaped grain and basked in the admiration of wholesome and fecund young peasant women.

Hitler, Stalin, and even Marshal Pétain shared this strategy of linking the call for national renewal to reinvigorated masculinity and properly controlled feminine domesticity and fertility. In France propaganda satirized young independent working girls in the figure of the dangerously androgynous "garconne," while Italian Fascists inveighed against the "crisis woman" with her cigarettes and nylon stockings as an example of sterile and neurotic individualism brought on by pernicious foreign influence. The pronatalist, right-wing interwar ideal of the family removed the woman from waged work, blocked her participation in politics, denied her access to birth control, abortion, and higher education, and placed her firmly in the role of housewife and prolific childbearer. The disappointed and bitter men who called the Treaty of Versailles a "stab in the back" or Italy's part in the peace process a "mutilated victory" also donned their brown shirts and black shirts in an effort to restore their masculinity and reclaim their positions as family wage earners, virile fathers, and undisputed masters of the hearth and home.[2]

Among the many causes of the rise of Fascism it is surely important that this war between the sexes—or war against women—raged so powerfully in the interwar years; it also appears not at all coincidental that Fascism jealously defended a threatened masculine primacy while portraying democracy as effeminate.[3] Indeed, democracy *was* feminized, but not in the way Mussolini said. Rather, in the aftermath of World War II's destruction and Fascism's fall, democracy would be reborn and enhanced thanks to women who fought in the Resistance, and, once victory was achieved, fought again to attain the right to vote and wield political power. The women whose stories are told in this book claimed that female heroism and sacrifice had defeated Fascism and saved democracy. And, in some unexpected and counterintuitive ways, they were right.

Raised and educated in the two decades Italy was under Fascist rule, the first female members of the Italian Parliament secured the vote for women, ran for and won national political office for the first time, helped write the nation's new constitution, steered the party system towards a politics of mass consensus that courted women voters, and passed more than eleven major laws guaranteeing women's equal rights in the two decades following the regime's fall. They were a group of women who were both exceptional individuals and the products of their environment, who sometimes fearlessly called for radical change and sometimes accepted old conventions about women's roles and identity seemingly without question. The paradoxes surrounding their story extend even to their personal biographies. To take three examples, Teresa Noce, despite the fact that she identified herself as "ugly, poor, and communist," happened to be one of the most successful politicians in postwar Italy. Lina Merlin was a veteran socialist with a magically captivating voice who championed a law that laid bare all the public's worst fears about prostitution and disease. Maria Cocco humbly insisted she was merely called to serve in the Christian Democrats' anti-communist crusade, yet passed a law in cooperation with her Marxist sisters that cleared the way for the most ambitious women's rise to power in the Italian state. The change they fomented created Italy as the democratic republic it is today, paradoxes and all.

The Lost Wave also tells the story of another woman: the symbolic woman who had achieved equal rights of citizenship. She would not be exceptional like the first forty-five female members of Parliament, but would be quite ordinary, a model of femininity accepted by all. She would be a mother, a worker, a member of political associations and trade unions. She would be a participant in building a new democracy and reconstructing a dynamic economy and society. She would have dignity and individuality, but she would also be the moral pillar of a stable, happy family and the anchor of a productive community. This was the constitutional woman that the first forty-five worked to create as an image that could gain mass consensus in Italian and international politics. She was the cumulative and aspirational product of the legislation written and passed during more than fifteen years of activism by the very real women who entered government after the end of Fascism and World War II.

Although Constitutional Woman never had a name, she played a role akin to that of France's Marianne. She was meant to be not only an encouragement to Italian women to assert their rights, but also a patriotic, even nationalist symbol of the female citizen and of democracy that both men and women could support. The women politicians used various models of femininity in Italian postwar and Cold War culture to forge a legislative path toward achieving the rights of such a woman. Mining existing tropes of femininity such as the Resistance heroine, the working mother, the sacrificial Catholic, and the nationalist "mamma Italiana," they searched for social consensus for women's equality that could reach across religious, ideological, and gender divides. Although those gaps proved more resilient than they had imagined, their effort nonetheless illuminates important aspects of the period and answers vital questions about twentieth-century feminism and its legacy. Through the dual lenses of their self-fashioning as Parliament members and the passage of specific new laws regarding women's rights, women politicians navigated gendered political identity as they picked and chose among competing models of femininity in Cold War Italy. In so doing, this book argues, they forged a political legacy that in turn affected the rights and opportunities of all Italian women.

The work done by this cohort represents one of the key moments in the definition of modern citizenship and reveals how crucial the spoken and unspoken ideas men and women held about manliness and womanliness were to shaping the category of citizen in postwar democracy. The challenges of Italy's transition to a peacetime, consumerist pro-American democratic society were understood by contemporaries in highly gendered terms.[4] The aspects of past gender roles that female lawmakers embraced, the shameful sexual politics they rejected, and the image of the Constitutional Woman they aspired to create reveal the issues at stake in reconstructing Italian government after Fascism and a devastating war and in the context of the developing Cold War.

So why isn't the story of these women better known? How did they become a "lost" wave of feminism? Postwar European history has been so focused on the dominance of the international diplomacy of the Cold War that it has often overshadowed the domestic politics in Europe.[5] The influence and urgency of the United States' and, to a lesser extent, the Soviet Union's interests and their ability to throw their weight around financially and militarily are frequently seen as posing severe constraints on local politicians. This book avoids portraying Italy as completely dominated by foreign relations or as cunningly exploiting American aid for domestic agendas unrelated to the struggle against communism. Rather than relying on communism and anticommunism as opposing binaries in all political situations, it instead highlights a complex "*intreccio*" or intertwining of foreign and domestic politics. Italy's role was unique in that it stood as a frontier between East and West, North and South, and had historically served as a laboratory for political experimentation given all its "cleavages" along socio-economic, geographic, and religious—and gender—lines.[6] To convey how these transitions occurred on the ground, *The Lost Wave* focuses on the personal formation and political belief systems, tragedies and triumphs of particular individuals whose stories enrich our understanding of this moment of complex historical change. But this book also contextualizes these women's lives and political achievements in an examination of how political and social power was structured and restructured along gendered lines in this period. Women both influenced and were influenced by political discourse in this period; their gender was central to others' redefinition of democracy in Italy, and they themselves were protagonists in that process.

Democracies are built locally, by the formation of citizenries. Any abstract consideration of national politics leaves the impression that citizens were gender neutral. Amidst this, the women of Italy's Lost Wave have not received attention, other than perhaps a footnote on Italy's backwardness in not awarding women the suffrage until after World War II. In this case, though, the relative lateness of women's achievement of political rights in Italy—1945 as opposed to 1918 in Britain or 1920 in the United States—paradoxically highlights the problem of gender for the building of a democratic citizenry. Italian women had not been backward and unchanging compared to their Anglo-American counterparts; like them, they had organized as feminists throughout the nineteenth and early twentieth century, and like them, they had participated in the larger trends of expanding education and employment for women. Further, they had experimented with the ideology of Fascism and had spearheaded the civil resistance during World War II by which Italians reclaimed sovereignty from the Nazi-Fascists and then from the Allied occupation. This was far from a static conservation of old-fashioned gender roles; it was a conflict-ridden, extremely fluid, and innovative transformation.

Women activists understood that making citizens in a new democracy required careful, assiduous work at the grassroots level as well as leadership of institutions. They formed nationwide women's organizations, a movement known as women's associationism. They flowed into political parties, boosting their membership and their representative power in government. And a smaller core of them became candidates and elected officials at every level of the state, rebuilding city councils, schools, and infrastructure, framing a new law of the land in the Constitutional Assembly, and helping to convert the pre-Fascist Parliament of clubbily elite old men into a radically mixed space in terms of gender, age, and class.

In the process of legislating and campaigning for women's rights they also created crucial new links between the mass of ordinary voters (the majority of whom were now women) and the hierarchies of the political parties and government (which were bastions of masculine power). These ties were the foundation of the new mass parties, notably the Christian Democrats and the Italian Communist Party, an enlargement of political participation that may be the single most crucial innovation of postwar politics. Women leaders and voters and their issues therefore shaped the newly forming postwar state so powerfully that it can be characterized as a feminization of democracy in the postwar era, or, to use the argument they sometimes did, of women and their model of active citizenship as the "bulwark of democracy" against either a return to fascism or the worst excesses of the Cold War.[7]

Gender and Citizenship

This book's story brings together constitutional history, the history of Italian society and politics, the history of women in Italy, and the history of feminism and women's rights. Beginning with Simonetta Piccone Stella's groundbreaking work *La prima generazione*, which discussed growing up in the 1950s as an experience of instability and bewildering new opportunities and roles for both sexes, rather than the stereotypical quiet if oppressive long snooze before the youth revolution of 1968, more and more scholars have been taking on the challenge of reexamining the postwar period through a lens of change, reopening to the world, and social and economic upheaval.[8] Other scholars have used women's and gender history to clarify, on the one hand, the narrative of how a progressive trend in legislating women's rights was common to European nations, both East and West; and on the other, how the economic and industrial drive to reconstruct and then surpass prewar levels of prosperity dramatically changed both standards and styles of living, in a story that puts women at the center of new kinds of growth in service and information economies and in new practices of consumption. [9]

Above all, *The Lost Wave* aims to interpret the history of citizenship in postwar Italy as gender history. Scholarly investigation of key historical concepts like citizenship, the public sphere, the welfare state, and political representation has highlighted the ways that a gender history approach reveals the discourses of gender and the sexual order that underpinned the making of these political and social institutions in different ways across time and space. It has also, importantly, asserted that these institutions and discourses are shaped as individuals have mediated and articulated them, while debating and struggling over the conflicts that arose as they changed.[10]

While I use both, I have tried to be careful about distinguishing between the categories of women and gender, since even when the women of the Lost Wave were not fully successful in their attempts to achieve women's equality, the widespread sense of challenges to the gender order motivated the legislative intervention and political mobilization of both men and women. Nor should the use of the categories of women or feminism suggest that all women share the same subjectivities, political motives, or locations in hierarchies of power. In addition, gender as a way of understanding difference and signifying power strongly shapes the kinds of choices people make and the way they award their political allegiance, even when there are no women present. Finally, gender as a category of analysis highlights how historical subjects made decisions and understood their own identities in specific contexts, allowing for a better mapping of changes in political power and social difference over time. In this way, gender history is for this book a particular approach to women in history, asking about their experiences and their own subjectivities. It is also a particular approach to the history of politics, asking about how gender difference shaped and was shaped by rights, laws, parties, and state institutions.[11]

In tune with gender's illustration of power and difference, gendered histories of citizenship treat citizenship not merely as the condition of belonging to a state, particularly a nation-state, but as a practice and as a set of rights and obligations.[12] These rights and obligations are not fixed or unchanging; both citizen and those excluded from citizenship define it by a series of participatory claims. Citizenship is a set of legal prescriptions, but also a number of historically specific experiences and identities. It is by definition an ongoing arena for struggle, debate, redefinition, and new inclusions and exclusions. In some moments, such as the period of postwar reconstruction (and the Cold War was one of those), citizenship becomes a primary category of identity as people participate in politics with special energy, determined to shape a new identity as citizens and to imagine a new democratic representation after the disintegration of a militarized state.[13] By focusing on citizenship, this book shows how the claims of Italian women, prompted by their experiences of Fascism, war, resistance, and deprivation in the years leading up to the creation of the new republic, helped to determine the institutions and ideals of that state. Not only did they frame their own citizenship rights around women's issues, but their interventions also made citizenship an ongoing arena for conflict over identity, rights, representation, work, sexuality, welfare, and other aspects of society and popular culture for both men and women well after the particular women of the Lost Wave no longer held office.

The surge in numbers of women in the early legislatures of the new Italian republic was in step with an international phenomenon reflecting women's increased visibility in civil society and "reward" for their good citizenship during the war years. There are parallels in France, where women also enjoyed the suffrage for the first time after the war, and in West Germany, where a democratic government needed to court new women voters in order to establish its own legitimacy in a post-fascist context. But Italy retained higher numbers of women in Parliament for a longer period of time than either of those two countries, and those female legislators successfully pressed for more laws in support of women's rights. They did this primarily by demanding the unfailingly consistent application of the Constitution. They insisted that the democratic republic created by the Constitution would only become reality if all of its articles, especially those concerning women citizens' equality, were implemented. They also made women's rights inextricable from the overall health of the state. These claims were not mere rhetoric; the legal transition from Fascism to democracy was slow and inconsistent. The Allied occupation government and the emerging domestic political leadership were reluctant to disrupt a fragile peace by purging Fascists too energetically. As a result, the entire judiciary and much of the civilian and military bureaucracy was left intact, while the laws that the judiciary and bureaucracy enforced were those already on the books, including the entire revised penal code installed by the Fascists which defined both birth control and abortion as crimes against the race.[14] The women subjects of this book insisted that Italy would become a democracy only when *all* these laws were expunged or rewritten. This insistence on the reconciliation and adaptation of the entire body of the law to the principles of the constitution, which I call constitutional rights feminism and Italians called *adeguamento,* was the basis of Lost Wave activism.

In the postwar period a number of European countries recreated themselves as social democracies. Between their constitutional conventions and the creation of the U.N. Charter and the Declaration of Human Rights, the language of rights was very much in the air. In the aftermath of World War I there had also been a wave of rights talk and constitution writing, one that under the influence of Woodrow Wilson and the League of Nations focused on protecting the rights of minorities as groups within nation-states. After 1945, in contrast, given the racially-motivated genocide and the vulnerability of civilian populations during World War II, focusing on the rights of individuals without regard to their minority or national group identification was a natural preference. And the Atlantic alliance against communism, quickly spreading at the urging of the United States, believed the same guarantees would prevent Soviet influence from taking hold. Finally, collapsing minority rights into individual human rights proved most acceptable to the Big Three of Great Britain, the United States, and the Soviet Union, which sought to avoid scrutiny of their own contradictory policies regarding imperial colonies, African-American segregation, and ethnic minorities.[15] Given this confluence of moral and political motivations, in a short but intense period—roughly 1941, the year of the Atlantic Charter, through 1945, the year of the UN charter, to 1948, with the UN's Universal Declaration of Human Rights—the language of human rights became universal rhetoric; protecting the individual also served the interest of the superpower governments.

Despite the cynicism that underlay the idealistic rhetoric, the triumph of human rights as the basis for postwar rights regimes was a promising one for women. Writing new constitutions created a rare and precious opportunity for European women to assert their full citizenship. The adherence of all political hues of the antifascist spectrum to the language of universal human rights made it difficult to reject their claims. This atmosphere explains the sense of naturalness and necessity that accompanied the achievement of women's suffrage in Italy in 1945, as women were "given" the vote by decree. But if this seemed a passive milestone, a reward for their wartime service and sacrifice and a promise of Italy's future conformity to the standards of modern democratic nations, women activists were not to stand on the sidelines going forward.[16] Women's suffrage immediately became a determining factor in creating the new Italian democracy as one of mass party politics rather than the liberal elite model from which Mussolini had seized power. Italy's Parliament could not just pick up where it had left off in 1922, because in 1946 women created an entirely new mass democracy. The "feminization" of postwar society which would be so visible in the consumer revolution of the economic miracle (the name often given to the period of sustained economic growth and dramatic rises in the standard of living in the 1950s and 1960s in Italy and throughout Western Europe) was already present in 1945–1948 in the popularity and campaign activity of the mass women's associations, the first national elections, and the progressive guarantees of women citizens' equality written into the constitution.[17]

Women's demands for social rights as well as political ones inverted the relationship of all citizens with institutions of the state and with state power. Rather than serving the state, as Italian subjects had been expected to do in wartime and under Fascism, now the state would serve its citizens. The commonly shared sense—first enunciated by the head of the Italian Communist Party (PCI), Palmiro Togliatti—that women's emancipation and the stability and longevity of a democratic republic were mutually dependent, led to a pursuit by all the political parties of women's votes and women candidates for political office. It was this pursuit that made the election of the "first forty-five" possible. Thus the Cold War reconstruction of political institutions, women's rights, and Italy's democracy are inextricably linked, and their stories should be told together.[18]

The Lost Wave focuses on the period from 1943 to 1963, stretching from the start of the Resistance as an armed conflict with large numbers of women militants to the end of the last legislature in which large numbers of the cohort of women from that movement served. In between key events such as women's suffrage, ratification of the Constitution, and the crisis years of the Cold War, illuminated the importance of gender in European political development. This book intentionally disrupts the standard chronology that celebrated 1945 as a "zero hour" when one era of history ended and an entirely new one began. According to that narrative, the years 1914–1945 represent Europe's "Age of Catastrophe," when the ostensibly civilized West descended into the primitive brutality of world war, totalitarian regimes, and the Holocaust. The Allies joined in World War II to liberate Europe from Fascism and Nazism; in 1945 peace was established and democracy and prosperity promptly resurrected. This took place with the leadership of the world's preeminent democracy, the United States, and the cooperation of friendly powers under the UN's charter and the Universal Declaration of Human Rights. It is a neatly packaged story, and in Italy the mythic status of 1945 was very useful: those who had opposed Mussolini and fought in the Resistance had redeemed Italy from its Fascist past by proving that the true Italian passion was for freedom and democracy, and all those who had not opposed Fascism could safely focus on the future and put the past behind them. This easy periodization, in other words, served to tidy up and sweep away difficult problems in Italian history.[19]

But these issues could not be dismissed so easily, and women in many ways bore the brunt of those haunting remainders of Italy's past, since their transition into this brave new Italy did not occur so speedily. Women may have gained the suffrage and helped birth the Republic in their first vote (the 1946 referendum on whether to retain the monarchy), but they continued to live under an old legal regime that declared them the dependents of their fathers or husbands and denied them the ability to make decisions about where they would live and work and if and when they would bear children. Divorce was illegal, and adultery and domestic violence were punished lightly, if at all, when committed by husbands. But a wife's act of adultery was considered so heinous that "honor killings" were still condoned in some communities and would not be prosecuted by the courts. Quite apart from the legal system, Italians still lived in a society dominated by the Catholic Church, uneven industrialization, widespread poverty, and the dislocations and pain of dictatorship, war, and occupation. In 1945 any Italian under the age of 35 had no or very limited memories of life before Fascism, including no experience of voting. The population overall was still powerfully influenced by the gender norms and social mores Fascism had championed during its interwar rise to power and what I characterized as "the war of the sexes." None of these conditions changed in 1945, and they arguably affected people's day-to-day lives and decisions more powerfully than any political rights could.

At the same time as discriminatory laws remained in place, long-term trends had reshaped Italian (and all European) lives and offered women new opportunities. Family size decreased, female education rates improved, literacy rose, and radio, film, and television spread (radio broadcasting began in Italy in 1924, television in 1954, and both were monopolies of the state).[20] The first women graduates of medical and law school had begun practicing in the 1920s, and women had come to dominate teaching positions in elementary education. From the turn of the century several feminist organizations had struggled for women's suffrage, equal education, and professional parity; the Fascist regime itself had aided in giving women a more "modern," if not more emancipated, role in public life and leisure activities. Developments in housing and domestic technology were slow in coming, however, so women's time was consumed by a great deal of housework for which they remained nearly solely responsible. Only 20% of homes had flush toilets in the 1930s, and only the rich had washing machines, refrigerators, or other domestic appliances, so the very onerous weekly task of doing laundry by hand and the daily tasks of shopping for (or, during and just after the war, scavenging for) and cooking fresh food remained a heavy burden on women's time.[21] The war devastated agriculture, housing stock, and infrastructure, and left many families bereaved and scattered, further worsening the situation. No wonder, then, that only about a third of women were officially recorded as employed (though the inclusion of informal labor—and prostitution—would make this percentage significantly higher), a percentage that, having grown to that number with the mobilizations of the two world wars, stagnated until the early 1970s.[22] At the start of the period covered in this book, women had just been through bombings, rapes, forced labor, retaliatory strikes by occupiers, and near starvation; often they were still alone in facing the prospect of rebuilding their lives, as other family members, especially the men, took years to return from prison camps or never returned at all. Having suffered years of hunger during the war, Italians still had the lowest average food levels in Western Europe in the spring of 1947.

Women's weak status was reinforced by the Catholic Church. Despite the increasing activism among laypeople, particularly women, that had made Catholic associationism the most common and powerful form of civic participation in Italy in the twentieth century, Pope Pius XII's official declarations continued to uphold the authority of husbands and women's sacred mission of motherhood and domesticity, and the unsuitability of women in the public sphere.[23] The new Constitution preserved the so-called "Lateran Accords" Mussolini's regime had negotiated with the Vatican, which gave Catholicism the status of official state religion. Despite the Left's wish to found a secular state, Togliatti led the PCI into a compromise on this issue in order to prove the Communists' mainstream credibility, a failed effort as PCI members were expelled from the cabinet in 1947.

The task of recomposing families and relations between men and women was urgent on both personal and political levels. This everyday reality would be quickly overlaid and complicated by postwar trends of modernization, urbanization, and the events of the Cold War, decolonization, and globalization in an international context.[24] However, there was also a powerful countervailing force in favor of women's claim to move center stage in politics. Fascism was so thoroughly discredited by the time Italy emerged from occupation by both the Germans and the Anglo-Americans that many Allied observers mistrusted the Italians' suitability and maturity for democracy. The Fascist "new man" had been defeated, the hungry Italian supplicant of American loans and reconstruction funds seemingly stripped of his virility and potency; Italian women were more eligible for the role of partner in democratic reconstruction as mature democratic subjects uncompromised by Fascism. Women's strength and heroism in the democratic crisis was seen, paradoxically, as the necessary element in the eventual reconstruction of a "normal" gender order in which men could regain their authority and independence as leaders of a respected democratic nation. For example, much of the initial Euro-American encounter took place between local women and American GIs, so that women came to symbolize the national honor and well-being and capacity for autonomy of their nation. This was often negative in that women who traded domestic and sexual favors for material goods from occupying forces were shameful proof of the dependence and decline of the nation. Americans too took from their relations with women their ideas of how dependent and how morally lax Europeans were. These encounters "confirmed that the loss of national self-determination extended to the sexual order." Italian men, particularly those charged with negotiating Italy's position in the new international order, felt anxious as they tried to fathom how "a people whose recent history consisted of defeat, occupation, liberation, and retribution" could find autonomy and respect among the world powers. The Anglo-Americans' contempt for Italian political and sexual honor "provoked... the deepest sense of exposure and helplessness."[25] That is, Italians were uncomfortable with dependence, a feminine condition incompatible with full democratic citizenship status. So, as this book shows, women helped provide a buffer between the strong come-on of the Americans and the vulnerable Italians as they tried to reconstitute a social, political, and economic order that could restore them to masculine independence—all of which were predicated on the restoration of sexual order. Women cooperated in this but used the opportunity of increased visibility to renegotiate some of the terms of the sexual order. The women of the Lost Wave were in a sense taking on the task of restoring an entire nation's self-esteem and legitimacy.[26]

Most ordinary Italians, though, simply craved a return to "normalcy," although normal would have to be reinvented as much as any other aspect of life after Fascism and total war. The aspiration to normalcy was best symbolized by family: a stable harmonious family with a working father, a nurturing mother, and children who would be well-fed, well-dressed, and, above all, safe. The extreme disruptions of the war years would be overcome through the work of creating new families on the personal level, but also on the larger symbolic level of the "family" of the nation.[27] The prosperous harmonious nuclear family imagined as the balm to all these wounds had not been the norm anytime during Italy's twentieth century, but with the take-off of the "economic miracle" in the late 1950s, a period in which televisions, refrigerators, cars, and indoor plumbing quickly spread to a majority of Italian homes, it would come to seem possible and even taken for granted. This turn to domesticity might have been more aspirational than lived, but it was an important part of the postwar and Cold War processes of "re-feminization" of women as serene managers of children, households, and budgets, and "re-masculinization" of men not as soldiers but as fathers and providers.[28]

The promise of safety, prosperity, and strong families was the refrain of every political party and social policy advocate all across postwar Western Europe, and it was predicated on working women moving aside to let the men return to their jobs and their own embrace of domesticity. Women did indeed embrace the idea of a return to peace and family harmony, and they did play crucial roles in the transition of Western Europe to American-style consumption-based economies.[29] But they did not accept that those roles as mother, housewife, and household budget chief limited them to the private domestic sphere; rather, as this book highlights, they claimed and made use of political rights as part of their social and public contribution to the nation's recovery and success. That the simple and cozy story of a return to normalcy did not reflect the messy reality on the ground is easy to grasp, but what the story of Lost Wave feminism contributes to an understanding of this transition period is how gender worked to redefine and shore up the social and political power structures that enabled that transition—and just how complicated and full of failures to break with the past it was.

The Lost Wave, while it focuses on the political narrative of rights and legislation, also strives to take into account how the economic and social context functioned in reshaping women's roles at work and in the family. The book begins by providing a collective biography of the first female members of Parliament. It analyzes the nature of women's political militancy in postwar Italy in order to identify the characteristics of the first forty-five. Although they came from diverse families, regions, and social classes, they shared a way of understanding the historical events of their early lives that led them to a common political and theoretical viewpoint about how to fight for women's rights and which issues to choose as priorities, despite difference in party lines and opposed ideologies regarding communism and capitalism, East and West. The chapter identifies the key moments of their shared politicization, which came during the war and Resistance, and in the widespread growth of women's volunteer organizations in the first half of the twentieth century. Finally it focuses on these specific women's roles in the institutional beneficiaries of these new forms of civic participation, the two postwar mass political parties of the Christian Democrats and the Communists, and the two mass women's associations, the Union of Italian Women and the Italian Women's Center.

After evaluating the personal meaning of militancy for women of these years, it addresses how the first forty-five translated the popular activism of the women's movement translate into concrete legislative reform for women.

The decisive factors for Italian women were their stronger presence and politicization in the Italian Resistance, and the strength of women's associationism in the postwar period. This associationism, what Patrizia Gabrielli has called "the Club of the Virtuous," drew on that Resistance experience as well as the uninterrupted legacy of Catholic Action volunteerism, and functioned on both the Left and the Right.[30] The fundamental outlook shared by the "two churches" of Italy, the Catholics and the Communists, centered on a spirit of solidarity, a distrust of unlimited capitalism and consumer culture, and the sense that the destinies of women and democracy were interdependent; and it was this common ground that allowed the women's rights movement to move forward in its work. The second chapter, "Gender Roles in Italy's Elections and Constitution," is focused on a comparative context of the successful rise of women activists to representative office and their contributions to constitutional law in the immediate postwar, exploring their more specific experience of navigating party politics, elections, and the corridors of legislative power in the national parliament. It shows what set the Italian women's movement apart from those of other European nations, analyzes their successful cross-party cooperation, and questions how their ambitions for political equality became so unlimited, while their willingness to divert from strict codes of personal behavior and respectability remained so very limited.

From the larger group, the book turns to more focused case studies from different political parties and different five-year legislatures. Each chapter follows a woman member of parliament through her sponsorship and passage of a law for women's rights, interweaving the stories of her career, the issues her law addressed, the negotiations between her and her party and fellow legislators and interlocutors in the women's associations, and the history of the legislature in which the law passed. Chapter 3, "Legge Noce for Working Mothers: '*Madonna Tempesta*,'" takes Teresa Noce as its subject. A veteran of the Communist Party and Resistance heroine, Noce was an infamously argumentative loudmouth whose contemporaries dubbed her "Our Lady of the Hellstorm." Noce never thought of herself as a politician for women only, but she spent much of her career championing laws to improve women's treatment and opportunities, particularly in the workplace. Though her own experience of motherhood was difficult and marked by tragedy, she never separated the role of mother from that of worker in her definition of women's lives and contributions to society. The chapter examines the passage of her first and foundational law (passed in 1950 during the first legislature of 1948–1953), which guaranteed maternity leave and employer-provided daycare for working mothers. The passage of the law marks the gendered ideologies present at the creation of the welfare state. It demonstrated for the first time both the extent and the limits of the cooperation among the first forty-five that was to become characteristic of constitutional rights feminism. The chapter makes clear how high the stakes would be for the Lost Wave, as activists, working mothers, union leaders, national politicians, medical experts, and employers all struggled to control the process of redefining family and individual, home and work, private and public that accepting pregnant women and mothers as workers with equal rights necessitated.

Chapter 4, "The Merlin Law against the *Case Chiuse*," focuses on the Socialist senator Angelina Merlin. Like Noce, she was already in her fifties and possessed international stature by the time of her campaign against regulated prostitution during the second legislature, 1953–1958. Unlike Noce, she had long reflected on the problem of gender and citizenship and devoted most of her energies to solving it. During the decade-long fight to pass her law, which closed the state-run brothel system in Italy, her initial presentation of the reasoning and possibilities for reform behind her proposal to deregulate prostitution got lost and oversimplified amidst the noise of the controversial debate. Though the law eventually passed in 1958, nearly all of its accompanying feminist analysis and prescription for women's equal rights failed to survive, as this chapter shows. While Italian politics had taken an extremely progressive turn in the postwar, social mores and sexual proprieties showed a remarkable continuity from the Fascist period. Women might become citizens, but only through a compromise in which they asserted their respectability and turned on prostitutes and other "deviants" to help discipline them and uphold social order.

The final case study moves forward to the end of the third legislature, 1958–1963, to address the work of a young Christian Democrat from Sardinia named Maria Cocco. In 1963, during a session primarily concerned with the crisis-laden rapprochement between the Christian Democrats and the social democrats known as the strategy of *centrosinistra*, Cocco championed a capstone law that acknowledged and made complete the many inroads women had been making into civil service. Her law focused on allowing women to become judges, and coincidentally its passage was eased by the landmark first ruling from the newly functioning Constitutional Court. The ruling confirmed that the Constitution was legally binding to speedy implementation (rather than simply a set of aspirational abstract goals), thereby justifying fifteen years of calls by women for constitutional implementation and making it clear once and for all that no legal grounds remained for reserving certain career opportunities to men. Cocco's law was both the victory lap of Lost Wave feminism and a foreshadowing of its demise: Italian women's employment rates remained at a lower percentage than nearly all other Western nations, as they still do today. Clearly women's economic inequality was a result of more than just legislative discrimination. Women activists began to agitate for more radical critiques of inequality and its origins and to show more anger about masculine privilege in social customs, marriage, and family relations. In just a few years feminists would revolt against formal politics altogether, denouncing the promise of equal rights as a trap and dedicating themselves instead to the discovery of an authentic feminine identity and voice completely autonomous from the patriarchal structures of the state, the university, the workplace, and the family itself.

Although many other women's stories and women's rights laws fall under the rubric of the Lost Wave's strategy of constitutional rights feminism, these three accounts offer a representative sample of the major parties, political commitments, and personal backgrounds of the first forty-five. The range of issues they negotiated in the legislative process, and especially the very real and very widespread passion and activism of a women's movement before second wave feminism, demand new attention. The focus on institutions and formal politics characteristic of the postwar women's rights movement was not the result of a lack of sophistication in their feminist analysis. By choosing a constitutionalist strategy that recognized sexual difference as a real division in the categories of male and female citizens, women activists were accepting a framework that did not encourage radical transgression—much less erasure—of mainstream gender norms. It did allow them, first, to cooperate in spite of political differences and, second, to effect political changes in women's rights, and thus in the nature of their democracy. Indeed, they made those changes by disrupting the very notion of a clear oppositional boundary between the public and private spheres. Women as mothers and workers are inhabiting both spheres at once; women as state-regulated prostitutes certainly problematize notions of private sexuality and public commerce; and women as judges, diplomats, and soldiers bring their gendered bodies into the most masculine redoubts of state power and legitimation. In each of these cases, women also remind men of the importance of the private for their own masculine public identities and actions.[31]

The constitution, through compromise and through the reality of social mores in Italy, did not and could not fully confront the contradiction between citizens' *de jure* equality and women's *de facto* inferiority. This both reflected the reality of postwar society and conditioned the future.[32] Constitutional rights feminism was a legislative strategy practiced by women at the Parliamentary level, as well as an attempt by women activists to control the conflicting rhetoric about women's issues and women's identities in a period of crisis, and to keep it on the track of mass consensus.[33] It was also an effort to claim the multiple mantles of worker, mother, wife, antifascist, activist, consumer, and citizen without any one being to the detriment of another. In doing so, women as political subjects did ultimately develop more power. But it was by no means a simple process, and it did not have a singular, easily evaluated outcome.

A mystery originally inspired the research that led to this book: why were women elected in such high numbers to Parliament in the early postwar years, only to virtually disappear from Parliament later? Even a 2003 constitutional amendment and a 2004 law instituting quotas only managed to bring their numbers to about 16% of the total. In solving this mystery, I began to see that surge of women in the first legislatures as a lost wave of feminism: a mass women's rights movement spearheaded by a cohort of political leaders who created and defended laws that redefined and asserted women's citizenship on a basis of democracy and equity. But their presence and representation were lost when they were not replaced with a new generation of political women, and their movement came to seem compromised and uninspiring to later feminists. The concluding chapter brings these elements together in a discussion of the complicated and emotional world of Italian memory politics and its relevance for today's profoundly ambivalent sexual politics in Italy. Looking back at the years of the Lost Wave reveals the fragility of the restoration projects of the period—including the restoration of a sexual order—rather than claiming their success or completion. In this process the first forty-five present a legacy for understanding subsequent feminism, gender politics, and citizenship, in Italy and beyond. This book is an attempt to turn the personal political and the political, personal; as a productive way to discover a lost chapter of Italian history, and also a new way of telling the history of Europe's postwar and the Cold War more generally. Struggles over sexual difference and the law are flashpoints for the entire organization of power in the state as well as among states, and they reveal what is at stake and what is in play across the spectrum of political models.

1

"An Essential Way of Life"

The Political Awakening of Women Militants

> "... above all the battle [is] to make women understand, even through the most banal and most simple initiatives, that politics is not intrigue and scheming, but an essential way of life."
>
> —Ada Gobetti, *Diario partigiano, 1949*

On a warm June day in 1946 twenty-one women gather in Rome for a group photo, each holding a rose in her hand. A curious passion animates their faces, creating the momentary appearance of a family resemblance. Their suits, though respectably clean and modest, are worn and cut in styles from before the war. All are thin and their old suits look sizes too big for them; in 1946 recovery and reconstruction haven't advanced enough to satisfy the demand for even the most basic foodstuffs.

Physically, there is nothing else to tell us why these women belong together as a group—they cannot be of the same class, given the differences in dress and grooming. They are deeply divided by age, with several white-haired women seated in the front of the tableau and several standing behind who look to be in their twenties. They are the first women ever elected to public office in Italy by the first women ever to vote in Italy. Their unifying passion is politics, and their politics are motivated by a common experience of over two decades of Fascism, war, and resistance. They will make up only 21 out of 586 members of the Constituent Assembly, the body charged with writing a new republican constitution, but these women are among the most famous figures of their parties and of the Resistance, and they will make their voices count.

Angelina Merlin, fifty-seven years old, dignified and attractive, her wispy graying hair pulled back in a chignon, smiles impartially at the whole group; she is already well-known and established as a leader both in her Socialist party (PSI, *Partito Socialista Italiano*) and among the women, many of whom she directed in their Resistance activities. A dark-haired woman with big glasses and protruding teeth ignores the smile, already raising her voice in argument with the genteel and quietly commanding lady with the large crucifix on her chest next to her. She is Teresa Noce, known for her temper and her passion throughout the Communist Party (PCI, *Partito Comunista Italiano*). The target of her anger shakes her head but doesn't respond; Maria Agamben Federici is already practiced at the balancing act between cooperating with leftist women colleagues and making this cooperation palatable to the Church fathers who oversee her as president of the Italian Women's Center (CIF, *Centro italiano femminile*), an organization committed to politically organizing Catholic women voters. Noce will hear soon enough that Federici and Merlin have already agreed on a first cooperative initiative: passing the constitutional article that will guarantee women's equality as citizens.

Their faces, proud and happy on this day of celebration and relative quiet after the election and before the political and legislative work begins, betray the great fatigue and strain of recent months. The June 2 referendum was extremely hard-fought, and they were sent by their parties all over the country to campaign and to exhort first-time women voters to their new civic duties. Merlin's smile may be conciliatory: in this year of Cold War intensification, there were ferocious campaign tactics pitting Marxist left against anticommunist right. The communist women especially have suffered, and indeed there is a physical separation even in this photographer's grouping between Communists and Christian Democrats. Merlin and the other Socialists and members of smaller parties are left to fill the gap in between, a configuration that foreshadows the political maneuverings to come.

The rose each grasps is attached to a printed card which articulates the reason for this gathering: the Union of Italian Women (UDI, *Unione donne italiane*), a leftist-sponsored organization dedicated to educating new women voters from across the political spectrum, has invited them to tea and a reception to congratulate them on their election to the Constituent Assembly and to remind them that, among their constituents, women need special representation from them. The new constitution of the Republic must respect women's status, says the card's text: legal equality with men in every field, recognition of the right to work (including access to all schools, professions, and careers), the right to protective legislation that "permits a woman to fulfill her task as a mother," and equal treatment and equal compensation for equal work.[1] These will indeed be the articles women constituents go on to fight for and largely win.

As the photographer signals for silence, twenty-one eager faces turn toward his lights. From this moment on, everything these women do will constitute a historical first.

In the parliamentary elections of 1948, elections made legal by the constitution finished and submitted for ratification in 1947, additional women were elected to office, so that a total of forty-five women shared the distinction of being the first female parliamentarians of Italy. If twenty-one women wrote the constitutional articles that enabled this movement to exist and forty-five women represented that movement's goals in parliament, the generation of women active in the women's rights movement of the 1950s and 1960s numbered in the millions and spread across all of Italian society. This chapter provides a collective biography of this Lost Wave, using their life stories to illustrate their motivations and to explain the nature of women's political militancy in postwar Italy. Despite the many differences among them, they acted as a cohort when it came to the question of women's rights, drawing on a few key shared moments to create a vision of gender equality as the crucial linchpin in a new Italian democracy. That shared vision is at the root of the strategy of constitutional rights feminism.

Communism and Catholicism, the specificity of women's participation in the Resistance, and associationism were shared parts of the earlier experiences of the Lost Wave and set the stage for the emergence of the first forty-five from this cohort into the Constitutional Assembly and first Parliament. Although the ideologies they subscribed to shaped these women, their agency resided in not just submitting to ideology—of the Cold War, of gender, of labor—but in insisting on participating in defining it from women's points of view. This biography underscores both the commonalities and the rich diversity present among these women, the products of different locations, networks, and political systems.[2]

The presence of women "*in piazza*," going into otherwise masculine public space to protest at times of crisis, especially times of famine and want, is familiar from the revolutionary years of 1789 in Paris and 1917 in Moscow. In Italy, even before the watershed of the postwar feminist movement, women's protest had already taken on a more consciously political bent in the years before World War I, the interwar *biennio rosso* (the red biennial, the two years just after World War I of factory occupations and general strikes in the North), and the violence of Fascist *squadrismo*. Italy had a strong socialist movement and a growing feminist suffrage movement in the two decades around the turn of the century: the oldest women of the Lost Wave had participated in such actions as the factory occupations in Turin and the demonstrations against entering World War I, and the youngest remembered their mothers and aunts participating. That family connection played a significant role in motivating women to become political activists; for most women, with lower literacy rates than men and without the vote, the family was the first and most influential site of politicization. Neither the Liberal nor the Fascist governments had succeeded in their attempts to fully nationalize Italy since its 1861 unification, and especially during the Fascist regime most Italians found that the family was a necessary resource in worsening economic circumstances, a safe haven for expressing one's opinions in a harshly punishing regime, and the best place from which to resist the fatherland's increasing demands on one's daily life and activities.[3] Rarely did a woman's choice of political loyalties and militancy contrast with her family's traditions, and many women *staffette*, or support personnel, followed their fathers, brothers, or partners into a partisan brigade during the Resistance. Of women elected to the Constituent Assembly, many had male relatives in positions of leadership. Giuliana Nenni's father was Pietro Nenni, the leader of the Italian Socialist Party (PSI); Teresa Noce was married to Luigi Longo, and Rita Montagnana to Palmiro Togliatti, both leaders of the Communist Party (PCI). Lina Merlin felt her family's tradition of military and civil service to Liberal Italy was her most important formative influence, and Angela Guidi Cingolani's entire family held leadership positions in various Catholic organizations in Rome.[4] Carla Capponi, a deputy in the second legislature, was a member of the city partisan forces, the GAP, and set the bomb in Rome's Via Rasella that killed 33 German soldiers and led to the Nazis' retributive massacre of 335 Romans at the Fosse Ardeatine. She recounted in her autobiography: "Searching within myself, I felt that it [my political choice] had been born in the isolation of my family, within which a sort of separate 'culture' had reigned, some sense which for years had kept us different from, and distant from, the Fascist reality."[5] Her family, in other words, had served as a school for politics at a time when the Fascist regime's totalitarian aspirations had infiltrated every other mediating group between the individual and the state.

The women of the Lost Wave emerged from antifascist families with one of three main political identities: the *anziane* or "old guard," the *leva della Resistenza* or "Resistance recruits," and the *Cattoliche* or "Catholics." The *anziane* were the veterans: communist, socialist, and independent militants whose political experience began in the *biennio rosso,* the pacifist movement, or Catholic social work, born between 1880 and 1900. Later in the postwar period other even less complimentary nicknames were given to this cohort: some spoke of them as *le draghe,* the dragons of emancipation. From the ranks of these veterans came nationally famous leaders such as Lina Merlin, Teresa Noce, and Maria Federici. The older women had much longer histories of militancy within their parties and their experience with the Fascist regime had been adversarial from the beginning. The Liberal state had been severely weakened by working class radicalization and the vexed question of Italy's entry into World War I. From about 1919 a revolutionary atmosphere of everyday violence by the thuggish blackshirts, the Fascist paramilitary squads, drove many to participate in protests, strikes, and union organization. After Mussolini's rise to power in 1922 and especially after the outlawing of all non-Fascist parties and civil society groups in 1926, Italy became a one-party state and political activities were severely curtailed. Communist activist, teacher, and author Tina Pizzardo recalled in her memoirs, "It's laughable what a poor thing we called the struggle in those years [of the regime]: a little bit of assistance [*soccorso rosso,* the aid association for communist prisoners and their families], not giving in [to the Fascist regime], trading books, banned newspapers and news from the prisons and from abroad; and above all, endless political arguments. Nothing more, but that was enough to send you to jail."[6] Indeed, many of these women spent a great deal of the 1920s and 1930s in exile, in jail, or in *confino,* the internal exile created by Mussolini to isolate dissidents and render them harmless without jailing them. Those with experience abroad, like Teresa Noce, who led a party cell in France, edited the Communist newspaper in Barcelona during the Spanish Civil War, and was sent to party functionary's school in Moscow, later credited that education with their wider understanding of women's rights as constitutional and human rights issues.

The PCI lost many leaders during the struggles of clandestinity (when all non-Fascist organizations were outlawed, forcing the parties to go underground and operate in secrecy), the Spanish Civil War, and the Resistance. Those young women partisans who had shown leadership skills and promise became their hastily groomed replacements. These *leva della Resistenza* or "Resistance recruits," were overwhelmingly Communist and born around 1920. *Leva* literally refers to military conscripts, and the name was also used for men in the immediate postwar period as a derogatory way of identifying partisans who had not joined through antifascist conviction but through cynical opportunism, waiting until it was clear which side would win, so they could secure their piece of the rewards. But for women of the *leva* the term was really an indicator of youth; they had fought in the Resistance as little more than teenagers and barely passed the minimum age requirement of twenty-five for the Chamber of Deputies in the Parliament in 1948. For them, politics was literally a life-or-death choice made in the face of dictatorial oppression and total war. Less aware of feminist history than the *anziane*, they were nonetheless equally determined to make their sacrifices count in the postwar period. Normal politics had not been practiced in much of Europe as they came of age. Young men and women of this age cohort often envisioned postwar politics as a seamless continuation of their wartime activity, since secret activism was the only public life they knew.[7] While in one sense all Italians would experience "normal politics" and citizenship for the first time after 1945, the *leva* women represented an extreme version of that initiation.

Gina Borellini's story is both heroically exceptional and generally representative of the Resistance recruits. Born October 24, 1919 in San Possidonio near Modena (part of the "Red Belt" of Italy, the traditional stronghold area of Leftist voters), she was one of five children, two boys and three girls, of a farming family. Her father had been a socialist for a long time; the children all joined the Garibaldi brigades (the Communist-sponsored partisan bands) and then the Communist Party.

The siblings were all encouraged to be militant, without regard to gender. In fact during the Resistance she, a brother, and a sister fought as armed partisans, traditionally a masculine role; the remaining brother and sister both worked as *staffette*, or couriers, traditionally a feminine role, carrying messages, arms, and money. Borellini and her husband were arrested and condemned to death three times; they escaped twice, but the last time she was let go and he was executed. Leaving her children with her family, she fled to a Communist partisan formation and fought with them until Fascist soldiers discovered their camp. Although she was injured during the attack, she managed to hide and later crawl to a doctor. Her leg had to be amputated but she survived and was decorated with the Gold Medal of Honor for her heroism and courage.[8] She was elected to the Chamber of Deputies for all of the first three legislatures, in 1948, 1953, and 1958. At the same time, she served as president of both the Veterans' and War Disabled Association of Modena and of the Union of Italian Women of Modena.[9] Her career, in other words, demonstrates how the youngest women of the Lost Wave reconciled the masculine and feminine worlds of antifascism. The Resistance was such an urgent and *sui generis* movement that Borellini and young women like her were valuable and celebrated in capacities that would previously have been denied to their gender. This would however frequently mean that the transition to peacetime was more difficult for them, as they had never known anything other than the intensity and elasticity of social identities in an extraordinary moment, than for the veterans or the *cattoliche*, both of whom had more continuity and experience with a traditional social and gender order.

The *cattoliche*, or Catholic activists, were a group mixed in age and unified by an institutional culture different from that of the Left. In this case, the women came from families whose antifascism was nurtured within a religious context, and their political experience was usually in leadership in the Church-sponsored Catholic Action (*Azione cattolica*, AC), an organization dedicated to social work among Catholics, religious education, and providing a moral context for leisure activities among young people. AC had had almost total continuity during Fascism because only Catholic organizations had remained legal alternatives to the regime's youth, women's, and after-work organizations. Catholic women had had time to pay their dues and rise slowly into leadership positions in AC; unlike activists from outlawed organizations, their oldest leaders had not been dispersed through prison and exile, and the relationships between older and younger women, while marked by hierarchy and obedience to elders, were often close and involved spiritual mentoring as well as other kinds of direction and instruction.

Separation by gender was both traditional in the church and useful for producing women leaders, who could gain a great deal of experience rising through the many possible ranks of women's associations. They did not have to compete with men for leadership roles and had the benefit of a practical education in how to navigate the contradictions of big hierarchical institutions to guide them in their initiation to government.

Identifying these women as "Catholic" may be somewhat misleading; nearly all Italians in the period were Catholic. Indeed even the most dedicated Communists or anarchists might also call themselves Catholic. Italy's systemic, cultural Catholicism was also one of the most important ways the Fascist regime was different from fascist movements elsewhere, especially the Nazi regime. Mussolini had no choice but to compromise with and seek approval from the Catholic Church in order to get and retain power, so Catholicism was imbricated not only in the Resistance but also in the very thing that they were resisting. Yet the term "Catholic" is a valuable descriptor for this segment of women of the Lost Wave for a number of reasons. First, unlike Communists and Socialists, these women had no other dominant category under which they organized. They cannot be referred to by their party affiliation because, although the Christian Democrat party was the de facto political party of the Church, its membership was never completely coterminous with nor completely controlled by the Church. Many of the women who were Catholic political activists were not members of the DC party; some were not members of any party. Second, although one association, CIF, and one party, the DC, were the hegemonic civil groups of the center-right, the women in this group did not all belong to both, and sometimes not to either. While the *Gioventù Femminile* (Female Youth) of *Azione Cattolica* (Catholic Action)—the branch of AC for young women during the Fascist regime—was the proving ground for nearly all the women in this group, many leftist female militants had also spent time as members of the GF of AC. Third, to simply distinguish between political left and right, or liberal and conservative, would be anachronistic and even more misleading, since there were many threads of Christian Democrat and Catholic activist politics, some of which were decidedly progressive, like the social democrats Alcide de Gasperi and Amintore Fanfani, who both served as Prime Minister in early postwar governments. Thus, "Catholics" refers to those women whose antifascist formation and political militancy were identified with anticommunism and with a Catholic-inspired vision of solidarity, human dignity, and women's role in private and public life. The *cattoliche* were determined that women should ensure Italy's stability as a democracy through their refusal to succumb to extremisms, be they communist revolution, a return to Fascism, or runaway American-style individualist consumption.

One representative *cattolica* was Angela Maria Guidi Cingolani, the woman who appeared at the start of this book as she became the first to speak in an Italian legislative session. She was born in Rome on October 31, 1896 to a family of the Catholic bourgeoisie. In 1909 her mother was shot and killed by a stray bullet when she looked out her window during a demonstration in the piazza below. Around 1914 Guidi Cingolani met and befriended M. C. Giustiniani Bandini, a noblewoman who had founded the Union of Catholic Women in 1908 as one of the subgroups of AC. She began to participate in the Union's activities, and by 1918 was a *propagandista* and then a director of the Roman section of the *Gioventù Femminile* (GF). In 1919 she was among the first members of the newly created *Partito Popolare Italiano* (PPI; a party of Christian inspiration, the DC was the direct heir of this party) and became the secretary of its Roman women's section. She was particularly active in organizing Catholic trade unions. In 1930 she became vice president of the International Congress of Professional and Business Women in Geneva.

In 1935 she married Mario Cingolani, who had been a parliamentarian for the PPI in the 25th, 26th, and 27th legislatures of the Liberal state and would become a senator in the postwar Republic. He was a widower thirteen years her senior, with three children, to whom they added one son, Mario. They were both extremely active throughout the Fascist period in promoting Catholic activism and making it more independent from the Vatican; the two became a main reference point for the Catholic antifascists of Rome, choosing the battle names of Eugenio (hers) and Pollione (his). The names were both clever references to classical times: Eugenio is an ancient Greek name meaning well-born or noble, and Pollione was an ancient Roman proconsul made famous in the Bellini opera *Norma*. With such naming practices Resistance members reclaimed the patriotic history of the Roman Empire and Italian national identity. Appointed to the *Consulta* in 1945 where she gave that noteworthy address described in the introduction, she went on to be elected to the Constituent Assembly in 1946 and then in 1948 to the first legislature; in 1951 she became the first woman in a government cabinet as Undersecretary in the Ministry of Industry and Commerce. Guidi Cingolani thus represented the aspiration of the *cattoliche* to reconcile three missions: their spiritual effort to "resurrect" the morality of Italian politics, their quest for leadership and autonomy as female citizens, and their embrace of traditional gender roles as helpmeets to husbands and religious authorities.

The Female Youth of Catholic Action (*Gioventù femminile*, GF) was the primary legal civic organization to which most antifascist women belonged during the years of the Fascist regime.[10] The *Gioventù femminile* was the group for young women within the larger association of Catholic Action, a national group whose main activities were social and charity work. Through their experience with GF, young women from all over Italy got to travel, speak in public, meet new people, and improve their minds. Because these activities took place under the aegis of the Church, in a strictly single-sex and closely supervised atmosphere, their experiences were not seen to be in conflict with young women's modesty or piety.[11] It was, in other words, ideal training for the balance between accepted gender norms and feminist political activism that women of the Lost Wave would later work to strike. Begun in the early twentieth century by Armida Barelli, GF was the largest mass organization still intact in 1945 at war's end.[12] As such, it had a powerful influence on the members' sense of themselves as women in public: very liberated with regards to relatively radical ideas and debates and the entry into formerly forbidden geographical and cultural spaces, but quite intensely conformist in their understanding of bodies and sexualities as needing to be strongly marked by feminine respectability to properly represent gender in the national and social collective.[13]

Even girls who would later join parties of the Left often experienced their first civic participation in GF: Olga Prati, who fought in the

Resistance with the Action Party's partisan formation *Giustizia e Libertà* and joined the Communists after the war, confirmed that in Ravenna, her hometown, the parish group of GF was the only one left after the regime dissolved all other sports, youth, and professional groups there. It was "the only place that offered us the possibility to meet our peers, and everyone from my generation, some motivated more than others by religious sentiment, attended."[14]

Women who participated in GF developed a sense of personal responsibility within the public sphere that not only spurred many to participate in the Resistance when the situation arose, but set a foundation for their understanding of and desire to renew female citizenship.[15] Their training in GF provided them with a common ethic and moral, if not specifically religious, outlook: whether they joined Communist or Catholic politics afterwards, women of the Lost Wave were influenced by a populist brand of Catholicism that valued good works, humility, and brotherly love. Power and leadership were not to be chased for one's own ambitions, but were seen as the means to serve one's fellow citizens.

This early linkage of public works and private dedication took on a new, more radical, and feminist connotation when the Resistance began in earnest. The transition from associationism to Resistance, and its accompanying articulation of a new role for women in politics, happened very quickly. In July 1943 Mussolini was removed from power and imprisoned through the cooperation of King Victor Emmanuel and Fascist leaders, who had turned against Mussolini as the military situation became ever more disastrous for the Axis powers. The king appointed General Badoglio to lead the government and negotiate an armistice with the Allies. Taken by surprise when the September 3 armistice was announced publicly only five days later, many Italian soldiers had to flee from Nazi troops as they turned from allies to enemies in an instant. The Nazi occupation of the Italian peninsula was lightning fast and brutal; in mere days Italian civilians had to decide how to react to this reversal, and thousands of women all over Italy improvised an operation to stop or divert military and prison transports and rescue, disguise, and hide deserting Italian soldiers and escaping Allied POWs before the Nazis could hunt them down. Historians Anna Bravo and Anna Maria Bruzzone dubbed this women's action of spontaneous transformation from soldiers to civilians and collaborators to resisters after September 8, 1943 as a "*maternage di massa*," or "mass mothering,"[16] and argued that the most important aspect of the Resistance was the civil resistance of women.[17] Women partisans not only protected and nurtured others but also began to recognize the value of taking action for oneself, as protagonists in what had clearly become a defining historical moment for individuals as well as for the nation as a whole. In this role they grew in self-awareness, pride in their physical and mental abilities, and a sense of belonging and being important, of "making history," that was partly coming of age, partly politicization, and partly raw courage.

These sentiments were not always initially connected to any emancipationist female awareness for women, especially because the culture of the Resistance was so strongly egalitarian. Partly in reaction to the chauvinism of Fascism but mostly because of the crisis conditions and the awareness that everyone involved was constantly running the risk of death, conflict between the sexes seemed offensive.[18] Nonetheless, the choice to resist and to fight created space for a feminist awareness to develop and to crystallize. The biggest novelty of becoming a militant for a woman was learning to trust, alone and in sometimes very dangerous situations, one's own ability to make a decision, to think quickly, to move in public with confidence, aware of the life and death consequences of such actions and decisions. This new self-awareness could be the first step in thinking more about the condition of women in general and about the freedoms and autonomy they were denied in more conventional times. But this feminine consciousness in the Resistance was accompanied by darker fears and violence. The largely female *staffette* often faced greater danger than the largely male guerilla fighters, since they carried messages, money, and arms from place to place in cities and on trains where they could be stopped and searched at any time. When they were part of a military action, they had to be the first to arrive, to set up contacts and reconnoiter, and were the last to leave, still holding the contacts, usually the local telephone and telegraph station, until all the partisans had escaped. If women were captured and discovered, they expected torture and interrogation to quickly take a turn towards sexual abuse and rape. As Marisa Ombra, *staffetta* in the communist Garibaldi brigades and postwar women's activist and journalist, put it, "We knew it, we [women] talked about it among ourselves often. We asked ourselves up to what limit we would be able to stand it."[19]

A woman who joined or aided the Resistance, whether as fighter, courier, or supporter, had taken responsibility for her destiny in a way that was unique to the feminine experience of Resistance. There were higher stakes in the Resistance for women than for men, their voluntary participation was a more conscious choice, and the discontinuity from their previous lives was more marked. All this led to divergent experiences and memories of what the Resistance meant among women versus among men.[20]

Laura Ingrao, a Communist urban action organizer, emphasized the feminine version of the story this way: "The women of Rome—in diverse situations, in a political struggle at many levels—were inside, not outside or at the margins of, the Resistance. They created the basis—we felt it more every day that women participated in the national political life."[21] Because men's mobility and visibility were so constrained during this period, an unaccompanied woman went from being a symbol of immodesty to a normal sight. Her freedom of movement became a precious ability: women traveled miles out of cities and towns to gather rationed food and supplies, they filled jobs vacated by missing men, and they became the key to the survival of the Resistance by carrying concealed messages, money, supplies, and ammunition. *Staffette* hid underground newspapers or other material packed into a false belly under their clothes to pass safely among Nazi officers too chivalrous or prudish to search a pregnant woman. By trading on the most normative stereotypes of femininity as fundamentally passive, women gained subversive power. Fascism, by insisting on women's subordination and their essential lack of independent initiative, had provided them the perfect cover stories through which they found new kinds of liberation.

Not all women in the Resistance were *staffette.* Women like Gina Borellini also fought side by side in armed guerilla bands with their male comrades. Others became influential journalists and publishers of underground newspapers and propaganda; Anna Garofalo became a radio celebrity who broadcast news and commentary into Italy on clandestine channels. Ada Gobetti, widow of philosopher Piero Gobetti and co-founder of the Action Party, frequently crossed the Alpine border between France and Italy to lead refugees to freedom and served as the primary liasion between the Resistance in Northern Italy and the exiles and French *maquis* on the other side. Women who would later become national leaders in politics and culture also filled important positions of command in the Resistance: Gisella Floreanini helped liberate Piedmont ahead of the Anglo-American troops' arrival and was the Minister of Health and Welfare during the forty days of independence during which they declared the area the Republic of Ossola; Teresa Noce entered the Central Committee of the Communist Party as one of its directors; and Marisa Rodano helped to elaborate the philosophy and founding party platform of the so-called *cattocommunisti* (Catholic Communists), the Party of the Christian Left.

Women in the Resistance, then, were motivated by much more than the maternal instinct invoked by Bravo and Bruzzone's coinage of the term *maternage di massa*. Their powerful individual experiences of independence and competence made them rethink their hopes for the outcome of their struggle. They both exploited and transgressed accepted gender behaviors in their activities and gained awareness of the need to reform and broaden definitions of femininity in order to overcome Fascism and create democracy. Instead of wanting only peace and to rid their homes of occupying foreigners, they began to articulate claims that women's contributions to the Resistance proved their readiness for political equality with men. In this context a new form of associationism was born: the Women's Defense Groups, (GDD, *Gruppi di difesa della donna*).[22] These groups were sponsored by the PCI but were designed to have women militants from all the antifascist parties as organizers to reach out and recruit Italian women from all walks of life to Resistance work. The leaders of the GDD wanted to start even in the midst of the war a national women's association to educate women for their citizenship in the republic to be created with the peace they worked toward. So the propaganda of the GDD urged women to help oust the Nazi oppressor, as well as emphasized that women resisters fought for women's suffrage, for their right to work, for equal salaries and protection under the law.[23] The GDD both helped to politicize the acts women were already undertaking and offered those acts an ongoing meaning that could last through peacetime. It was never very large, but it introduced women's rights as citizens into the rhetoric and reasoning of the Resistance and helped women transition from family or individual involvement into the world of political association. The GDD would become UDI after the war, and most of its leaders went from GF to GDD to UDI without interruption; while the acronyms changed, the women who populated the movement remained the same, merely deepening their commitment to a uniquely feminine role in social justice. Despite the cataclysmic discontinuities of the time, from Liberal state to Fascist regime, from peace to total war and back again, and from partner to enemy among the Axis and Allied powers, the women of the Lost Wave sustained a remarkable continuity of purpose and association.

There is also continuity between the Resistance and the postwar period in the paradox of women's gender identities. A great deal of women's activism, including its most radical forms, intersected with and even passed under the cover of conventional gender roles. Women used gendered assumptions to their advantage to participate unobtrusively in the activities of antifascism and the Resistance, which contributed to their roles being defined as stories of assistance, rather than leadership, of subordination rather than revolution. While the women themselves never showed anything but pride in the ability, moral and physical courage, and independence they demonstrated, the dominant postwar narrative of their roles obscured their transgressive acts by casting all women's participation in an assistance-oriented, maternal light. The first accounts of the Resistance focused on a very masculine, military movement which, if it included women at all, did so only as nurses of fallen soldiers and mothers of future ones.[24] This sense of women's marginality to the Resistance was reinforced by the fact that of the 200,000 people formally recognized as partisans by the Italian government and therefore eligible for veterans' benefits and pensions, only 35,000 women were granted the status of *partigiana combattente* (fighting partisan) with a full claim to a pension, and another 20,000 women were recognized as *patriote* (patriots), a title with no material benefits.[25] When historians first began collecting oral histories from the women themselves they usually helped them to obscure the transgressive aspects of their experiences; even as they reclaimed for women the fundamental nature of their support of the Resistance, they characterized much of the Resistance as civil and not military. But in fact these women were "rebels," officially labeled as such by the Nazis when they were arrested, interrogated, and condemned to concentration camps and execution. And these rebels made their own countrymen anxious as well: in April 1945 when partisan bands marched through the liberated cities of Italy in celebratory parades, their female members were forbidden to march with them because they were not considered respectable women and might damage the Resistance government's legitimacy in civilian eyes.

Only recently have historians begun to look at the ways in which the Resistance served as a form of political preparation for women, as training in militancy and citizenship for that generation which had known neither during Fascism.[26] In the twenty-first century even official government-issued history started to make connections between the Resistance and the birth of a feminist consciousness. A pamphlet for schoolchildren from the National Committee on Parity, a government group charged with improving women's equal opportunities, called "*Ragazze vi racconto la nostra storia*" ("Girls I'll Tell You about Our History") argues that women joined the Resistance out of

> . . . a strong desire for action and citizenship experienced alongside and complementarily to the masculine one, which exalts her own individual being as free, responsible, and self-determining. The effects on her character are physical courage and mental stamina, the need to quickly make decisions on her own, the ability to analyze and operate in unknown fields, and a new linkage between the public and the private. The effect for society is the continuation after the war of the networks of assistance for veterans, refugees, and children which characterized the first political activities of women and the popular presence of the great women's associations just being born, UDI and CIF.[27]

This quotation testifies to the popularization—indeed the normalization—of women's heroism during the Resistance. Yet the connection between that period's female protagonism and women's roles in the postwar period is only acceptable when linked to "networks of assistance," the nurturing feminine roles that do not challenge the conviction that women's nature is to be subordinate and helpmeet. The evocation of a "new linkage between public and private" barely hints at the true import of women's participation in the Resistance, that they behaved in transgressive ways including military defense of the nation, and that it was autonomy and agency that they brought to the postwar democracy. The ideal of social work as political work that had been elaborated in women's associations from the GF to the GDD effected an important postwar transformation. While their platforms called for women to enter political life and achieve equality as democratic citizens, their grassroots activities transformed transgressive young partisans into nurses, cooks, and aides, much more reassuring roles for a society in reconstruction.[28]

The women of the postwar movement came to political life with a passionate, idealistic, and deeply moral belief that they had been called to unite private and public, individual and civil society, family and "national family." Women, as they had during the Resistance, were ready to enter fully into society. They were committed to cleansing and renewing the institutions of public life in ways that were both antifascist and broadly democratic. It is the mass character of women's participation that gives a unique flavor to this moment. While a relative minority of women were militant activists vis-à-vis those who merely signed membership cards, and a vast majority remained "apolitical" yet were a target audience for the Lost Wave's imagery and narrative, the GDD counted 70,000 members. It was this spirit of women's collective emancipation that motivated the founding of UDI and CIF and assured them a mass membership in the postwar years: by 1949 UDI claimed one million members, and by 1954 CIF claimed two and half million.[29]

Formed by antifascist families, steeped in totalizing political and religious subcultures, politicized and in some cases radicalized by the Resistance, women transformed their postwar activism into a politics with a distinctly feminist purpose. Though they had learned through their membership in GF, *Gioventù Femminile,* to work in the context of single-sex associations and to think of their mission as enlarging women's participation in civil society, the Lost Wave only emerged as a movement for feminist equality with the founding of UDI and CIF in the aftermath of the war. UDI and CIF were overlapping but competing organizations deeply enmeshed in the dynamics of the Cold War in Italy.[30] Their ideological foundations were fundamentally opposed, yet their practical effect was to call attention to women's inferior position in society and to popularize the ideal of the new woman citizen.[31]

Women's associationism had a history of rooting itself in communities and in women's loyalties by doing social work. Activities such as summer camps for underprivileged children and creating free or inexpensive cafeterias for poor workers remained a basic mode of participation and outreach that overshadowed explicitly issue-based political organizing. Women continued to be addressed as wives, mothers, and community-wide nurturers; associationism did not substitute those identities, but it added another claim to women's work and time. Instead of confronting or challenging the "double shift" of paid outside work and unpaid domestic work, the associations usually supported the image of an emancipated woman who would handle both of these with aplomb and take on responsibility for political activism. No wonder then that these protagonists would seem "dragons" of emancipation—mythically powerful but singular and forbidding—to their daughters' generation of second-wave feminists.

Still, associationism by its very definition sustained the ideas that women as a group were distinct from, and had different interests than, the male-dominated mainstream society that women had the responsibility and the right to defend. Through its unobjectionable but growing influence in society, it asserted that women should enter the civil sphere. Association women's activities in food banks, classrooms, political demonstrations, and journalism were an indispensable step on the road to citizenship. At the national level, UDI and CIF not only created women voters and educators of women as citizens, but also served as training grounds for women leaders. Both organizations recognized the need for a class of women politicians; both made efforts to quickly train organizers and executives through crash courses in politics, government, and history for its most promising young women. Both organizations also made repeated pleas for female candidates and pledged continuing support for those women who answered the call and ran for seats on their local city councils, school boards, and public health commissions.[32]

It was a universally held belief in the women's movement that women's emancipation was necessarily a mass phenomenon, and that only the mass entrance of women into civil society could guarantee a democratic society in Italy. So in addition to creating leaders from a politicized avant garde, women's associations also had to reach out to the mass of ordinary women. In practice these associations were far from neutral about political loyalties. The Italy of UDI and CIF was one of deep divisions between two hegemonous subcultures, the Communist and the Catholic. These institutions did not merely signify how one voted or how often one went to church, but also denoted where one went after work for a coffee or a drink and with whom, in which town or village festivals one participated, what sports one played and with which team, to whom one gave charity, how one dressed, which newspaper one read, where one's children went to school, and who they socialized with. Christian Democrat and GF or CIF membership was closely linked; and the PCI leadership was quite blunt about seeing UDI as an auxiliary organization and a reservoir for collecting party votes.[33] Additionally, the typical class makeup of each group's membership could be a source of division: in the early years UDI members tended to be working class, while the typical CIF member was a middle-class or formerly aristocratic housewife, though over time membership in both groups expanded to include the mass population.[34] Both main women's associations would struggle with their paternal parties and the question of loyalty—to all women or to the party line?—throughout the period. Not only did the associations compete for some of the same women as members, but the DC and the PCI also competed for the same people as voters. Tolerance and compromise were essential; this is a further way that women's citizenship helped build mass democracy as a reality in Italy. But their calls were not entirely successful in the Cold War atmosphere that produced, in 1949, the Church's decree that those who voted for the PCI were committing a mortal sin and could not take communion or confess.[35]

UDI was initially unsuccessful in portraying itself as independent of the Communist Party, nor was it in hard fact, and so struggled to convince previously unaffiliated women who feared Communism that they should join. PCI leaders Palmiro Togliatti and Velio Spano issued instructions about UDI's tasks and propaganda and were also married to women in UDI's leadership, Rita Montagnana and Nadia Spano. The stereotypical image was that of subordinate wives carrying out their husbands' wishes, working in parallel on the same agenda. Furthering this impression, UDI explicitly endorsed the PCI as part of the Popular Front coalition in early elections and reproduced much of its platform verbatim in its own propaganda. After the 1948 elections, UDI suffered from the defeat of the Popular Front by losing all of its state subsidies, while CIF received 300 million lire from the state. Another 600 million went to the *Pontifica opera di assistenza*, the papal charity umbrella organization, from which CIF also claimed funding.[36] The 1949 excommunication seriously challenged UDI's work at the grassroots, where it wanted to appeal to all women, including Catholic ones. In order not to alienate potential Catholic members, UDI obeyed the PCI's directive that it was not to publicly promote the recognition of children born out of wedlock, birth control, or divorce.[37] This was a losing strategy: anticommunist women mistrusted UDI anyway, and those Leftist women who were the base of UDI's activists increasingly asserted those issues in internal meetings and bulletins.

Recognizing the need to prove its autonomy in order to secure women's trust, by 1953 UDI showed increasing signs of refusing the party line in social and cultural issues. For example, it used its magazine *Noi donne* (*We Women*) to conduct national surveys on public opinion of divorce, women's education, and birth control practices. After 1956, when Krushchev's report condemning Stalin became publicly known and many communist sympathizers were horrified by the violence used in putting down the Hungarian revolution, UDI declared its autonomy from all other organizations, rejecting the PCI and staging a walk-out in protest of the Soviet influence on the Congress of the Women's International Democratic Federation (WIDF).[38] In the 1958 elections UDI included only women's issues in its platform and enumerated election goals that mentioned no particular party but called upon all candidates to more frequently debate women's issues.[39] Nadia Spano wrote of this new phase after 1953 that: "From now on, the bills on spousal equality, ending *patria potestà* [the law giving the husband or father complete legal and juridical control over his household members and their property], and the civil status of children born out of wedlock would come out from 'semi-secrecy.'"[40] The UDI slogan for the birth control debate from that time forward was "As women we determine how many children we want and when we want them." By the 1960s and 1970s the women of UDI were proudly marching in demonstrations for the legalization of divorce, contraception, and even abortion.[41]

CIF had even more would-be masters from whom to free itself, in the triangle of the Vatican, the Christian Democrat Party, and Catholic Action. The leaders of CIF, while nominally autonomous from the Christian Democrat party and the Vatican, did officially answer in frequent meetings to priests and executives from the hierarchy of Catholic Action, who were in turn always closely entangled with the Vatican and the DC. As happened with UDI, the men in the Church and party hierarchy who saw women's associationism as simply an auxiliary and a reservoir of obedient votes would clash with the women they appointed to lead the organization. Those female leaders would push for more than formal independence and for their mission to educate newly voting women in becoming citizens with parity of rights.

The relationship between CIF and the Christian Democrat party was conflicted from the beginning. Although a good number of the female members of Parliament from the DC, especially the older women, worked closely with both organizations, much of the rank and file of CIF wanted to avoid the rough-and-tumble of party politics and focus on a more neutral mission toward women in civil society. A letter from a local chapter president in Fano to the national president Maria Federici shows this:

> Dear Federici,
>
> Have patience if I bother you every so often, but my job is so new that I need occasional help. What is our real relationship—as CIF—with the Christian Democrat party?
>
> I lose my voice repeating that CIF wants only to ensure every woman deepens her social and political responsibilities, and that it acts in this field in complete good faith. Is that true? Nobody believes me. The communists certainly don't believe it. What do you say to all this? Frankly if it were true that we are just christian democrats camouflaged and masked, I would prefer to resign, and if I really felt the vocation I would subscribe directly to the party. But I hate every form of hypocrisy, even for a good cause.[42]

Maria Federici agreed with her colleague in Fano that the goal of women's associations was to promote women's citizenship, not any one political party. She spent four years struggling to end the symbol of that "hypocrisy" as embodied in the membership cards for CIF. The Vatican had initially imposed a rule that CIF could only award membership to women who already belonged to pre-approved groups within the Catholic Action hierarchy, adding its stamp to their cards rather than issuing its own. Her act of protest was to issue membership cards directly to individuals throughout Italy from the CIF headquarters in Rome. By making public this conflict between the Church wanting to keep control over the organization and only allow pre-screened and ideologically correct members, and CIF's desire to attract a larger mass of women through a more open and democratic format, Federici drew the ire of Catholic Action leaders, who forced her to resign in 1950.[43] After that, CIF, unlike UDI, did not openly rebel against the party that wanted to control its votes, nor did its members show any desire to take more controversial positions on issues like birth control, abortion, or divorce. CIF retreated from the conflict by not issuing election platforms at all after 1952 and recommitting itself to social work. But CIF's campaigns, including its support for working women's rights and for the deregulation of prostitution, both Left-led legislative proposals, demonstrate that these women refused to take the Christian Democratic bait of vicious anticommunism and remained willing to cooperate with other women's associations when their goals were aligned with Christian ideals and to invite women of all political persuasions to join. Indeed, in city councils and other local forms of governance, women from the DC and left-wing parties frequently cooperated when the issue was discrimination against working women. When in 1954 the Cisa Viscosa factory, a textile production firm in Rome, tried to dismiss its mainly female workforce, women politicians worked together across ideological and party lines. The proposed factory closing had met with a long and energetic strike from the female workforce, which had been supported by public opinion. The city council debated a resolution opposing the firing of 150 women workers from the factory, citing not only their familial responsibilities as breadwinners but also the dignity that they had earned as organized union members and as human beings. The resolution also mentioned that such an obviously discriminatory mass layoff would contravene articles in the Constitution. Introduced in cooperation by two councilwomen of the DC and one of the PCI, the resolution was passed unanimously on November 16, 1954.[44]

Pope Pius XII himself walked a fine line between affirming women's traditional subordination in the Church and calling on them as a new kind of public protagonist. In November 1945 he gave a speech to the women of Catholic associations that has been remembered as a milestone for Catholic women's autonomy. In it he called upon them to embrace a new, more public role in the life of Italian society. He underlined the personal dignity of women and their unbroken link to the continuity of tradition; he told them that it was women's responsibility to combat the vices of the modern world. He defined women's role as the defenders of the border between *casa* (the home) and *mondo* (the outside world). But, he said, women had an important new role in a democratizing society; he invited them to live in both spheres as exemplars of that personal dignity Christianity should preserve even as the world modernized around them. This message was probably deliberately ambiguous: on the one hand the Church continued to portray women's roles as sacrificing helpmeets and mothers, but on the other hand there was clearly a need for women's activism in mass society to keep a majority vote out of the hands of the Left. The Catholic Church saw itself as threatened not only by communism, but also by the worldliness and materialism of American-style modernity; women, defenders of tradition and piety, would have to work on both fronts. The Church preferred to encourage women not to take paid work outside the home. Nonetheless, part of mediating women's entrance into mass society was not just recognizing their new political rights, but the inevitable fact that women were and would continue to work outside the home and therefore gain access to education and careers. In this same period women began to win the right to be consecrated virgins and yet live alone and unconnected to any convent or institute and unsupervised by a male priest. Female DC leaders from Tina Anselmi to Rosy Bindi would embrace this new choice, one that allowed a woman to live a solitary life as neither wife nor mother, yet consecrated to God, and in total engagement with the world and the civil community.[45]

Pius XII's ambiguous message reflected the Church's growing, yet guarded, acceptance of new forms of feminine identity and thus the paradox that would trouble Catholic women's political activism over how to simultaneously defend new and traditional gender roles for women. The Cold War undoubtedly played an important part in inciting the competition for women's loyalty to one or the other polarized ideological loyalty, as well as providing two broad models for the new Italian woman. American propaganda of this period emphasized the importance of a liberal capitalist model of society with a nuclear family characterized by a gendered division of labor: a companionate marriage anchored by a breadwinning father and a cheerfully efficient consumer-manager of a mother. At the same time the Soviet model of an emancipated and educated working woman was extremely attractive to many on the left who saw in the new people's democracies a better model for social justice.

These choices may have been extremely fraught for Catholic Italians, who were clear about their anticommunism and their embrace of American modernity, but who were troubled by the consumerism, racial and class inequality, and media-inspired violence and oversexualization that seemed to characterize American culture. Indeed, Italian women did not wholly or uncritically embrace either Soviet or American gender models.[46] Given these ambiguities, women of the Lost Wave who had already chosen public roles and who had therefore been, like Maria Federici, guilty of disobedience to the Church's wishes, felt relieved that Pius XII had sanctioned their activity. At least the Church had sent a positive signal: the previous admonition to women from a pope ran in the old folk rhyme *"La tasa, la piasa, la staga a casa"* ("Let her be quiet, let her be pleasing, let her stay at home").[47]

Angela Guidi Cingolani, first female speaker in the *Consulta,* took the Pope's *"casa"* versus *"mondo"* trope farther to unambiguously defend women's political activism. "Woman is the home, and the home is the world," she argued in an article published in the Catholic journal *Il Popolo* in 1945, "and the participation of women in political life is justified by her indisputable duty to make her mission as spouse and mother as effective as possible."[48] This call to "political life" was not limited to the Catholic point of view; the entire Lost Wave seems to have embraced this version of women's rights discourse. The women of UDI also articulated their wishes for constitutional equality as being composed of legal equality, the right to work, and protection for mothers. Though the women of the Lost Wave were of course fulfilling—and reshaping—roles far more complex and non-traditional than "effective spouse and mother," that definition of their public role could attract women (and men) more conservative than or less politicized than they were, and so sustained the mass character of associationism.[49] CIF continues to this day to frame its social mission in political terms, affirming the importance of women's contribution to the *res pubblica*, and the need for their dignity and equality in civil society in order to preserve a democratic state.[50] Guidi Cingolani and the women of the Lost Wave did not reject the conventional identities of wife and mother; but they directed their activism toward enlarging those identities until they encompassed every possible opportunity; denying the Pope's division between the public and private spheres, affirming that all Italian citizens deserved women's care and that the whole world had become women's home to claim.

|| 2 ||

Gender Roles in Italy's Elections and Constitution

The "first forty-five," the group of women elected to the first Republican Parliament of 1948–1953, was an exceptional group of highly educated, accomplished, radical, militant women. This select group of women was responsible for creating and carrying out the dominant legislative strategy of constitutional rights feminism. First by blazing the trail for female political candidates and election campaigning, then by writing women's citizenship into the new constitution, and finally by serving in the early Parliamentary legislatures to pass new women's rights laws, it was the first forty-five who truly wrote the Lost Wave into history as a feminist movement. Yet these women could not stand apart from the rest of Italy's female citizens. They needed to build constituencies, campaign networks, and paths to mass participation in politics among women throughout the nation.

If the postwar women's associations had trouble establishing autonomy from male political hierarchies, the first forty-five parliamentarians' negotiations among colleagues, association, and political parties often proved even more fraught. Party hierarchy and electoral platforms played such a key role in the recruitment of candidates that the aspiring woman politician could seem at times like little more than a pawn of party politics.[1] In part this reflects the challenges of the transition to mass democracy in a parliamentary system based on multi-party proportional representation. In 1946 the PCI had about 240,000 women members and the DC 253,000.[2] For most of the postwar period, in a voting public where women were 52% of registered voters and had a turnout rate of around 90%, women comprised about 25% of total PCI membership (a figure of 2,225,000, so women would have been around 550,000) and about 35% of total DC membership.[3] The DC obtained almost 50% of the entire national 1948 vote but in subsequent elections always garnered around 40%, while the PCI averaged between 19 and 26% of the vote in the 1948–1963 period.[4] The DC could not rule alone without a pure 50%-plus-one majority so always had to form coalition governments. The PCI needed to attract as many voters as possible to remain a relevant opposition voice, and also tried to keep the rest of the parties of the left in its orbit (and out of DC coalitions) while dominating them with its larger numbers.[5] Because of these electoral goals, the two most important parties of the Cold War struggle in Italy were also the two most similar parties in terms of structure and strategy. While minority parties like the Liberals (PLI) or the Radicals (PRI) appealed only to their own narrow bases and counted on the few parliamentary seats they won in Italy's proportional election system to be the veto voice of coalitions, the DC and the PCI pursued a politics of mass democracy, casting as wide a net as possible rather than posing as ideologically pure organizations.[6] The DC and the PCI also controlled vast resources to recruit, reward, and discipline candidates. Useful party boosters received patronage jobs in local administration, generous donors were awarded lucrative construction contracts and energy licenses, and candidates who were faithful to the party line were placed at the top of electoral ballots, guaranteeing them first pick of the parliamentary seats won by the party. Since voters marked their party preference first and then had a limited number of preferential votes to award to individual candidates, most candidates could not afford to count on preferential votes and had to depend on their party to gain office.

Female voters were indispensable to the parties' claim to enact mass democracy in the new Italy, so the parties used campaign rhetoric aimed at what they considered female interests and offered many female candidates on their ballots in early elections. Women politicians continually had to maneuver to take advantage of the party's aid without succumbing to its instrumentalization. Keeping the progress of women and women's issues alive required considerable horse-trading on the part of a parliament member. Just as the party hierarchy required her to project a positive public image for the party if she wanted to be on the ballot, so she required her party to support her legislative campaigns if it wanted her to deliver her female constituents' votes and membership cards.[7]

Each party emphasized the primacy of the family, an aspect of the image campaign that particularly impacted women's political careers. The DC and the PCI competed to promise the best road to recovery after the war and Fascism, and both deployed the symbol of a happily reunited, stable, and prosperous family unit to sway voters. The demand that candidates fulfill this image of respectable and serene patriarchs and matriarchs circumscribed politicians' personal lives and weighed more heavily on women than on men. PCI women in particular suffered from the party's defensiveness about Catholic attacks on communist immorality. Its (not entirely unjustified) paranoia about persecution and spying from the state and the American intelligence community resulted in strict rules of behavior, originally designed to protect conspirators in clandestine conditions in party cells, well into peacetime.[8] The personal lives of women in the PCI had to be completely above reproach, and no personal matter was considered private. Women in the DC could emulate two main models and still appear respectable: one was the good wife and mother whose politics came from her maternal duties, the other the chaste virgin who dedicated herself to the service of others. It was harder for PCI women to be single and escape suspicion; if they weren't married and/or old, they were likely to be seen as sexually promiscuous and morally loose. In her autobiography, antifascist militant Tina Pizzardo recounted the splash she made upon her arrival in Rome when the Communist party was still underground and she initiated contact with her new cell members:

> "Here's our Torinese comrade," [my host] announced with a little smile to a table exclusively of men. That little smile and the surprising warmth of my welcome, a noisy festive exclamation—it would have been totally different back in puritan Turin—are explained right away by my new comrades themselves: everyone knows that women in the party are all ugly and malformed and usually old to boot. Imagine what they were expecting from [my description as] a comrade from Turin with spectacles and a degree in mathematics! They would never have imagined me . . .[9]

This episode is told with some self-deprecating humor, but heralds an image problem for women politicians. They needed to erase the stereotype of old ugly women being the only ones who would be party members and replace it with an image of the politically active woman as attractive and natural. Yet that attractive image could not be overtly sexual, a stereotype with equally damaging potential. The lovely and sensual Pizzardo suffered politically as well as emotionally for her affair with the antifascist author Cesare Pavese, who blamed "the husky-voiced woman" for his arrest by Fascist secret police. Her beauty and personable manner, combined with her unmarried status, made her sexually suspect, leading her comrades to accept without question that she had been at fault.

The unsubtle personal chauvinism of one's own comrades was difficult for a woman politician.[10] An obvious double standard operated as male politicians pursued their romantic lives freely yet demanded that female politicians maintain respectable public images as desexualized wives and mothers. Male activists and elected politicians went relatively unpunished for changing partners, companions, and marriages, partially as a result of the displacement of war, but women whose companions or husbands left them, or who merely remained single and childless, found their names removed from election ballots, for fear that they would expose the party to accusations of supporting free love and the dissolution of the family. The Communist Party Secretary Palmiro Togliatti was relatively immune from criticism when he left his wife Rita Montagnana and made public his relationship with the young Nilde Iotti around 1949. Although this had made the party vulnerable to accusations of immorality from the right, he was protected by both his powerful position and his masculinity. But both Iotti and Montagnana, previously easily elected to the Constituent Assembly in 1946, had trouble getting renominated. Indeed Montagnana's political career was essentially over by 1950. Iotti went on to have a fabulously and historically successful career, but she only became a member of the party's central committee in 1956, after Togliatti's death, and even then many party colleagues crossed out her name on the list when they voted. While most men in the party said they supported the idea of women's emancipation and legal equality as a measure of modernity and democratic legitimacy, they did not perceive how those goals should change their own behavior and expectations about women or their relationships with women. Even though she was a standout in the party after having served as the first woman minister of government during the liberation in Piedmont, Gisella Floreanini was not even made a candidate in 1946 because she was separated from her husband, having gotten a divorce in Switzerland that was illegal and unrecognized in Italy. Teresa Noce was certain her removal as the executive of the party was due to the controversial way Luigi Longo had left her and obtained an annulment of their marriage without her knowledge or consent. His leadership position was unaffected.[11] Women's marital status, in other words, played a key role in their perceived fitness for political office in a way it simply did not for men.

The double standard also applied to forms of service to the party. Women were officially encouraged by their parties to create initiatives, to recruit more women, and to campaign for women's issues, but they were to do so in their own associations or auxiliary groups. What's more, while they were called off their own projects to work for general campaigns whenever an important election or parliamentary vote approached, they could expect little or no help from the men of the party for "women's work," and often had to provide their own funding. Women had learned long before that social assistance could be an effective form of grassroots political work and saw it as a way to expand mass participation in democracy. But the men of their parties associated such work with their memories of clandestinity and the Resistance, when politics were restricted to hidden and informal activities. They were eager to leave that period of humiliating impotence behind and reclaim the formal halls and chambers of government. Party culture was an important part of the political apprenticeship of the first members of Parliament, but it was far from the supportive, liberating experience provided by the partisan brigades of the Resistance and the women's movement. The women had to become part of a very masculine world, assimilate to its ways and especially its arcane rules, and quickly complete their apprenticeships in political life while the men were already accustomed to and privileged in it. The women ran the risk of becoming only "living statues," monuments to women's courage in the Resistance and pretty images of patriotic motherhood, and losing hold of the very initiatives they prioritized out of their Resistance experience.[12]

Although success in the first elections was often a lonely victory for these women, it positively influenced their leadership of the Lost Wave movement. Their lack of patronage from their parties explains their reliance on the support of associations and the strategy of going to the voters, particularly the women, to expand grassroots participation, win legislative campaigns, and achieve re-election. The solidarity of women in politics became a fundamental part of the Lost Wave's practice and vision of democracy. As historian Mariuccia Salvati describes, in the aftermath of Fascism and in the context of Italy's competing ideological subcultures, political organizations portrayed themselves not just as defenders of the family but as extended family structures, "emphasizing the feeling of belonging."[13] Women's associations deepened the connection between social work and politics, expanding the realm of the political to all those social and cultural practices that were characterized by collective action and decision-making.[14] The need to belong, to rebuild trust in mass institutions of civil society and of politics, and to find aid from community social services was an important aspect of reconstruction in postwar Italy. Lost Wave women made use of the distinctly feminine role of nurturing and assistance available in traditional gender norms to enlarge their political participation and to garner mass consent for women's activism.

In addition this connection between the social and the political helped anchor a more fruitful understanding of rights and citizenship: that rights are not possessions, that the privileges and duties of citizenship are relationships among people. Female activists promoted the view that rights are those rules that govern what people can do in relation to each other; having them means moving from an understanding of oneself as acted upon by the state and towards an identity as a protagonist, a woman who makes government respond to her.[15] It was the first forty-five's relationship with ordinary women citizens, not with their respective parties, that made the difference between women having political rights and actually participating in democracy. Women may have had rights but they were invited to abstain from using them as either voters or candidates for political office by their lack of support from their parties, money, extra time, autonomy, and authority relative to men.[16] The fight to represent women citizens and to fulfill women's constitutional rights would help bolster a global redefinition of citizenship as "active": participatory, grassroots, open to all and beneficient to all.

For many of the first forty-five, it was thus more important to be the "women's representative" than it was to be a representative of the party. While making party politics fraught, this would have the positive effect of insulating these women from some of the divisiveness of the Cold War and allowing them to continue cooperating in ways their male colleagues, who were inextricably bound to the patronage structure of their party, simply could not afford.

For all these women politics were central to the course of their lives, and they shared a passion and a certainty that they were making history in being a part of the national Parliament. Also common to all was the growing understanding that women's issues were urgent, important, and integral to the continuing strength and development of that institution as part of a democratic system. This urgency led many to accept sacrifice of personal priorities as a necessity of political leadership. "I intend to harmonize my life as a militant with the rest of my life," Gisella Floreanini insisted in her writing; but that attempt at reconciliation of public and private in the lives of a cohort of women with an intense passion relationship for politics was a wrenching aspect for many.[17] Even those who married, stayed married, and had children—and who used marriage and motherhood as part of their public and political image—would later admit that they had had to give the raising of their children and the care of their husbands to housekeepers and grandparents. Floreanini argued that the very fact that it was a painful choice for women made women's political militancy morally superior to men's and led female politicians to always tend toward the revolutionary, while men could afford to be reformist because they could live politics in continuity with the rest of their worlds.[18] Ada Gobetti, elected vice-mayor of Turin upon Liberation, wrote in her diary of her anxiety as she contemplated the governance of the city: "when I think of the responsibility I am about to assume before a disoriented population in need of everything, materially and morally, of the difficulties of every type that will arise in the resolution of every little problem just to return the people to a modest level of civilization after years of forcing them to live by the law of the jungle—I confess that I lose my breath." She described meeting the men who had been elected to other city offices: "I thought that my future colleagues—even if older and more expert than me—must be feeling the same worries. The two I met with today were instead tranquil and satisfied like heirs who finally take over possession of a patrimony to which they have always had right and about which all doubts have at last been removed."[19] Her sentiment is also descriptive of the first impressions of the first women members of Parliament when they entered Palazzo Montecitorio. Awed by the responsibility and authority of the office they were about to assume, they were both shamed and angered by their male colleagues' attitude of entitlement.

The Lost Wave women's creation of a public persona, an image used to approach voters and to invite consensus for women's rights, was therefore critical. To play the role of powerful parliamentarian, confident and comfortable working in an overwhelmingly masculine environment, in an institution with its own obscure traditions and etiquette, women needed to reinvent some of their gender identity. PCI representative Lalla Festa confessed in a 1979 interview: "When I entered the party I had in me all the disadvantages, all the limits of being a woman. To begin with, not knowing how to speak. I succeeded in conquering it, but I did it by learning the language of politics, learning to speak as a man."[20] The women parliamentarians had extremely full professional schedules and little time for a personal or family life. In addition to being in session in committee and assembly, and traveling to campaign for the party, most needed to remain intensely involved in associationism. They had to be representatives, networkers, liaisons with institutions, and publicizers of parliamentary policy, while at the same time constantly exhorting other women to be involved in local initiatives.

Most of the women deputies learned to juggle these expectations, no matter the personal cost, and even to use them to construct public images that they offered as new gender ideals. During electoral campaigns, they compensated for a lack of newspaper space by doing interviews and photo shoots for women's magazines. Election rhetoric exalted the maternal and feminine qualities of female candidates, showing them in photos with their babies in their arms whenever possible. In order to communicate a universally understandable and sympathetic image, even "professional revolutionaries" presented themselves as mothers and wives.[21] As Marisa Rodano put it, "You have many children, you are fat and you have long hair. A women's leader has to be that way."[22] Women practiced various forms of self-fashioning to attract voters with their respectable femininity and their non-threatening ambition. The Roman resistance heroine Carla Capponi was surprised when her former partisan comrade Adele Bei, who "made a show of being nearly illiterate," became a member of the Constitutional Assembly and revealed that she was capable of speaking, as well as reading and writing, English, French, and a bit of Russian as well as Italian.[23] Miriam Mafai described the search for a woman who could be everything to everyone, saying that women activists had to be double personalities, "having the qualities of both a man and a woman": both a militant and a good mother, intelligent, expert on party policy, with the stamina to last through all-night meetings; but also modest, self-effacing, and more self-sacrificing than a man. Laura Diaz famously joked that the PCI leaders wanted "Lenin's brain in Marilyn Monroe's body."[24]

Some of the women of the Lost Wave avoided the demands of the idealized maternal image and the pitfalls of sexuality another way. They sought to expand the category of femininity through emphasizing other aspects of their identity, particularly the modern image of the working woman. This worked particularly well in the Communist party, whose theory held that women would be emancipated together with men as a class, and therefore needed to be encouraged to work outside the home. Some women traded on their very lack of conventional femininity to avoid accusations of feminine weakness or emotionality and to more easily fraternize with their male comrades. To take an extreme example, Teresa Noce's national fame derived from her celebrated ugliness and aggressive, combative nature. Liberated from the trap of Rodano's long-haired maternal stereotype, Noce possessed a reputation that meant she did not need to hide her anger or disguise her impatience. That ugliness also made her the frequent subject of political cartoons, further contributing to her instant recognizability. She emphasized her working-class background and the fact that she had begun working as a young girl. She preferred being identified with her title as union leader to the honorific "*onorevole*" which was her right as member of parliament. The rest of the first forty-five also proudly presented themselves as workers and educated professionals. The first line of the official biography of Bianca Bianchi (PSIUP) stated that she had dual degrees in philosophy and pedagogy; Lina Cecchini (DC) noted that she had completed a doctorate. In total, thirty-four of the early women members of parliament had advanced university degrees listed in their official profiles. While nearly every member listed her marital status and the number of her children if she had them, nearly every one also listed a profession other than politician/activist; only two women self-identified as housewives. In the draft of a publicity profile submitted to her for approval, Gina Borellini (PCI) made no changes except one: at the very end, she crossed out the biographical note describing her as a housewife and, with an irritated question mark, wrote in instead "*bracciante-mondina*" (field hand-riceworker).[25] Borellini wrote "*bracciante*" because she wanted voters to see her as being qualified to citizenship and representation through her identity as a waged agricultural laborer, not as a dependent. Yet she also chose to add the strongly gendered term "*mondina*" because the popular image of the seasonal riceworkers was of extremely free, strong women who withstood the worst working conditions and had been among the first to renew labor protest after the Fascist regime tried to permanently suppress it. Given the choice of two stereotypical feminine tropes—housewife or riceworker—through which to present feminist claims, Borellini tried to make use of the one that came closer to requiring equality in citizenship, and the one that would elicit sympathy and recognize heroism.

Another role the first forty-five negotiated as part of their public images was that of the Resistance heroine. All the women jealously insisted on the recognition of the partisan experience that gave them legitimacy in their parties and in the Parliament. Every single woman in Parliament who had participated in the Resistance (forty-three of the first forty-five had official recognition as partisans, and all could claim impeccable antifascist credentials) had her *nome di battaglia* listed next to her real name in every official biography and index entry for at least the first two legislatures and, in some cases, beyond. Nadia Spano was Renato, Angela Guidi Cingolani was Eugenio, Nilde Iotti was Egidio, and Teresa Noce was Pietro and also Estella. This must have served a practical purpose, since throughout clandestinity and the war these women had met many people who would have known them only by their nom de guerre. But it was also a way to signal their Resistance credentials. The women of the Lost Wave never relinquished their Resistance-based claim to a new politics. Borellini showed her flair for public relations when, during the 1953 election campaign, *Noi donne*, the women's magazine of the Union of Italian Women, had a ten-page spread on the women candidates for Parliament, dominated by a full-page headshot of Borellini with the headline "*La santa rossa*," the "Red Saint." The accompanying article noted Borellini's heroic service as a partisan in the Resistance which led to her "sublime sacrifice" of a leg in battle against Nazi attackers; her simultaneous leadership of the women's association and veterans' league groups in Modena; and her political activism as an act of enduring dedication to the women of Modena.[26] Other articles follow this same hagiographic tone: Giuliana Nenni (the daughter of Pietro Nenni, leader of the Socialist Party) is identified as "the sister of all of Romagna's women," who is tireless in her dedication to that ultimate and universal maternal desire for peace. A profile of Ada Alessandrini, literature professor and representative of the Christian Social Movement party, celebrates her "faith in the Bible and in Socialism."[27] The images published in the early issues of *Azione femminile* (*Women's Action*), the periodical of CIF, were consistent with these themes. Beginning in 1944 every issue included portraits of women, including partisans and many nuns, who had lost their lives in the Resistance. These continued to be a feature at least until 1947, as Catholic women activists engaged in a memory project similar to that of their Communist counterparts to elevate the image of the heroic female partisan as a role model for all women citizens.[28]

This practice of Lost Wave women to create role models for the woman citizen demonstrated their own pride and solidarity as a group of exceptional women. Yet the connection they created with ordinary women voters was a two-way relationship with great symbolic value, because the inventiveness and practicality they showed in making good use of limited materials and resources was a skill celebrated in Italian femininity. Every Italian could take pride in women's capacity to rebuild and repurpose after the misery and ruin of the war. [29] Like the love that is popularly said to be the secret ingredient that turns leftovers and scraps into the favorite family dish of *ribollita*, the passionate charge of emotion and care that fed the Lost Wave's activism reunited and nourished the greater Italian family. Passion is in fact a key word that recurs in every testimony, every autobiography, every description of these women and their political careers. This term carries a distinctly gendered sense of the emotion a woman brought to politics, but it was a trope of femininity the women of the Lost Wave wielded as a strength. Although the identity of the female citizen and political leader remained anchored to her traditional role in the family, her identity was also reinvented and enriched with new values. Among these were the profound conviction that it was a feminine mission to defend the institutions of a democratic state as the highest realization of antifascist and Resistance ideals, that women should associate to be the social and political foundation of such a defense, and that it was a rewarding and exalting act to choose public service over one's private comfort, and to sacrifice one's family life to make the party or the association one's spiritual family. For the Lost Wave, this mission to remake political gender roles would bring great victories as well as troubling conflicts.

The first test of female candidates' efforts to reach out to the mass of voters took place in the context of intense anxiety and speculation as to the destiny of Italy. In the elections of 1946, the first in which Italian women were able to vote, over 52% of the 24,947,187 voters were women (12,998,131).[30] International attention was riveted by the spectacle of a nation emerging from Fascism, with a large enough Communist party to make revolution seem a real possibility, whose fate might be decided by newly enfranchised females. *New York Times* journalist Anne O'Hare McCormick devoted several of her "Abroad" columns to the novelty and significance of a women's majority. In "Bulldozer and the Woman with a Broom," she argued that Europe's previous infrastructure, both physical and social, had been destroyed, and that the women who were primarily responsible for cleaning up were also going to be primarily responsible for restoring society. The implication was that the destruction had been wrought by men, the reconciliation and rebuilding would be more legitimately done by women. Yet she worried in another column that "their [women's] vote can swing the election, but in general they are so unaccustomed and indifferent to political action that it requires a country-wide campaign of education to wake them up to the life and death importance of the present issues."[31] The Young Women's Christian Association launched an Italian reconstruction campaign using a photograph of a young woman holding a baby in a voting booth captioned, "This young mother is casting her first ballot... a new privilege for Italian women. She needs YWCA guidance in democracy."[32] The campaigns of female politicians exceeded expectations, bringing out gratifyingly high numbers of voters as 89%

of eligible women voted in the 1946 elections. They returned a mandate for a republic in the institutional referendum, ending the monarchy. An accompanying vote for the delegates to the constitutional convention (the Constituent Assembly) to write a new constitution for Italy elected twenty-one women to that body. Local council elections also elected over 2,000 female city council members to office.[33]

The image presented by O'Hare McCormick and the YWCA campaign of woman as more legitimate guarantor of social peace and reconciliation, but also as mother needing guidance, recalls the history of citizenship in the nineteenth and early twentieth centuries that had developed into dual categories, one of independent bread-winning male citizens and one of dependent female nurturers and childbearers. The processes of industrialization and the growth of the modern state (in Italy the turning point was 1871, when national unification gave rise to the *stato liberale* which was a constitutional monarchy with a very restricted male suffrage) had worked in their own gendered ways to redefine the notions of work and the public sphere, spaces inhabited in the ideology of Liberalism by free, white, bourgeois and artistocratic men whose property and education, tax paying and military service—and their responsibility for dependents in the private sphere—gave them the capacity to engage on equal footing in the decision making and representation that were the privileges of the citizen. Working class men made their way into this category by emphasizing their own stake in the public sphere through the organization of labor and the ongoing redefintion of the worker not as a dependent on his employer but as himself an independent earner of a family wage that supported his own wife and children. Feminists and women workers had challenged the exclusion of women from the public sphere and political rights, but in this period the most successful arguments for women's rights had been through maternalist claims, which not only accepted but insisted on women's difference. It was the very uniqueness of women's mission as mothers, to oversimplify these debates somewhat, that they argued required social citizenship for women. With protectionist labor laws and the aid of the state to mothers and children, women entered citizenship not through individual independence but in this gendered category of mothers of the nation.[34] These categories were represented as natural and as part of a necessary sexual order at the levels of work, family, and the state. The 1948 Italian Constitution was written in a transitional moment of trying to reimagine citizenship for a republican mass democracy; but the long-term histories of industrialization, class formation, and the growth of the state had not lost their power to shape that concept. The constituents did not dissolve citizenship's gendered categories or reject the idea of a sexual order, but women activists did strive to redefine and re-equilibrate them. These ambiguities of past, present, and future would all appear throughout the constituent assembly and the text of the constitution itself.[35]

In this period of political transition, the courtship of women voters took on great importance, especially for the parties of the Left that wanted to overturn stereotypes of women as an inherently conservative voting bloc, piously obedient to Church guidance on how to vote. The parties took action not only by recruiting female voters but also by vying to prove their democratic commitment by encouraging women's entry into the polity. The parties sought out female candidates, particularly prizing Resistance heroines. Noce remembered, "The Party decided to present women as candidates in almost every district. Naturally those chosen were the most popular, the ones who had worked most in the Resistance, who had sacrificed themselves."[36] In 1946 and again in 1948, women candidates were in great demand, as PCI women's leader Nadia Spano's wry comment indicates:

> I entered the Constituent Assembly because I wore a skirt. If I think back to the Federal Committee of those days, to the direction of the Rome Federation, there were many male comrades of my level or better.... The party wanted a woman and so I passed in front of everyone. So in a certain sense not only did being a woman not hurt me, it helped me. There were relatively a lot of women in the Constituent Assembly and also in the first legislature, from the other parties as well. And they had great importance, which doesn't necessarily show through in the minutes enough. In the months during which there was no activity in the plenary assembly, for example, the women... became the representatives for all the women of their district and their region as well, an essential element of linkage between the voters and the

> parties and organizations.... To have a deputy [at the constitutional convention] was an element of strength, of prestige, a stimulus to other women, pride for the female comrades. The women considered you "their" deputy.[37]

Here Spano discounts the publicity campaign that the party ran by choosing many women candidates merely for "wearing a skirt" by emphasizing that once elected, the women had a non-partisan agenda based on representing women's issues, regardless of party membership or constituent locale. Yet she is highlighting an important point about the constitution and its making: the members of the constitutional assembly envisioned different categories of citizenship for bodies in skirts. This would become the most deep-seated of the many ambiguities in the Constitution of 1948: it would try to break with the past by creating equal, gender-neutral citizenship rights, but it would reenshrine the dual, sexed categories of citizenship by imagining different roles and obligations for male and female citizens.

Of the 226 female candidates for the Constituent Assembly, 21 had been elected. Twelve of them were also leaders in UDI or CIF.[38] The DC won a sizable percentage of the vote (35.2), but the PCI and PSIUP (Socialist Unity Party) garnered 18.9% and 20.7% respectively, making their cooperation as the Popular Front coalition the dominant force in the Assembly.[39] The delegates got to work writing a constitution that could be presented for ratification by the spring of 1948, when national elections would take place to form the first Parliament. The United States and the Vatican abandoned moderate rhetoric in their urgency to secure the anticommunist identity of that future government: Pius XII broadcast his radio homily expressly stating that the situation had already become a clear choice "either with Christ or against Christ!"[40] For Italy, the Cold War had become the main focus of both foreign and internal politics; the United States would continue to grant assistance according to anticommunist political rather than economic criteria, while the DC would continue to emphasize the danger of the communist fifth column. The DC's strategy endeavored both to draw domestic votes and to leverage its vulnerability for ever more aid from abroad, including by 1948 the Marshall Plan. In May 1947 the U.S. Ambassador to Italy, James Clement Dunn, sent a report that unrest was spreading across Italy, leading many to predict an imminent Communist insurrection. By November the National Security Council report was focusing the American gaze firmly on Italy as the primary area of urgency. Claiming that a Communist seizure of power was likely, it authorized the initiation of "psychological warfare" and authorized funding of ten million dollars to start a program for funding election campaigns, anticommunist propaganda, and bribes.[41] Despite the Church's intense anticommunism, its discomfort in fully embracing American-style modernity was also palpable. Both Catholics and Communists were pursuing a national identity for Italy that could be more autonomous from the Atlantic alliance, and it was becoming the special mission of Italian women to provide that buffer.

The first general election, in April 1948, represented much more than the birth of Italy's first parliament. It established Italy as a flashpoint and testing site for the Cold War, particularly for American endeavors to bolster anticommunist outcomes.[42] Although most American observers of Europe saw reformist social democratic parties and trade union moderatism as the best antidote to Communist influence, in Italy the political configuration was such that this description fit the PCI itself only slightly less well than it did the DC.[43] Still, the DC was out of necessity the beneficiary of the bulk of American hopes—and funds. According to the *New York Times'* Anne O'Hare McCormick, the election results were "a vital decision," a clear choice between "the Soviet system" and "western civilization."[44] Yet even in the heat of an ugly campaign, as priests warned parishioners that voting for the PCI was a sin and posters appeared that "revealed" the PCI symbol of Giuseppe Garibaldi to be a portrait of Stalin, while the Communists paired graphic photographs of victims at Mauthausen and images of lynched African-Americans with the admonition that "This is American Democracy!" and "Hitler's executioners are today at Truman's service!", women candidates had attempted to keep their tones more moderate. When Nadia Spano was sent by the PCI to run for a seat representing Sardinia, the authorities so feared she would provoke violent anticommunist protest that she was required to speak in empty piazzas flanked by two military policemen at her public appearances. Loudspeakers carried her voice to listeners kept out of the squares by police barriers. But, she recalled in her autobiography, she tried to speak as if she were not representing Communists, and as if there were no conflicts dividing her voters and barring them from attendance. Instead she chose to address herself to all Sardinian women: "I spoke as if to a great crowd; indeed I knew that in the nearby streets, from behind the windows, the women were listening."[45] They were. She was elected with a huge preferential vote in her district, proving to her that women were voting according to a different agenda. In choosing to vote for the solidaristic women's democracy Spano described in her campaign speeches and overriding the claims of Cold War scare tactics, female voters actively influenced political culture in Italy.[46]

Luciana Viviani, a Neapolitan PCI member and daughter of the famous playwright Raffaele Viviani, had the humor to appreciate the theatrical value of the spectacle, knowing that the novelty of women politicians combined with the hunger for news from Rome to make candidates' whistle-stops into festive village events:

> They sent me to a big town where, only days before, a priest, a certain don Fiori, had pronounced offensive words against Nadia Spano, the communist deputy elected in Sardegna, accusing her of having put the atheist and freedom-killing logic of communism before her duties as wife and mother. When I got there I found an unusually full piazza awaiting me: evidently it was a great spectacle that one communist woman should speak in public in order to "defend the honor" of another communist woman.[47]

Viviani's comments highlight the damaging combination of sexual deprecation and anticommunist invective leftist women faced. And yet during this season of feverish politicking the Constituent Assembly managed to work in relative serenity. Because the Constituent Assembly was weighted nearly evenly with delegates from Right and Left and took no orders from the DC-led acting government, it remained autonomous from day-to-day governing (and U.S. interference), united in shared antifascist sentiments and experiences from the Resistance and Liberation, and therefore insulated from the mounting tensions of the Cold War. The women constituents pushing the document towards more specific and progressive language in favor of women's equality had the advantage of uncensored, cross-party discussion to exert their influence. These constituents continued to work in the optimistic and cooperative atmosphere of the days of Liberation even as the spirit of the Committees of National Liberation faded away elsewhere.[48] Even as party politics became an ugly battle outside the doors of the chamber—under the pressure of the United States' withholding of loan money, the Communist ministers were kicked out of the government in May 1947—the male constituents could not disavow the egalitarian and progressive rhetoric in vogue since 1941, and their female colleagues were able to act in extraordinary cooperation across party and ideological lines to extract every last benefit to women's rights.[49] Women's assumption of the rights and duties of citizenship proved decisive in the ability of both major mass parties' leaders to steer a central course between both the superpowers' demands and their own cadres' more extremist politics, guaranteeing stability and the affirmation of a constitutionalist democracy in Italy.[50]

Of the twenty-one women constituents, four had been further elected by their colleagues to the "Committee of 75," a smaller group given the task of writing a constitutional draft for the entire Assembly to debate and vote upon. Nilde Iotti, Teresa Noce, Lina Merlin, and Maria Federici were key to articulating the theory of women's citizenship embodied in the Italian Constitution.[51] In particular Maria Federici and Angela Merlin cooperated again and again to defend the explicit inclusion of women and women's rights in the Constitution. Merlin proposed that Article 3 include sex as one of the factors on the basis of which a citizen could not be discriminated against. Federici argued in favor of Merlin's proposal on May 22, 1947:

> I remind you, and it is by now a principle recognized by all Constitutions, that sex must no longer be a discriminating factor for the enjoyment of civil and social rights. It is strange that women, who nevertheless pay taxes and support all the duties of social life, shouldn't also have the ability to follow their careers in conditions of equality with men. I hope this is the last time that a Constitution has to mention, in order to claim them, women's rights; the last time that women have to demand their rights from men.[52]

Despite setbacks and some resistance from male colleagues, Federici and Merlin insisted until Article 3 was accepted as part of the constitution. It read as follows:

> All citizens have equal social dignity and are equal before the law, without distinction of sex, race, language, religion, political opinions, or personal or social condition. It is the duty of the Republic to remove all social or economic obstacles which, limiting de facto the liberty and equality of citizens, impede the full development of the human beings and the effective participation of all workers in the political, social, and economic organization of the country.

In addition to this article, the women made sure that the draft presented to the plenary Assembly included Article 37, which guaranteed women equal rights in the workplace; and Article 29, which stipulated that spouses are juridically and morally equal. In both of these last two articles, when finally approved, inequality snuck in through the back door: Article 37 said these rights at work had to respect the necessities of "*l'essenziale funzione familiare della donna*" (the essential familial function of women), and Article 29 noted "*i limiti stabiliti dalla legge a garanzia dell'unità familiare*" (the limits established by the law to guarantee family unity). Nonetheless, the inclusion of explicit guarantees of women's citizenship rights in the Constitution made the entire strategy of the first three legislatures possible: the first forty-five could fight for women's rights by insisting on the unconstitutionality of discrimination, they could demand "*adeguamento costituzionale delle leggi*," that is that all laws be reconciled with constitutionality. Not only the statement of women's equality but even more crucially the phrase committing the Republic to "remove all… obstacles" to liberty endorsed this activist potential of constitutionalist politics. These women had not only guaranteed that possibility for formal political and civil rights but also equal rights in the realm of family and maternity. Maria Federici, who, as a Catholic argued for loans and insurance to protect marriage and for family salaries instead of, like Noce and Merlin, more guarantees for working women's independence, still defended the social value of women's unpaid work and of maternity as topics belonging in the Constitution. She even argued for state salaries and pensions for motherhood: "The old age of mothers must be guaranteed in conformity with the principle that the maternal mission and domestic work are not less important for the collective than any other possible productive activity." She went on to argue that the state should also pay for the health care costs of pregnancy and abortion for every woman; Federici thus demonstrated how her Catholicism was not an obstacle to her feminist beliefs.[53]

In Italy women's antifascism enabled them to cooperate across Cold War lines and fight for women's rights as the guarantor of emerging democracy. Since France and West Germany shared the same context of emerging from fascism and creating a democratic constitution, it seems logical they would produce similar feminist results. While this is not precisely the case, the comparisons are illuminating.[54] In the fall of 1948, sixty-five representatives were delegated by state legislatures in the British, French, and US zones of occupation to meet in Bonn, Germany to formulate a Basic Law, the *Grundgesetz* (as a symbol of their hope for a reunification of the two Germanies, the West Germans preferred not to call this a constitution in order to reserve that name for a document founding that future state). While only four of the representatives at Bonn were women, in terms of percentages women were better represented there than they were in Italy's Constitutional Assembly. As in post-Fascist Italy, all of the delegates to Bonn agreed in a basic sense that the Nazi regime had been misogynist, and that Germany needed to make a clean break from its past. A democratic Germany would explicitly guarantee women's equal rights. But beyond this, there was little consensus. While some called for an explicit guarantee of women's equality in all respects, others felt that there should be no significance laid upon sexual difference, not even for the special protection of women in some areas, like maternity. Some delegates argued that the equality of male and female workers followed directly from their equality as citizens, while others again warned that it must be explicitly articulated in each separate case. There was disagreement as to whether the private sphere was different, or subject to the same laws as the public. Many felt that the power relationship of husbands and wives, mothers and fathers could not be and did not need to be legislated.[55]

Elisabeth Selbert, a fifty-two-year-old lawyer and expert in constitutional affairs from the Social Democratic Party (SPD), argued in the Parliamentary Council for the inclusion of Article 3 guaranteeing sexual equality in the Basic Law like that defended by Maria Federici and Lina Merlin in Italy. She pointed out that the women who during the war years had stood atop the rubble and replaced men at the workplace had earned their moral right to have equal rights to men. She was, however, wrong to assume that everyone agreed that the recent experience had proven women's equal citizenship. The first time it came to a vote the Council voted down the article. Only an impassioned response on the part of the public, in the form of delegations to the council members and letters to the editor in newspapers, prompted it to reconsider and then approve it. This public response signaled women's sense of their new citizenship in a democratic Germany. Women had gotten the vote in Germany in 1918 with the Weimar Republic's constitution, but after the apocalyptic destruction of the war they were deeply engrossed by the effort to clear the rubble and reconstruct their lives, and were therefore somewhat apolitical and apathetic about the constituent assembly. A poll in March 1949 showed that 48% of West German women declared themselves indifferent to the constitution (over 30% of men felt the same way). Yet public opinion did make itself known when it came to defending a woman-friendly formulation of Articles 3 and 6 (Article 6 placed marriage, motherhood, and the family under the particular protection of the state).[56] Selbert was suddenly revealed as a major spokesperson for women's interests.

Although the delegates to Bonn were overwhelmingly male, the women delegates played a crucial role in pushing the language of the document to more explicit and progressive guarantees. Like their Italian counterparts, they anticipated a hard road ahead for women's rights if they failed to include the basis for implementation in the Basic Law's articles. But the Basic Law set a time limit for laws needed to make the civil code conform to its articles. If new positive laws were not passed by March 31, 1953, all laws that did not conform would become invalid. This automatic abrogation of unconstitutionally discriminatory laws would hand power over to the courts for the final decision on each individual aspect of the civil code as it pertained to women. This deadline was in fact activated as German legislators failed to rewrite civil code laws, and a number of interesting court cases were brought to force clarification of women's and family rights until the *Bundesverfassungsgericht's* (Federal Constitutional Court) sentence in 1959 redefined the relevant parts of the Civil Code.[57] As in Italy, the final effect of the council at Bonn was to commit abstractly to a progressive constitutional guarantee of women's equal rights in the political and economic realms, but to leave untouched the legacy of patriarchal family regimes and prioritization of motherhood before all other women's roles in the private sphere. The work of actually achieving women's equality and reconciling public and private standards was abandoned by legislators and left to the individual citizens themselves.

The low numbers of women delegates and the overall sense of apathy towards formal politics reinforced a major difference between the German and Italian experiences. All of the German parties made direct appeals to women voters, but despite protestations from women party members, none included corresponding numbers of women as candidates to the Bundestag (the West German parliamentary body). The male candidates simply presented themselves as effective advocates for both genders. A total of only 29 women (out of 402 total seats) entered the first Bundestag in 1949, split almost evenly between Social Democrats and the conservative coalition, with 2 from the FDP, Free Democratic Party.[58] In Italy a cohort of women politicians became the representatives of women's interests in the legislature and, sustained by a mass movement of women in the associations, advocated for those rights left imperfectly defined and unfulfilled. In West Germany there was no such reciprocal relationship between grassroots coordination and parliamentary representation, and no united women's lobby emerged.

In France the immediate postwar experience was also comparable to Italy's: both countries were emerging from fascism and occupation, and both had provisional governments that used women's first suffrage as demonstrations of their commitment to widening political participation to ensure true democracy. Even before Liberation, the Consultative Assembly in Algiers had voted to enfranchise women on March 22, 1944; and on August 25, 1944 General de Gaulle issued a decree that gave women's suffrage legal force.[59] French women, for their part, had participated to a great extent in the Resistance and in wartime civil society and felt that they had provided ample proof of "deserving" their full citizenship. As in

Italy, the assumed naturalness of the suffrage at Liberation papered over the radicalism of the suffrage fight conducted for decades by first-wave feminists and the intensity of opposition that they faced. According to the government's version of this milestone, women's suffrage was not a feminist issue but simply a conventional proof of governmental legitimacy in the modern West. Though the fascist government in Vichy from 1940 to 1944 had tried to turn back the clock on the achievements of the prewar Third Republic, the Resistance had reinvigorated the Left, especially the Communist Party (PCF in France). In France as in Italy, Resistance ideals dominated the imagination of the constitutional framers so that the document guaranteed equal rights to both women and men, and made a great leap in enlarging social rights for all citizens. But as in Germany, the political and social equality guaranteed to women as individuals again conflicted with the articulation of family policy; married women remained legally subordinate to their husbands, who continued to be considered *chefs de famille* as in the Napoleonic Code, and patriarchalism was presumed to be the continuing norm of the private sphere.

Like Germany, France moved more quickly to uphold some of these principles than did Italy: the right of equal pay for equal work was confirmed by Labor Ministry policy in June 20, 1946, and the minister of state, Maurice Thorez, on October 5, 1946 issued a statute ensuring women equal employment opportunity. Indeed both decisions were made by the Popular Front government before the ratification of a new constitution or the opening of legislative business in the National Assembly.[60] In Italy, women activists would campaign and negotiate for years before obtaining either of these rights: Teresa Noce spent virtually her entire career on various aspects of women's employment equality, while the young Christian Democrat Maria Cocco's fight for women's access to the magistracy wasn't successful until 1963. Lina Merlin, who effected legislation on state-run brothels, had her French counterpart in the senator and Resistance hero of nearly the same age, Marthe Richard. Yet while Richard successfully demanded the end of state regulation of prostitution in 1946, Merlin's fight lasted ten years. In France, male government leaders were ready to behave as a progressive, if authoritarian, avant garde whether or not the population agreed; in Italy, though these laws took longer to pass, they were passed by grassroots campaigning, indicating that they reflected the opinion of the populace and were a result of the ongoing practice of active democracy. French laws reforming family hierarchy were slow in coming: only in July 1965 was marriage law reformed to create equality between spouses in the administration of common property and in moral and material responsibilities.[61] Indeed, between the years 1946 and 1965 no law specifically addressing women's rights was passed in France. The elected legislatures of the entire Fourth Republic (1946–1958) did not improve women's rights, nor did General de Gaulle show interest in the problem upon his return and the foundation of the Fifth Republic. And even those early victories occurred more by decree than by legislative consensus. From this, it appears that women's rights in France remained more a rhetorical instrument for the government than a passionate issue of the people.

The nearly two-decade legislative gap in France does not reflect the real amount of debate and activism over women's issues in those years, but it starkly contrasts with the constant flurry around implementation in Italy during the same period. An explanation lies in the difference in women's representation and the strength of a mass women's movement supporting those women politicians in Italy as compared to France or Germany. Not only did men keep a stranglehold on party politics in France, but women's politics did not take hold in the postwar popular imagination either.[62] Women came together to agitate around individual issues several times, for example the legalization of birth control, which saw the 1956 organization of the *Mouvement Français pour le Planning Familial.* Yet a lasting and unified national movement for women's rights, which defined those rights as essential to overall democracy, regardless of the specific issue, did not materialize until after 1968 with second-wave feminism.[63] It thus appears that Italy may claim the distinction of the most grassroots and democratic push for women's rights.

Returning to Italy, a moment during the days of the Constituent Assembly takes on new relative significance. During a committee meeting to discuss the formulation of those articles dealing with the family, Piero Calamandrei, an august figure of Italian politics and culture who had been professor of jurisprudence at the University of Florence, a founding member of the Action Party, and one of the most influential legal experts in the framing of the Constitution, was against including the equality of spouses in the Constitution and in favor of affirming within it the indissolubility of marriage. After presenting religious and moral arguments in support of a patriarchal view of the family, he added that since the entire corpus of current law was against spousal parity, it would need to be entirely rewritten if the Constitution were to proclaim equality—something he said simply couldn't be done. Maria Maddalena Rossi, a Communist who had been a partisan fighter and was at that time president of UDI, fired back, saying she was putting Calamandrei on notice that in fact there was now a force in Italy with the intention to change the entire civil code, and that force was Italian women.[64] The other women on the committee had already been complaining about their male colleagues' willingness to compromise by resorting to generic formulations with the proviso "according to the conditions established by law," rather than confronting the specifics of controversial women's rights questions. The reliance on established law was essentially an acceptance of the Fascist and Liberal regimes and specifically their sexist, but also authoritarian and antidemocratic, tendencies.[65] The women constituents, on the contrary, saw their work in the assembly as precisely what Calamandrei wanted to avoid: the formulation of articles that would require positive laws to be written anew, the creation of a constitution that would abrogate those old discriminatory laws and found a new, antifascist and democratic state. So it was important to them to insist on specific language as often as possible and not to consider themselves bound by extant law or legal tradition.[66] As it happened, the amendments and compromises of working politics meant that women constituents rarely succeeded in getting their own extremely specific language approved, but they continually pushed their colleagues to more rigorous formulations of rights which explicitly affirmed the framers' intentions to guarantee equality among all citizens.

Maria Federici argued that the women constituents understood their election by a prevalently female electorate as a mandate to guarantee women's interests: the affirmation of women's rights, the rights of women workers, and reform of family law. In addition to the recognition of individual rights, "the legal freedoms," she said, women wanted to be able to affirm their social influence, their equal access to the workplace and marketplace, and their right to protection from exploitation of their work and their property.[67] This meant that the Constitution had to affirm women's equal rights not just of citizenship but also as workers and within the family. It was crucial that social rights become as valid as political and civil rights. It is one of the peculiarities of the Italian Constitution that it so strongly emphasizes labor rights as citizenship rights. This is clear from its opening line, which states, "Italy is a Democratic Republic, founded on labor." As the constituents saw it, labor rights give concrete reality to the social rights of citizenship just as the vote gave concrete reality, a voice, to the political rights of citizenship.[68] Working in the Constituent Assembly's Third Subcommittee, which wrote Article 51,[69] Teresa Noce was put in charge, along with Maria Federici and Lina Merlin, of the article dealing with economic and social guarantees for the family. Federici had proposed that the rights of women workers, especially if they were heads of family, would be best protected by the following text: "Female workers who are heads of family are assured the same rights as male heads of family, to be integrated with social services dedicated to the safeguarding of maternity and infancy." This and other proposals on women workers by the three women were eventually subsumed into a proposal that there be a section of the article which read, "Women workers have all the same rights in labor relations as recognized for male workers." This was approved.[70]

This very attempt to simultaneously uphold both a "logic of solidarity," that is, the rights of social groups, and a conception of individual human rights as the basis of citizenship highlights the ambiguities in the rights of women as defined by the constitution.[71] Teresa Noce had to contend with Article 37's wording that working women have equal rights but that working conditions must allow women to carry out their "essential role in the family." Maria Cocco had to argue that Article 51's similar qualifying phrase was not meant to affect its assertion that women were eligible for all public offices. One article in particular created a conflict between women's freedoms and the state's interest in enforcing family stability. Article 29 reads, "The Republic recognizes the rights of the family as a natural society founded on matrimony. Matrimony is based on the moral and legal equality of the spouses within the limits established by law to guarantee family unity."[72] This articulation represents a major compromise between the Catholic and leftist forces in the Assembly. While women like Maria Maddalena Rossi, herself an unmarried Communist, had successfully fought against declaring marriage's indissolubility, the

Catholics had forcefully demanded that the family must be defended as the natural and most basic unit of society. This unit, they argued, could function in equality but only "within limits;" the law should establish in the final instance a head, or representative, and this head of household they assumed to be male.[73]

The Italian Constitution, then, is an extremely progressive document, given its adoption of human rights discourse, the sense that women's political rights were natural and inevitable as a postwar condition, and the understanding of women's participation as a fundamental guarantee of democratic government. It is a document that enshrines solidarity, community responsibility, and social rights in the fundamental definition of the Italian republic.[74] But it also displays the founders' ambivalence when it came to evaluating and making concrete the ways that asserting women's equal rights would and should affect family law, the rights of labor, and programs of social services and social citizenship. Ultimately, it was not so difficult to find approval for women's rights as individuals. But in those areas where women's equality seemed to necessitate changing the entire legal approach to family, to marriage, and to the workplace, there was decided and immovable resistance.

Though the pressure applied by Noce, Merlin, and Federici as well as the other women of the Constitutional Assembly did not entirely succeed, it laid the foundation for at least the next fifteen years of the women's movement in Italy. The conflict over a maternal identity was not so much whether to accept it as a dominant form of identity for women, but that Lost Wave women tried to define it as an identity that was not oppressive or limiting. As Nadia Spano later said, "There were 21 of us, we worked a great deal, and I believe not too poorly; since the Constitution has never been an obstacle for women's battles. We were looking to the future."[75] She was understating the case, but the sentiment is powerful. The Constitution has been an aid, not an obstacle, for the women's rights movement.

The political contributions of women also better explain how the tensions in Cold War Italy exacerbated by international conflict and internal opposition were in the end resolved without succumbing to violent ruptures.[76] The complexity of Italy's struggles for a new national identity and for international acceptance as a ranking democratic power, passing through not only a test of loyalty to democracy and constitutionalism but also a new commitment to European integration and a special partnership with the United States, were both eased and made more concrete by the contributions of women activists smoothing out the gender gaps at the political, institutional, and socio-cultural levels.[77] Subsequent chapters will show how this process worked on the quotidian level of proposing, campaigning for, and passing three specific women's rights laws.

3

Legge Noce for Working Mothers

"Madonna Tempesta"

> I had little legal or judicial knowledge. I had to study the Chamber's regulations, the Parliamentary records, the law codes from before Fascism and those from the regime... But as a worker, as a professional revolutionary, as a partisan, I had a set of experiences lacking in many of my male colleagues, even if they were professors or former parliamentarians.... I considered myself the representative of all women workers, of any political tendency, and I had to oppose those colleagues when, all too often, they forgot about women's problems.
>
> Women, to liberate ourselves as women or as workers, must first and foremost learn to say no; to say no to teachers and to fathers, to say no to bosses, no to husbands, no to colleagues when they are sure they are in the right. We must fight for our own beliefs, defend them; and never think that men, whether companions or bosses, are always right just because they are one rung higher than us in the hierarchy of power.[1]

Teresa Noce was the main proponent of the 1950 law for working mothers, which guaranteed paid maternity leave and other benefits for working women. But Noce herself presented a contradictory image which was hard to press into service as a role model for Italian women. She considered the creation of a special women's section of the PCI and Togliatti's encouragement of UDI to be a segregation of women from general politics and denounced it as "women's work." Rather, she believed that women's rights were a question of social justice and needed to be a priority for men and women working together. Yet she participated as a leader in UDI and, through her union work, formed another parallel kind of associationism. This was a woman who never consented to live at the margins. Her insistence on "saying no" made her some enemies, but she refused to let anyone forget about the women she represented and their problems. In her vision of women's citizenship, in her own embodiment of militancy, and in her indefatigable struggle to pass the legislation for working mothers, she was undeniably a woman of the Lost Wave.

This chapter narrates activity during the opening of the first Parliamentary legislature, but much of the politics of labor organization Noce was involved in was shaped by the transition from Resistance to Republic. One of the great political aims of the Resistance had been to liberate Italy ahead of the Allied armies' arrival and to prove that the various partisan brigades as represented by the Committees for National Liberation actually constituted themselves as a legitimate democratic state. Then the occupying forces would have to treat Italy as an antifascist partner. Accordingly, the initial government ministers dealing with the Anglo-American forces were appointed from the Committees for National Liberation and were carefully chosen to represent each of the political strands of the Resistance: Communist, Socialist, Action Party, Liberals, and Catholics. This was an uneasy union from the beginning, and it began to fall apart almost as soon as hostilities ended. At the local level, old scores were settled as partisan bands performed summary justice; at the national level, American anticommunism found a willing interlocutor in the Vatican and factions of the Christian Democrats. Both sides distrusted and largely disregarded official corridors of justice and state bureaucracy, correctly viewing them as bastions of twenty years of Fascist appointees. The Americans did not push hard to purge ex-Fascists, and Togliatti, as head of the Ministry of Justice, followed suit in order to pursue as much mainstream consensus as possible for his party. Though this strategy would indeed gain the Popular Front (the coalition formed by the Communist and Socialist parties) success at the ballot box, neither the U.S. State Department nor the Vatican were reassured. After the communists and socialists were expelled from the government in May

1947, mostly due to American pressure on the DC, much of the initial postwar spirit of antifascist cooperation faded throughout the political world. The April 1948 elections took place in an atmosphere of crisis, with Americans and anti-communist Italians fearing that a PCI success could mean that Italy would be drawn into the Soviet sphere of influence, as Czechoslovakia had been in February. Only the Constituent Assembly and its Lost Wave women persevered in their antifascist unity, resulting in a constitution that was the concrete, but staggeringly difficult to implement, artifact of Resistance consensus.

The opening of Italy's first Republican parliament on May 8, 1948 was a flurry of celebrations, speeches, and the serious work of committee assignments and strategy meetings. The Christian Democrats, with 456 seats of the 916 total in both the Chamber of Deputies and the Senate, formed a government, and the center-left DC leader Alcide de Gasperi was elected prime minister.[2] This near-majority was the highest percentage of the vote the DC would ever gain. Although the Popular Front coalition won 31% of seats, no Communist ministers would take—or be offered—government portfolios. Luigi Einaudi, august leader of the small Liberal Party, became the first president of the Republic. The three parties that received the most votes, the DC, PCI, and PSI, were also the delegations with women members: sixteen women from the Christian Democrats sat in the Chamber of Deputies, twenty communist women were Deputies and two were Senators, and the Socialists had two women each in the Chamber and the Senate.

The proud establishment of democratic legitimacy was overshadowed, however, by the weakening of Resistance-era cooperation. One very concrete symptom of the sectarian hostilities of this time was the *scissione sindacale,* the dissolution of the antifascist labor union into multiple unions corresponding to the mass parties.[3] Given the weakening of labor that this divide and conquer strategy represented, workers, especially women workers, who had fought so hard to regain the right to organize and to strike after Fascist prohibitions, suddenly confronted their vulnerability and lack of political protection all over again. Under these challenging circumstances, Teresa Noce, hardline communist and veteran of political activism since before World War I, impressively managed a very successful national mobilization of women workers, activists, and members of parliament between 1948 and 1950 to support the elaboration and passage of her law. The law, number 860 of 1950, guaranteed a number of protectionist benefits to working mothers in order to secure more balanced labor conditions between men and women, but its most famous and lasting effect was the very generous terms it set for maternity leave. Given Teresa Noce's contrarian personality and her strident opposition to segregated women's organizations, it seems somewhat contradictory that she dedicated her first parliamentary battle to maternity leave. But in the context of the period, with Italy's precarious position both politically and materially, there were many good reasons to address the question of women's entry into full citizenship through the discourse of motherhood.

Just as women's transgressive participation in the Resistance was made more palatable by presenting their motivation as a national "mass mothering" and their role as nurturing *staffette* rather than violent and warlike guerilla fighters, so too did these new citizens demanding rights and equality seem softer, more traditional, and reassuringly asexual as mothers seeking to protect their families. The image of the self-sacrificing mother helped the public accept that women would remain in the workplace despite calls for demobilized men to be given jobs. The woman as worker and mother, simultaneously inhabiting the productive and reproductive spheres, meant that she was disrupting the boundary between public and private. Yet after Fascism had sought to control Italians in both spheres and the war had wreaked havoc with traditional gender roles, the working mother presented by the Lost Wave offered a positive and unthreatening hybrid of public and private. The Lost Wave hoped to present this legal reform in favor of increased women's rights as a source of confidence and optimism in this period of moral anxiety.[4]

Despite the stereotype of the Italian *mamma* as a sentimental, self-sacrificing, and perhaps smothering figure, especially toward her sons, the effects and uses of the maternal image are complex and sometimes contradictory.[5] Further, the lived experience of motherhood was extremely varied and frequently diverged from that stereotype. Women of postwar Italy were able for the first time to alter and build upon this image in ways that could reflect their varied experiences and advance their goals. In the case of Noce's law on maternity leave, the strategy of constitutional rights feminism could allow women of the Lost Wave to sidestep arguments about women's proper place in society by presenting their waged work as unthreatening, even stabilizing to Italian society, and the law's urgency as a legal necessity rather than as radical gender subversion. In part, Noce's law illustrates just how central the implementation of those constitutional articles guaranteeing women's equality as citizens and as workers were to the fulfillment of the new democratic republic in Italy. On a more revolutionary level, the first thing Noce and her fellow women's rights constitutionalists did in Parliament was propose a bill to confront head-on the ambiguity of those constitutional articles that promised equality with one hand while taking away women's identities outside their "essential family function" with the other. The law did not depict women in the older maternalist vein as needing protectionist intervention by the state because of their dependence on male breadwinners or their health and medical needs; rather it asserted their rights as citizens to choose how and when to work, and how and when to have children. In requiring protection for working mothers, the Lost Wave was not eschewing political citizenship for social citizenship, but fulfilling a vision of female citizenship in which the good she did for society as worker and as mother was part of her political participation.[6]

Women's employment was an extremely topical subject in the reconstruction period, given the ambivalence about women's roles during the war and in postwar rebuilding as male soldiers, partisans, and displaced persons returned slowly and in a scattered fashion to their homes and jobs. Within Noce's own party, the economic analysis of work and the working class, when focused on women, produced the "emancipationist" line of the PCI in regards to women's liberation, the belief that women's liberation could only come about in so much as they belonged to the proletariat and shared in the liberation of the proletariat. Therefore the party had a duty to encourage women to join the workforce.[7] This was considered the "*linea togliattiana*," Togliatti's policy, which at its worst equated women's rights with the right to work, but at its best represented a diverse and ongoing commitment to ensuring women equal access to all jobs and equal treatment in the workplace.

Given the centrality of work in the new constitution, Noce was not the only deputy who looked first to the workplace when searching for a bill to propose. As many as four other women parliamentarians also proposed laws protecting various categories of working women or maternity rights.[8] But only Teresa Noce had the background and the personality to propose the reform and to galvanize a mass campaign from the grassroots. How she came to wield so much power is less well-known than its impact. Her life has been obscured by her own prolific autobiographizing. She wrote three book-length memoirs and gave numerous interviews and testimonials, detailing her political awakening as a young working-class girl in Turin; her first job delivering bread to workers on construction sites at the age of six; her first strike at the age of eleven; her role as a socialist youth group leader in the protests and occupations in 1919–1920, the so-called *biennio rosso*; her arrests, beginning in 1923; her many years abroad in exile in the Spanish Civil War, France, and Russia; her clandestine reentries into Italy and her participation in the Resistance as "Estella" and her internment in concentration camps in 1939–1941 and 1943–1945. She was less straightforward about her courtship, marriage, and eventual abandonment by Luigi Longo, a PCI leader; her struggles as a woman in the party to gain power in her own right; and her relationships with her sons, whom she often had to leave in the care of others to do her political work and one of whom died in infancy. These she tries to gloss over as either self-evident in their meaning or humorous opportunities for her to display her single-mindedness.[9] When asked by the journalist and second-wave feminist Camilla Cederna in an interview what kind of difficulties she had as a woman in the party, Noce replied: "Absolutely none. With my character, if I ran into difficulties I was happy because they stimulated me to conquer them. Maybe by arguing and fighting my way madly through, because I have always been a fighter. But it's important to remember that at the beginning it was the women to act; in Torino in 1917 it was we women who protested against the war, barricades and all."[10]

Noce's autobiographic tone is firm and without hesitation; she rarely admits to a doubt or preoccupation, constantly referring to her "*caratteraccio*" and "*testaccia dura*" (difficult character and hardheadedness). She uses the autobiographical form to assert that her life has been a completely coherent one, "always the same taut thread, from when I was ten years old and fought for working women until I was fifty and fought for right of working mothers . . . a continuous battle."[11] But the autobiographical form requires fictionalizing, choosing, and omitting details and events in order to construct a meaningful linear narrative. Indeed, a woman's choice to claim a public authorial voice, to write herself into history, changes the meaning and narrative of her life.[12]

Omissions and fictionalizations abound in Noce's works of autobiography. For instance, nowhere in her books did Noce address an incident mentioned in the Cederna interview. Once during a train trip she was overheard complaining about the double militancy of women who served both in the party and the women's organization of UDI, saying that as far as she was concerned the reason UDI women referred to themselves and each other as *amiche* (friends) and not *compagne* (comrades) was that they went to bed with the husbands of other *compagne*. The interviewer assures the reader that "Naturally, now everything has changed"; that is, Noce has been brought around to the politically correct stance on feminism. But at the time it was a scandal for which she refused to apologize and which embarrassed many of her colleagues. Although Noce insulted women who deserved to be taken seriously as fellow politicians, her hurt and suspicion are understandable in light of Longo's multiple dalliances with other women.[13]

From a young age she was involved with Luigi Longo, who was older and already a party leader when they met. A national hero for his bravery and leadership during the Resistance, he never seems to have suffered from public knowledge of his affairs, but Noce's career may have. Although she recounts some of the difficulties of the relationship and eventual split, admitting to her hurt and betrayal, she certainly never admits to the kind of cynicism evidenced by what was apparently a favorite later saying of hers: "Whenever she heard a woman criticize her husband for being a womanizer, [Noce] would lean a fraternal hand on her shoulder and say, 'Remember, comrade, behind every man hides a Longo.' "[14]

As a further humiliation, Noce read in a newspaper that her marriage had been annulled and wrote an angry letter to the editors denying it before finding out that it was in fact true. Not only had Longo applied for the annulment without her knowledge or permission, but the central committee of the party had agreed to it and helped to falsify her signature. This was especially surprising for leaders of the PCI, since getting an annulment meant spending a great deal of money to have one's case heard and approved before the judges of the ecclesiastical tribunal known as the *sacra rota*. As a result, Noce lost her seat on the party's executive committee and her favored placement on the next election ballot since she was seen as morally—and therefore politically—compromised by her status as an unmarried mother. Noce relates this story as one of victory and vindication, because she then won a plurality of votes in her constituency in the next election by appealing directly to voters rather than depending on her party. Since her district contained a very large convent, Noce joked that all the nuns must have voted for her. Noce recounts this episode in full in *Rivoluzionaria professionale*, without explicitly noting that her personal experience was shared by many other women comrades. In the course of postwar reshuffling and reunions of families and relationships, it was not uncommon for a male comrade who decided to legalize his position with his new lover to suffer no repercussions in his public life, while the party became reluctant to allow his former partner to continue in public roles. Noce's party saw her sexuality as disruptive once she was no longer married and used the opportunity to remove a gadfly from their leadership, but it still found an unmarried Longo a politically useful figure. Yet the voters perceived Noce as the victim of a disloyal and oversexed husband and rewarded her at the polls for her feminine constancy and chastity. In this way the otherwise overweening influence of the mass parties' male leadership was bypassed by a woman politician. It seemed that Noce's gender representation actually reassured voters that female politicians could promise sexual discipline. [15]

Whatever Noce's feelings about public understanding of her personal life, she repeatedly states that she is not embarrassed by her reputation for having a terrible temper and for being ugly. On the contrary, she is fiercely proud of her persona, seeing it as the legacy of the women of the proletariat of Torino. Like them, she is a fighter and a survivor, ingenious at getting results with few resources and sometimes by pure force of will. In her autobiographies she proudly listed her nicknames: *Madonna Tempesta* (Our Lady of the Hellstorm), *Brutta, povera e comunista* (ugly, poor, and communist), even *Brutto Muso* (ugly mug).

While celebrating the many results earned with her brazen manner, she fails to acknowledge as openly that this image was far from universally admired. To many she apparently remained a negative stereotype of the communist female, rough, off-putting, devoid of maternal feeling, and worst of all, unattractive. Women's historian Marta Boneschi described her public image as such:

> For those who hated her she was forever "*brutta e comunista.*" During the electoral campaign of the spring of 1948, in Piazza Colonna in Rome, a passerby heckled a speaker from the PCI by yelling "May you marry Teresa Noce!" Without any grace, beauty or delicacy, during the Cold War in Italy Teresa became a symbol for all the anti-communist invective: here everyone, these are the women the "Reds" desire [for Italy].[16]

Noce may be forgiven for putting the best face on her personal life and identity in her own memoirs, but occasionally she was also dishonest about details of her public and political life. She insisted she voted against Togliatti's posting to Moscow as new head of Cominform in late 1950–early 1951, when Stalin tried to bring him, and by extension the Western European Communist parties, back under Soviet control, although she did not. Also, she wrote that during the Constitutional Assembly, she knew that the PCI had decided to compromise and vote for the controversial article 7, the text of the Lateran Accords signed by Mussolini making the Catholic Church the official state religion. Including them not only preserved Fascist law in the very constitution of the new republic but also guaranteed the hegemony of the Church and thereby the DC within the state itself. Noce wrote that she couldn't ratify anything done by the Fascist regime and that she abstained from the vote. She claimed that when Togliatti didn't protest, other party members also felt free to vote their own conscience instead of the party line. "The party's imposition is just a story. I have always done and thought just as I felt was right.... I once wrote an article... whose title was 'Learn to say NO' and it was addressed to women. Say no to your father, your boss, your husband and your comrades. If you never learn to say no, even to the secretary of the party, you'll never be free."[17] Nonetheless, Togliatti only explicitly approved the decision of two other PCI constituents to vote no. Noce may have abstained, but since the Parliamentary records don't show a roll call vote, we only have her own word on that. Her collegue Nilde Iotti pointed out that in either case, a yes vote with the party line or an abstention, Noce did not in fact vote no on article 7.[18] Clearly there was a struggle on the part of both women to be on the right side of history after the fact.

Perhaps Noce alienated many of those with whom she negotiated; the eagerness Nilde Iotti showed in her biography to expose Noce's clay feet seems to attest to that. Given that the truth of her private life cannot be known, only the identity she presented, analyzing her political career and legislative legacy is the best way to discern her intentions and understand her victories for women's rights. Two quotations summarize her sense that women's rights were universally important rather than as part of a "woman question" that men could separate from general politics and safely ignore:

> Personally, I've never liked "women's work" (*lavoro femminile*) and I've always refused to do it, even though I've always been active in defense of women. It's the very concept of women's work that seems mistaken to me, as if it is opposite to or at least separate from general work. In my opinion, just as there can be no women's emancipation unless men are also emancipated, so in the Party there shouldn't be any organizations differentiated by sex.[19]

And this, concerning her fight for her law protecting working mothers:

> The women were all ready to fight to the finish for these rights. The men a bit less. So we had to conduct a vast effort to clarify and educate people on this issue, to make men understand that these were not just feminine problems, that maternity doesn't concern only women, but men too, all of them: not just because women don't make babies by themselves, but also and especially because these were problems of a general character, social and human, that affected the future of all workers.[20]

Virtually everything about Noce's experience of politics and women's equality up until 1948 tended to make her focus on women's needs as fellow-workers and bearers of constitutional rights; that is, as *compagne* and not as *amiche*. Noce and her peers, especially other women "veterans," had been formed in the party cell and the partisan brigade, where the emphasis was on egalitarian relations between comrades, individual sacrifice for the larger group, and extreme discipline in keeping one's personal life from interfering with the demands of party activism. Noce had spent virtually her whole life training herself to put political action first. Through difficult and sometimes humiliating experiences with Longo and her children she dedicated her life, public and private, and made sacrifices because she, like the rest of her cohort, believed that they lived in a crucial historical moment. Their reward for having fought against Fascism was that they now had the opportunity to recreate Italy as a free, democratic republic. She may have disdained separate "women's work," but she would put all her passion into making men and women cooperate to guarantee justice to her *compagne*.

Noce would therefore take a new approach in what was by then a venerable history of feminist activism to build a welfare state through protectionist laws on women's labor. These had usually been framed as necessary because of the vulnerability of women and children's health and reproductive capacities in the productive public sphere, and therefore as ways to shore up the integrity and health of the family unit.[21] Indeed discourses about child welfare, the morality of working women, and the dangers of industry to women's fertility and to the sexual order would be presented in the debates over this law as well. But Noce did not frame the target of the law as the woman-in-the-family, whether the domestic family or the family of the nation. She clearly defended the law as a citizenship right of the imagined constitutional woman.

Noce took a direct path out of the suffering of wartime and into leadership of both women's and labor organizations. Having survived both her son's death and her own internment, at the end of the war she was freed from Ravensbruck, the concentration camp for women prisoners where she had been detained since her capture by the Germans in 1943. She returned to Italy and was at the Fifth Party Congress in Rome as her comrades reunited. She was elected to the central committee, and, in recognition of her objection to "women's work," she was appointed to direct agitation and propaganda with Ruggiero Grieco, a co-founder of the party from Puglia who helped to promote the postwar occupations by landless Southern workers. She was also appointed to the *Consulta,* the legislative body charged with laying out the rules of the first elections and the Constituent Assembly's mission. She would go on to be elected to that body. At the same time she wanted to get into union organizing work, where she felt her pragmatic and insistent nature was better suited and where she knew women were scarce. Her election to secretary of FIOT (*Federazione Italiana di Operai Tessili,* the Italian Textile Workers' Union) in April 1947 with 297,000 out of 400,000 votes demonstrated that not only communist women workers but also those from other parties had voted for her.[22] It was in this position that she claimed to have invented "articulated strikes," where different factories struck at different hours and on different days so as to keep up pressure on employers. As proof of her ability as a union leader she cited her refusal to sign a bargaining agreement that wasn't up to par. Despite having obtained the agreement of the CGIL (*Confederazione generale italiano di lavoro*), the largest national union in Italy, the owners refused to go forward without Noce. Otherwise she was capable of calling her women to paralyze them all with just such a strike.[23]

Upon her election to the Constituent Assembly she asked to be on the further restricted Committee of 75 so that she could help to write the articles on economic and social issues with the third subcommittee. She was the only president of a union on that subcommittee; even her own party sent mostly professors and lawyers, she complained.[24] Characteristically, she made her presence count: "During the entire legislature of the Constituent, I spoke rarely in Assembly, little in the Committee of 75, and a great deal in the Subcommittee on economic and social problems." Noce's expertise emerged not only from her union work but also her experience as a working mother. With little help from Longo or his family and no family of her own during the 1930s and 1940s, she had struggled to raise her children while fulfilling her duties at work and with the party. She knew that many women were still without family support in the war's aftermath and, to her, the most pressing help working women needed was help with being mothers. In 1947 Noce proposed wording for the articles of the Constitution concerning the family that serves as a letter of intent for all her work to follow. Like her fellow women members of the Constituent, she hoped to make the Constitution an explicitly anti-discriminatory foundation law. She argued that the Constitution could not

> limit itself to affirming rights; it must also indicate how it intends to guarantee those rights to all Italian citizens. It is not enough, therefore, to solemnly affirm that the family is the base of society and that all citizens have the right to create one. To ensure the full enjoyment of these rights to all Italians, the Constitution must affirm: 1) that the State protects the family; 2) that the Italian Republic recognizes the social function of maternity; 3) that all Italian babies have the right to a minimum level of protection and care on the part of society, from the very moment they come to be part of it; after which it must translate these affirmations into concrete measures, for which I propose that the articles instead read: ... Art. 2 The Italian Republic recognizes that maternity is a social function and therefore of collective national concern. The Italian State guarantees to every woman, regardless of her social and juridical status, the possibility to procreate in good economic, hygienic, and health conditions by the following: a) for working women, a maternity leave, before and after the birth, paid at full salary; b) the institution of a pregnancy stipend for all working mothers; c) medical-obstetrical care for all pregnant women; d) the institution of a nursing premium. Art. 3 The Italian State guarantees to all children a minimum level of protection and care on the part of society, from the very moment they come to be part of it, by the following: a) creation of lactation clinics for every urban and rural zone; b) creation of nurseries in every workplace employing more than 50 women, as well as in neighborhoods and towns; c) creation of nursery schools, afterschool programs, and summer camps for all children ...[25]

The provisions Noce proposed were not included in the Constitution. Instead, the more general language that the family was the natural basic unit of society and that familial rights were to be protected stood and can be found in Article 29. But the "concrete measures" she advocated became those of the law she proposed immediately upon the opening of the first legislature in 1948. Indeed, she credited the Constitution and in particular her subcommittee's work during the assembly with the inspiration and the justification of the law. Noce explained that if the Constitutional Assembly's principal task had been to write the Republic's constitution, in the course of the debates the constituents were also preparing a series of issues that would have to be legislated by the parliaments to come: the protection of benefits for mothers, equal pay for equal work, pensions, work regulation, and so on. "All these laws, later passed or not, had their essential foundation in the Constitution's articles on economic and social problems, discussed in our subcommittee," she wrote.[26]

Noce had already been dealing with these problems as a union leader. Upon starting that job she realized immediately that the most important problems for women workers were equal pay and opportunity at work and maternity benefits, issues still governed by laws from the Fascist era. During the previous regime the attention and help available to mothers and young infants had increased from the Liberal period, due primarily to the creation of the National Agency for Maternal and Infant Welfare, ONMI (*Opera nazionale di maternità e infanzia*). This attention had a strongly pronatalist and repressive character given the regime's racist demographic campaign; nonetheless infant mortality had declined since ONMI's institution in 1925, and the postwar Republic recognized its usefulness by continuing to make it the umbrella organization for government welfare services to mothers and young families well into the 1970s. At work the Fascist mix of protection of and repression of women was even more pronounced. The regime's economic policy had aimed for both modernization and autarchy. Therefore women, a source of cheap labor, had to be encouraged to work in the great factories of the industrial triangle, the largely underground world of home work, and the still sizable agricultural sector. At the same time, the regime wanted to provide the means for men to be the sole providers and uncontested heads of their families; it therefore promulgated a number of laws which "protected" and excluded women from lucrative night work, overtime, and skilled jobs in the factories, reserved jobs in the civil sector for men, and encouraged women to work only when young and single but to leave permanently upon marriage and childbirth. The key legislation Noce had to contend with was part of a package, enacted in 1934, that not only prohibited all night work or excessive overtime for women, all work deemed dangerous or unhealthy (jobs which usually carried higher pay) for women aged fifteen to twenty, and all work for minors under twelve, but also covered most women working in industry and commerce with insurance funds guaranteeing two months of paid compulsory maternity leave (one before and one after birth), job security for longer unpaid leaves up to three months before birth and six weeks after, and time off on the job to breastfeed for a year. Families also received a bonus of 150 lire and unemployment benefits up to the equivalent of an average two months' pay. In 1938 women in agricultural work were covered as well. These measures were protectionist in intent but had the effect of discriminating against women workers, since employers would have little incentive to hire them legally. Nonetheless, in 1948 at the start of Parliament's activity, while certain categories of unionized women workers were engaged in gaining better benefits in their contracts, most women in Italy depended on a patchwork of local aid and family resources when they got pregnant, and many, if they had been working, were forced by employment policy or by practical necessity to quit work and to start anew when returning to the job market.[27] Moreover, although Marshall Plan aid was flowing to Italy by 1948, under the Christian Democrats these funds were channeled into infrastructure development and preventing inflation. Consumer goods were not encouraged, and food consumption was held down to prewar levels.[28] This reluctance to accept American notions and funds meant most working women were still hard-pressed to keep their families fed, making a change in the approach to the balance between motherhood and work more necessary than ever.

This situation was largely echoed in the other countries of postwar Western Europe. While maternity legislation had been expanding in Britain, France, and Germany throughout the twentieth century, this was usually done on pronatalist grounds, rather than in order to secure redistributive economic justice and independence for women. That is, maternity leave was part of a package of protectionist laws directed at working women that assumed their primary identity was as mothers. In the imagery of policy-makers, only incidentally or secondarily were women workers. State law aimed to safeguard a woman's reproductive health until she had children, at which time those same laws discouraged her from returning to the workforce. In the postwar expansions of the welfare state, new programs focused on the mother and her children's well-being within the family, such as free ambulatory postnatal and pediatric services, housing subsidies, free school meals, and increases in the family allowances instituted during the interwar years. Both Britain and Germany especially seemed to use social services to reinforce a male-breadwinner/ full-time mother and housewife family model; in Britain state functionaries were reluctant to diminish a man's role as provider, while "new" feminists followed Eleanor Rathbone in hoping that family allowances would take pressure off women in the workplace. In postwar Germany such a policy carried anticommunist and antifascist connotations, since both the Nazi regime and the East German state were perceived to use public nursery schools to take children away from their families and claim them for the state. France, which had long had a larger percentage of married women in the workforce, adopted a somewhat more flexible "parental logic" in its system of family allowances payable to mothers as well as increased public services and decrees guaranteeing women's equality at work.[29]

Women's work in Fascist Italy, in a difficult economy where jobs were scarce and the state was the most attractive employer but only for men, had been backbreaking and unfair. But the ideas its propaganda had helped to introduce to Italians, the expansion of modern welfare services to all working citizens, were more attractive than ever in a postwar democratic key. As a member of parliament Noce would fight for the primacy of the republican Constitution as a guide to creating new laws governing women's work and maternity. But first, as a union leader, she had to attempt to build on this mixed legacy. The first national union contract she helped to negotiate, in 1947, required a leave before and after delivery of a baby to be paid at 75% of full salary for textile union members and 66% for those not in the union; nursing rooms in the workplace; and child care in the biggest factories.[30] However, this contract was not being fully honored when Noce, as a member of parliament in 1948, began the battle to require all employers to provide maternity benefits. Even that contract, Noce recognized, had holes in it: the duration of leave wasn't specified, nursing rooms were not required, mothers would need regular absences approved during the first year after birth. She even wanted to extend maternity benefits to the unemployed and to wives of male workers. In addition, she knew that although the official percentage of "economically active" women was low compared to other industrialized nations, about a third of women aged fifteen to sixty-four, many more women worked under the table, often women in their childbearing years who were closed out of the formal labor market by employers' unwillingness to hire them or keep them on when they married and began having children. Further, the very factors that kept women's extra-domestic employment low could also be considered "work." In a state without a highly developed service sector and with a highly inefficient bureaucratic culture, every family needed someone available during working hours to shop in multiple food stores, wait in lines at banks, post offices, and government offices, and oversee the many forms, visits, and appointments required to manage household, finances, schooling, and health care. In most families the person tasked with all that management was a woman, and Noce believed, like the "maternalist" feminists of the generation before, that all mothers deserved the recognition from their government that motherhood is a vital social function.

In 1946, while working on the textile union contract, Noce created a study group to gather ideas about maternal leave reform from doctors, union leaders, and mothers. Noce pushed hard for the findings of the group to receive attention in contract negotiations and secured a meeting with Minister of Labor Amintore Fanfani, a co-founder of the DC. He examined the document Noce's group had produced and promised to present it as a *disegno di legge*. In the Italian Parliament, a bill presented by the prime minister or his cabinet, *il governo*, is called a *disegno di legge* to distinguish it from a *proposta di legge*, a law presented by a senator or deputy. Fanfani had guaranteed the bill would be presented before the Christmas recess in 1947, but the matter went no further until the first legislature began its work in the early fall of 1948 and Noce took matters into her own hands.

Noce probably would have been happier if the law had been presented by the government. She was more enthusiastic about organizing and motivating grassroots work than she was about writing and proposing the law itself. Nor did she strive to take personal credit for what she saw as a collective achievement. Although the bill was commonly referred to as the "*proposta Noce*" and later as the "*legge Noce*," she often referred to it as the "*proposta CGIL*," after the union. She was never the only sponsor or proponent listed as bill author on drafts; the bill presented to the Labor Committee also listed Giuseppe Di Vittorio, the founder and leader of CGIL and a fellow deputy in the Chamber; and the law eventually passed by the Chamber of Deputies listed just about every woman deputy, of every party, in the Chamber.

The debate over whether women's equality was better guaranteed through total legal neutrality in the workplace or through support for women's special needs was far from unknown in Italy. At the turn of the century Anna Maria Mozzoni and Anna Kuliscioff had famously disagreed over the help or harm done by protective legislation for working women when Kuliscioff helped pass the first law (1902) limiting women's factory work to days and non-dangerous tasks. The proposals of the constitutional rights feminists, however, did not reproduce this debate. Constitutional rights feminists were all firmly protectionist, determined to spread social rights in the new republic and to support maternity by distributing its burdens and costs throughout society. Teresa Noce saw compulsory maternity leave as a boon to working mothers and a check on bullying employers, not a discriminatory restriction limiting their earning potential and ability to advance professionally. In this sense, while the *legge Noce* was an innovation for constitutional implementation, it was a continuation rather than a rethinking of a much longer legacy, of protectionist approaches to women's work. In addition, it was part of the larger drive in the postwar years to create the social welfare system promised by all the European democracies to their populations as reward for the hardships of war and a way of preventing future wars.

In postwar Italy, life was especially precarious for many working women, given the displacement and separation of so many families, the destruction of physical plant and resources, and ongoing conditions of hunger and basic deprivation. While official statistics put working women at around 6,500,000 or about 26% of the total female population throughout the 1950s, and housewives around 60% of the female population, other statistics suggest that around 70% of the workforce in the grey and black markets was female. Overall the rates of women's employment were probably comparable to the 40–48% rates in other similarly developed countries.[31] Together with the postwar consumer revolution in durable household goods like washing machines and refrigerators and the twentieth century drive in the medical and social work professions to make motherhood a modern scientific vocation, the protectionist legal legacy and the party lines of both PCI and DC combined to encourage the 1950s stereotype of full-time housewife for married women with children. Like other stereotypes this carries a great deal of truth but by no means tells the whole story.[32] Still, the dramatic fears from the years of total war and Fascism of the dissolution of bodies—the social body, the body of the family, the bodies of women workers and their babies—were a powerful incentive to support this ideal and a law that could promise to prevent such damage.[33] While the Fascists had constantly urged women to have more babies for the Fatherland in their demographic campaigns without raising the birth rate appreciably, the baby boom was underway in the postwar period. This demographic optimism was really the first driver of the economic miracle to come.[34]

Noce was also drawn to the protectionist argument by her own experience of motherhood. In the 1920s and 1930s she had struggled mightily to raise her children with little help and often in dangerous situations. During her short stay in the USSR to attend party cadre school she had been overwhelmingly impressed by the free child care, health care, and community cafeterias that foreign guests of the party enjoyed, as well as by the (false) impression that all Soviet families had these same benefits. Noce, like many women, believed that motherhood was an exquisitely social function as well as a personally fulfilling one, and that every woman ought to be able to become a mother and all of society should help her child to grow to be a healthy and productive citizen. The law she wrote reflected these beliefs in every line.

Nearly all the women members of Parliament who participated in the debates about Noce's law would repeat again and again that because women worked at every other moment of their lives and contributed to the general productivity of the nation, no generosity at the moment of motherhood was too much or would go unrepaid. They also emphasized that all citizens should help bear the costs as they all benefited from the work that mothers did gestating, birthing, and caring for infants and children. In this way the chauvinist myth of "la mamma" and the feminist interpretation of the Constitution could appear not to be in conflict, but to reinforce each other. Article 37 in the Constitution states: "The working woman has the same rights, and, for equal work, equal pay to the working man. Working conditions must allow her to fulfill her essential familial function and must assure to the mother and her child a special and adequate protection." This was the crucial article to the constitutional implementation argument, for it made possible the argument that it was unconstitutional for employers to deny women adequate maternity benefits.

On June 2, 1948, Noce presented her bill, titled "*Tutela fisica ed economica delle madri lavoratrici*" (Physical and economic protection of working mothers). The bill called for five months of obligatory leave, two before and three after delivery, to be paid at 100%. For women who were unemployed or had no fixed hours, it mandated payments equivalent to what a formally employed woman would receive during her maternity leave. The cost was to be paid entirely by the employer, public or private. Although it was the first law presented by parliamentary initiative, Noce boasted that it was more important to call it the first law by "popular initiative," given all the people who had helped advise her and volunteered their services and ideas. "It was in fact, the first, if not the only, bill to be written by the workers it concerned, debated by them article by article, corrected and revised in great assemblies of women and mothers, and written finally by a committee they themselves had elected," she wrote.[35] This was significant because the prime minister and his cabinet finally presented a bill on the same topic, with much less generous terms for maternity leave. So from the start, Noce's popular, union-backed *proposta* competed with the *disegno* created by the cabinet and backed by employers. The women deputies from the PCI and PSI were fighting against the content of another proposal and at the same time fighting for their right to present laws. Both were constitutional fights: the fight to affirm democratic institutions and the fight for women's rights. This is what these women meant when they insisted that women's equality was essential to the existence of a truly democratic, antifascist state. [36]

The atmosphere by no means cooled in politics or society after the passionately contested 1948 elections. Noce called the turn of the decade the "Scelba epoch," after Mario Scelba's tenure as minister of the interior, to signal the worsening of Cold War tensions and interparty and interunion conflicts. Scelba was a Christian Democrat whose insistence on law and order earned him the nickname the "Iron Sicilian." While he pursued the suppression of ex- and neo-Fascist disturbances, he also purged the police and *carabinieri* of former partisans, then encouraged them to violently suppress working-class or peasant protests. He invented detached squadrons known as *celere*, who could move rapidly to impose law and order, but popular recollections are that they fired upon striking and protesting workers at the slightest provocation. Recalling the personal as well as political challenges of building consensus in this period, Noce described how she had to intervene to get her own son released from prison after his arrest during a demonstration.[37] The law itself would become a site for conflict as speakers from various arenas—medical and public health experts, church spokespeople, organized labor, employers, politicians, and women's associations—competed to define the needs and rights of working mothers and their children. Nothing less than the relationship between masculine and feminine in the workplace, the family, the community, the marketplace, and of course the state was at stake.

Noce and her PCI colleagues had wanted to get her bill discussed and passed to the assembly quickly, knowing it had better chances of getting interparty support there than in committee. The DC would not openly oppose her bill, but they kept it bogged down in committee. Noce admitted in her autobiography that this was due to her own inexperience at parliamentary procedure. Failing to foresee or understand all the tricks a majority party can use to slow down and sabotage bills, she lost a great deal of time. An additional complication arose when the government presented its own version, with Minister of Labor Amintore Fanfani as its sponsor, and a DC woman of equal stature to Noce, Maria Federici, as the proponent.[38] Both bills were sent to the Ninth Permanent Committee on Labor and Social Provision, where the government had the power to do two potentially damaging things: one was call the committee to order *in sede legislativa* instead of *in sede deliberante* (as a legislative body rather than merely an advisory committee to the general assembly of the Parliament), and the other was to insist on each bill being debated separately, with the government's bill allowed to take precedence. Federici, the senior woman deputy from the DC on the committee and a passionate advocate for the rights of working mothers, helped broker an agreement whereby the committee would combine the two texts into a workable bill to present to the full assembly for approval.[39]

The *proposta Noce* was applicable to all women, clearly specifying housewives, farm workers, state employees, and private employees; the *disegno* of the government said "*lavoratrici che prestano la loro opera alle dipendenze di privati datori di lavoro*," "women workers who work for private employers." They meant by this to exclude all agricultural workers (who were frequently employed as part of a family unit or crew and did not have individual contracts), home workers, maids, and wives of male workers who had health insurance. Given the numbers of women employed in the grey and black markets, this would virtually guarantee that the law would be unenforceable, as not applying to the great majority of women. The *proposta Noce* guaranteed 100% pay for three months before and six weeks after delivery and made maternity leave obligatory, while the government proposed 75% pay for six weeks before and six weeks after, and maternity leave was optional. Noce's bill outlawed firing pregnant women; the government's left open the possibility. The *proposta* required a whole system of lactation rooms and daycare centers, onsite and near workers' residences, to be created at the expense of employers; the *disegno* suggested that local labor inspectors "promote" the creation of local networks of daycare.[40]

Lengthy struggles took place in committee, as members considered both bills and decided what, if anything, to pass on the full assembly. Meanwhile Noce was re-energized by a public campaign that UDI sponsored, using the women members of Parliament as spokespeople. UDI conducted a "campaign for the protection of maternity" from region to region, collaborating with unions where possible, holding meetings, passing out flyers, collecting signatures on petitions urging Parliament and the government to support the bill. In Ferrara the women of UDI entered an allegorical float representing maternity and infancy in the parade for the *Festa della Stampa Democratica* (Festival for the Democratic Press, a PCI sponsored rally-cum-entertainment) which featured on one side "a miserable kitchen with poor sad babies, and on the other happy and well-fed babies in a daycare center, illustrated with slogans and the text of Article 31 [of the Constitution]—it was met with sympathy and enthusiasm."[41] Cremona's chapter organized a rally when Communist Deputy

Stella Vecchio Vaio came to speak about the bill, the Asti group did the same in honor of Gisella Floreanini, and Noce herself went to Florence on July 18. In June CIF included a special section in the association newsletter supporting the proposal. The women of CIF challenged each other to new heights of creativity, going beyond collecting signatures and donations to "bigger demonstrations, festivals, awards, and gift give-aways, tying the laws to the particular requests of women in each specific place . . . day care, a preschool, a clinic, a school."[42] In Bologna local women workers organized an ongoing protest of the DC's obstruction in committee by sending delegations of women every day during October to the prefect's office and to the local DC headquarters. With these campaigns the women of the Lost Wave illustrated their concept of maternity as a point of confluence between public and private: ideal motherhood emphatically did not take place in an isolated domestic place like the "sad kitchen" on the Ferrara float, but where the whole community could support the mother in all her forms of labor, productive and reproductive. The associations' intent may have been to compete for voters' loyalty to one or the other of the respective versions of the law and therefore to the Marxist or anticommunist bloc, but the overall effect was to widely disseminate public awareness and support for the mother-as-worker. Further, the presence of parliamentarians as the public voice of mothers in these campaigns underlined the connection between motherhood and the political achievements of the Resistance and the Constitution. Both maternity and politics were part of "women's work," they asserted; and both needed support and development to provide the stability and prosperity Italians hoped to restore.

The visiting delegation was a popular tool for citizens to rally behind. Noce related in her autobiography that a group of women workers from Bergamo made the trip to Rome to see their representatives in person. They first visited her to voice their support, and she invited them to go speak to Fanfani. He had his secretary say that he couldn't receive them, so the women waited for hours outside the main door of the palazzo until he left for the day and then gave him a severe talking to—in the best Italian *mamma* style—until he promised to accelerate the workings of the committee. The delegations that made the biggest impression, though, were the pregnant women who would come in groups to badger their representatives about the bill. Noce once overheard a DC woman deputy complaining just before going in for a committee meeting: "We must finish up with this maternity bill. We are overwhelmed by all the pregnant women the communists have mounted!" Noce wrote that the poor old maid of a deputy never understood why everyone around her burst out laughing at her unintended pun.[43] Women, whether politicians or ordinary citizens, were clearly still energized by the power and sense of their own abilities they had felt during the war and resistance. Eager to participate in this campaign, they were not at all hesitant in translating their authority as mothers into authority over political representatives. The power of the maternal figure meant that men like Fanfani accepted their harangues as good sons should; but the very ambiguity of maternal authority in the public sphere also allowed those same men to remain in denial over the subversion of traditional feminine identity performed by those women.

At the highest levels of government the wrangling over legislative details went on, a negotiation Noce and female constituents did not entirely succeed in dominating. After nearly two years of struggle, the IX committee on Labor finally managed to reach unanimous agreement on a bill that meshed the two proposals. It was closer in spirit to Noce's proposal, since it still guaranteed 100% pay during maternity leave, included farm workers, sharecroppers, and unemployed women and wives of workers; required one year's postpartum guarantee of immunity to layoffs; and required lactation rooms and day care centers at all workplaces with more than fifty women employees under the age of fifty. It was also a much more practical project, with different lengths of leave specified for different categories of workers and several articles specifying that all employers and all employees would contribute a percentage of their social security and health insurance taxes specifically to the fund for maternity assistance. In this way, it was thought, employers would not have any disincentives to hiring women of childbearing age, since the burden of paying their leave was spread across the entire marketplace. In return, the bill was called a *disegno*, marking it as a law sponsored by the government and therefore to be credited to the DC, and Maria Federici was named proponent of the bill to the full assembly. Noce was content with this agreement because it seemed that these compromises in committee had brought representatives of every party to unanimity and thus guaranteed a passing vote in the Chamber.

Discussion of the bill began in full assembly on June 27, 1950. As Noce expected, general discussion was very short and perfunctory, and Maria Federici's presentation was eloquent, focusing on the themes that united women deputies across the aisle. Vittoria Titomanlio, deputy from the DC and a member of the old guard, trained in the ranks of Catholic Action, and an ex-partisan, was the first to speak in general discussion. She reminded the Chamber that Article 4 of the new Constitution spoke not just of the right to work, but the responsibility to do so. If women were to be responsible citizens, they must work, and to be able to work they had to have adequate conditions to be good mothers and good workers at the same time.[44] In this debate the women deputies would repeatedly remind their colleagues that the Constitution had created a republic based on work and that this law was simply a fulfillment of women's needs in order to honor the Constitution. Maria Federici's presentation of the bill also highlighted the theme of women's rights as constitutional rights, citing the two places she felt the Constitution expressly promoted women's rights as mothers: in Article 31, which says that the Republic protects maternity, and again in Article 37 title III, which says that employers are responsible for providing to mothers and their children "a special, adequate protection." "I repeat, we were obligated to create to this law," she said. "The Constitution required it. The question whether to use the government's project rather than the parliamentary initiative presented days before as the template isn't important. The point is that we had to study this issue." Noce also spoke briefly, saying that the law was neither a majority nor a minority project, but "a law for Italian mothers by Italian mothers."[45]

These speeches were really only a formality, a celebration by the women deputies of their victory. The bill would pass. The assembly would vote on the articles of the bill, and the law would be approved and passed on to the Senate for approval in its Labor committee. Noce was happy that at least the bill had gotten in before the summer recess and would be finished within that session. But reading between the lines of the transcripts shows clear portents of more trouble to come.

Although Noce's Catholic colleagues had been cooperative in committee and union negotations and had indeed helped formulate many of the articles of the national contract and the legislation, the union split could not help but add to the ideological and party tensions. CGIL had been refounded in the immediate postwar period by Giuseppe Di Vittorio, Noce's original coauthor, as a representative of all forms of trade unionism: communist, socialist, Catholic, and anarcho-syndicalist. In 1948, the group split after the communists organized a general strike to protest an assassination attempt on PCI leader Palmiro Togliatti. The Catholics left to form CSIL, *Confederazione Italiana Sindacati Lavoratori,* and on March 5, 1950, the social-democrats would also depart, forming UIL, *Unione Italiana del Lavoro*. The women of Parliament continued to cooperate throughout these stormy events, but in hindsight Noce recalled a difference after the scission. Federici, in the course of her presentation, had mentioned almost as an aside that the government's version of the bill had given only 75% of full salary to women on maternity leave, and that she had supported it originally and felt that it might still be better to return to that number. Then the first male deputy to speak in general discussion, Repossi, who had been a member of the Labor Committee and presumably supported a bill he had helped to create, expressed his doubts that the bill could work in practical application. The bill tried to protect too many categories of women, he said, and the provisions for paying for maternity leave, not to mention the requirement of lactation rooms and day care centers, were too onerous for employers. "It's all very well, Honorable Titomanlio, that Article 4 of the Constitution states that the citizen has the right to work and the duty to work... but permit me to say that we must arrive one day at the point that the head of the family earns enough for the entire family so that the mother is never obligated to work, but can stay at home and raise her own children; the law it is necessary to create is the one that finally creates the family salary [for men] so that the woman may be truly liberated economically and attend above all to her duties as mother."[46]

Repossi, with his tone-deaf celebration of the version of motherhood the Lost Wave intended to do away with, seemed to imply that he no longer supported the bill, and Federici seemed to foresee more debate on the numbers. Even so when general discussion was closed, it was an unwelcome surprise to the opposition parties that a number of amendments were suddenly presented. It was a bitter betrayal for Noce that Federici herself, appointed proponent of the committee's exhaustively debated version, now stated her support for these amendments from her fellow party members and argued for returning many provisions of the bill to their wording in the original Fanfani *disegno*.

Repossi's rehashing of the family wage argument was a particularly disappointing sign for the long-term success of the Lost Wave. Originally women of Parliament, UDI, and CIF had confidently predicted that women's equality as citizens would be fulfilled right away, banking on the power of the new Constitution to bypass old arguments about women's proper place in society. This is why women with otherwise opposed opinions about women's responsibilities as mothers and wives and their subordinate status in the family and in civil society could agree on laws like Noce's. Repossi's failure to be silenced by the constitutionalist argument meant that women would have to fight the battle from both sides, arguing constitutional rights equality as well as the morality and fairness of women's emancipation. This meant that constitutional implementation was in a sense a failure as a strategy for reaching full equality. In this instance and others to come, the original intent of a feminist law was compromised by the amendments and political deals the women were forced to make to prevent their bills from being tabled. Nonetheless implementation remained a powerful motivation for writing the laws and for women to cooperate across party lines. Demonstrating their continuing faith in this strategy, Noce submitted a formal demand for a written response from the government defining just how article 37 of the Constitution was to be put into effect.[47]

The discussion of the bill in full assembly ended up dragging on until July 19, with multiple amendments and counter-amendments and, at one particularly low point, a motion to return the bill to committee for further elaboration. Noce knew that would kill the bill and fought desperately to keep her project alive, even forcing a roll call vote on many amendments in an attempt to shame the committee members and women deputies into honoring their alliance on the committee text. The longest and most hard-fought debate took place over three main points: first, the wisdom of including as broad a swath of women as possible versus excluding sharecroppers, piece workers, and the unemployed and wives of male workers. Due to a series of amendments from Repossi which the Labor Ministry and the DC supported, the final law no longer extended to wives of covered workers, nor to women in farming families, and only promised a law would follow to address piece workers from home. The second conflict was over the 100% of pay in Noce's bill versus the 75% offered by the government's bill. After five days of disagreement, a private meeting outside of the Chamber brokered a deal in which an amendment to provide pay at 80% was signed by a multipartisan group of twenty-seven deputies including Noce, Federici, Di Vittorio, Repossi, and nine other women. Once this was approved on the morning of July 19, the law was finally passed later the same day.

Third and even more disappointing was the resubmission of an amendment previously presented by the DC in committee and defeated that added the word *coniugate* (married) in the sentence in Article 11 requiring child care centers and nursing rooms in places of work with more than fifty women. Communist and Socialist deputies moved to erase the word but were rejected in the midst of a debate during which they were accused of wanting to delegitimize the Italian family and give Italian children up to the state to be brainwashed into communism. DC deputy De Maria justified the wording saying, "We want to formulate a law that defends maternity, but which defends it in its true and proper form, a form which creates a halo around a woman's head and makes her worthy of veneration on the part of men." Noce, perhaps stung by the reference to her own status as an unmarried mother by this point, retorted, "All motherhood is sacred!" The president of the Chamber had to call for order several times before the room calmed. Deputies from the left argued that whatever their morality, women did not have to be married to have a child, and their children were owed the same assistance from the state that legitimate children received. But Noce and her allies on the left were fighting a losing battle. The Constitution was as much a hindrance as a help in this instance, since it also stated that the family is sacred and is based on matrimony. As an article at the time in *Verso la mete*, the journal for Catholic Action, reminded the faithful: "Women must be subordinate, intelligent and affectionate companions for men.... It is this subordination that the woman must have in the family and in the Church, and which we can and must extend to her in the realm of civil society as well."[48]

Some women from the Christian Democratic party tried to soften De Maria's message, assuring the Chamber that the use of the term married was simply for statistical reasons, since it was easier to predict that married women would have children and thus that a workplace with at least fifty married women would have enough babies to activate the requirement for the lactation room and day care center. Why have those services if fifty single women worked there and none had children? And of course, once fifty married women and their children had activated the services, any single mother employees would be free to bring their children in to share them. Maria Federici demonstrated her commitment to being reasonable rather than partisan about the law by suggesting that the language simply be changed to refer to the number of children rather than the number of women; the civil state of their mothers wouldn't have to be considered at all. But her party wanted that specification, and they had the majority vote. The word *coniugate* was retained, 207 votes to 100, with 13 women voting for it and 11 against. But immediately after, in a compromise agreement, the number of married women required to activate the lactation room and day care requirement was lowered to thirty, a small victory that at least helped mitigate the possibility that employers would simply fire women upon marriage so as not to ever reach the limit.

A secret vote was held on the afternoon of July 19 after all the articles and their amendments were finally approved. The law passed, 309 in favor and 45 against. It was sent to the Senate's Tenth Permanent Committee on Labor in legislative session, which passed the law in one day of discussion, on July 28. The law was published in the Gazette number 253 as *Legge 26 agosto 1950 n. 860.*

The final law of August 26, 1950 was a true compromise, a more even mix between the Christian Democratic government's and Noce's texts than the committee's had been. In spirit and in its ambition it was still extremely generous. It required that women abstain from work for varying periods depending on their category of work (hard labor stopped six months before delivery and industrial work three months before, agricultural work eight weeks before, and six weeks for other categories), but in no case less than six weeks before the due date and eight weeks after delivery; and paying this leave at 80% of their full pay, financed through a national health insurance mutual fund. It provided protection of a woman's job for a full year after her return, and required two hours a day of breaks for nursing and care of the infant for that year, to be considered work time not break time. In any workplace employing at least thirty married women under the age of fifty it required a nursing room and childcare.

Although the law required nursing rooms and daycare centers, most employers did not institute them, and the law was not enforced against them.[49] Indeed, the law went unenforced in many aspects, especially the protection of women's jobs upon not only childbirth but also marriage, and required successive amendments through the years. For example, the law indirectly raised the number of women fired for getting married, since it outlawed firing a woman during or after her pregnancy; many employers assumed marriage meant pregnancy was imminent and required their female employees to leave upon marriage, often making them sign upon hiring a document promising to resign when marrying. This was later remedied by another constitutionalist law fought for by women members of parliament and led by Lina Merlin.[50]

Teresa Noce was rightfully proud that the law passed and that it was the most progressive maternity law of its time. Although she was furious at what she perceived as Maria Federici's betrayal and the "perfidy" of the Christian Democratic committee members who had reached unanimity on the bill and then proceeded to dismantle that consensus and bend the rules of parliamentary procedure by waiting until after general discussion was closed to begin amending the project, she believed ultimate victory was due to linking the parliamentary campaign with the popular one and to the fact that there was a high number of women in the first legislature. Other observers have additionally noted that the conflictual atmosphere made the differences between the two bills seem more ideological and irreconcilable than they were and that the final passage of such a protective law proves the essential agreement on both sides of the aisle on the issue itself.[51] As for Maria Federici, a woman who certainly was not afraid to defy Church or party leaders in order to cement women's cooperation, as her forced resignation from CIF had proven, it appears that she simply had a more centrist vision of the proper legislative approach from the beginning. Her constituents were less likely than Noce's to have a positive view of extra-domestic labor: a survey of 100,000 housewives undertaken by CIF in 1949 had shown that 90% reported they were content not to work outside the home. They saw jobs not as emancipatory but as a further burden on an already labor-intensive role; they dreamed instead of labor-saving improvements like domestic appliances and indoor plumbing.[52] For the Catholics the protection of maternity was more focused on the idea of valuing the unpaid labor of women; CIF's most energetic campaigns in the postwar years were for "housewives' pensions."[53] It is also interesting to note that her original proposal on the topic, lost in the committee choice to combine the Noce and Fanfani bills for debate, was quite close to the final 1950 law's provisions. She too had traded public recognition in order to secure concrete influence. The beneficiaries were and continue to be Italian working mothers of all political parties.

Noce, for her part, went on fighting for women workers, both as a union leader and as a deputy. She remained in the Chamber of Deputies for the second legislature, 1953–1958, and presented four more bills from 1952 until 1958, all concerning a further constitutional guarantee for women workers: salary parity. She hesitated to go back for the second legislature because she had so much union work and parliament required so much energy. Her family situation had also changed a great deal—Longo was truly out of her life, having started a new family with his new wife; her older son Luigi Libero moved to the USSR with his wife; and only her younger son, Putisc, was still in Rome. The woman who spent her parliamentary and union leadership career fighting to help mothers balance their work and their families had put her political militancy above all. In 1955 she decided to resign from being general secretary of FIOT, and, finally tiring of the constant battle, in 1958 she asked not to be a candidate for the third legislature. By 1963, at the age of sixty-three, she had relinquished all public offices and returned to private citizenship. She began writing again, producing multiple autobiographies. After suffering multiple recurrences of heart problems and high blood pressure, she died in Bologna in January 1980.[54]

Other women members of Parliament had also continued to propose related laws: Angelina Merlin proposed bills on December 12, 1950 and February 21, 1951 forbidding the firing of women for marriage or pregnancy, which eventually became law in 1963; in 1954 Maria Maddalena Rossi proposed a bill extending protection of working mothers to farm families; in October 1955 Adele Bei tried to impose the universal enforcement of the Noce Law on all employers; and in 1958 a law was passed which regulated work and leave for piece workers at home.[55] In 1971 law number 1204 of December 30, *Tutela delle lavoratrici madri*, extended maternity benefits to all Italian working women and extended the possible leave to a full year, and law number 1044 of December 6 finally did away with ONMI and created a national network of public daycare/preschool centers. In 1977, Tina Anselmi passed a law that affirmed the direct responsibility of fathers as primary caregivers and provided for alternation of absences between father and mother to care for a child.[56] In all of these legislative campaigns, fulfilling the Constitution's promise of equality continued to be women's main argument. In 1969 the CIF delegate spoke at the DC national women's convention: "The protection and advocacy [for maternity] is clearly required by the Constitution . . . In asking for the realization of the constitutional norm we do not mean to create artificial disincentives to female employment [but rather] to guarantee the possibility of a continuing commitment outside the home and . . . the fulfillment of all a woman's potential." The Noce Law continued to serve as an inspiration, both in its substance and in the courage its very passage was a testament to. As the CIF delegate continued: "Examining the evolution of the realization of Article 37, we can see that if in 1950 they had let themselves be guided by the paralyzing logic of today . . . we wouldn't even have had a law number 860. In 1950, in fact, female unemployment was higher than today, the economic miracle was still far away, and the dangers for women's employment were certainly more concrete."[57]

European countries still have differences in lengths of maternity leave, especially in compulsory leave, which ranges from only two weeks in the United Kingdom to eight in Germany but generally allows for voluntary totals around fourteen to sixteen weeks at 90 to 100% of normal pay; but the overall trend throughout the European Union has been a reduction of the protectionist aspects of women's work legislation and a slight increase in the balancing of leave and childcare benefits between both parents. In France and Italy around 80% of women now return to work within one year of taking a maternity leave—though the absolute number of women this represents is very small, given the low female employment rates in Italy.[58] Policies offering more generous parental leave vary greatly from employer to employer, and even within the same company each individual may be able to negotiate different benefits, whose terms are seldom made public to fellow employees. In Italy as elsewhere a continuing reliance on private employers to self-regulate has resulted in the lack of any coherent national system covering all working mothers and their infants.

Late in her life Noce had lamented that her law was not well enforced because it was still only women who cared about the issue or the law, and women's numbers were diminishing quickly in Parliament and elsewhere in government. "If we were to begin making the men wash diapers they would understand the weight of these problems, which are not just women's problems, and the laws would be enforced. Especially if the women were, as they ought to be, in the majority in town councils and neighborhood committees, in all the organisms of political power."[59] As always, Noce brought out the social aspects of her rights critique: not only should women come to share privileges, but men needed to relinquish their monopoly on privilege and share the burdens. The Lost Wave's feminism was defined by this refusal to be separatist and this insistence on the duties, as much as the rights, of citizenship. Though the problem of women's equality in the workplace is ongoing and still heavily linked to childbearing questions, the evolution of thought has been undeniably toward the fulfillment of this Lost Wave vision.

4

The Merlin Law against the *Case Chiuse*

Taking the State out of Sex, Putting the Sex in Citizenship

The Noce law was not the only major piece of legislation introduced by the first forty-five female parliament members in 1948. That same year Angelina Merlin introduced a proposal in the Senate to abolish the brothels or "closed houses" (*case chiuse*), the state system of regulated prostitution. She calculated that it would be an easy first victory for women's rights and a simple law to pass, since every person along the political spectrum would agree that prostitution was a social vice, that the state system of regulation of prostitution was a symbol of the defunct Fascist regime, and that the women trapped in state brothels and subjected to all kinds of indignities should be freed and brought into the polity along with their newly-emancipated sisters.

Despite her expectations that approval would come quickly, ending the system of regulation was not as straightforward an issue as Merlin had hoped. The passage of the Legge Merlin became a decade-long, highly complex battle. Involving women's rights, sexual morality, public health, and women's work, it questioned an entire collective imaginary of gender roles and identity, and how they were and ought to be tied to the politics of emancipation and citizenship. With severe restrictions on prostitutes' ability to choose a place to live, own property, and support a family, Merlin's law in its final form no longer liberated women from exploitation and state control but assured the continuation of the state's discipline of women's sexual behavior. She viewed reform of prostitution laws as a necessity to conform to the new constitution's guarantee of equal rights for women and join the Atlantic alliance of democracies. But many men (and women) saw prostitution as a moral weakness of the woman herself and an eternal reality, for better or worse, of the sexual order.

The women of the Lost Wave also began to see their fight to realize the Constitutional Woman would be longer and more difficult than they had hoped in the first days of the Republic. The "first forty-five" of the 1948–1953 legislative session turned out to be a record high. In 1958, when Merlin's law finally passed, the legislature was reaching the end of its second five-year session with only 37 women out of 833 members of Parliament, or 4%. Both the PCI and the DC had presented fewer women candidates, and both parties gave fewer women seats: five fewer Communists and all of them in the lower house of Parliament, the Chamber of Deputies; and four fewer Christian Democrats, also all deputies. Lina Merlin was the only woman who remained in the Senate long enough to see her bill become law. Though she worked hard to encourage the associations to campaign in favor of closing the *case chiuse*, and although the women of the Lost Wave stood in favor of her bill, in government her allies were few and not as powerful as they might have been in 1948. Despite lower overall numbers in the elections of 1953, the DC had a better hold on the reins of power: in 1955 Giovanni Gronchi became the new president of the Republic, the first time the Christian Democrats felt free to nominate one of their own to the position instead of the more neutral Liberal Party members Enrico De Nicola and Luigi Einaudi of the past. Although there were six different prime ministers during the second legislature of 1953–1958, they were all from the DC and rarely needed to form coalition governments to retain their votes of confidence.[1] Italy no longer appeared on the brink of revolution, reconstruction and the economic miracle were taking solid hold, and male leaders were reasserting themselves in a nation that didn't need women to serve as its only "bulwark of democracy" anymore.

Regulation of prostitution in Europe had been in existence since the turn of the eighteenth century, mostly a Napoleonic invention, and had spread across Italy in 1860 upon unification, as the system was extended to the entire nation.[2] But it held strong associations with Fascism, since the regime had made several highly visible "roundups" of women on the street and had confined them to state brothels where both clients and employees were required to obey strict guidelines imposed by the Fascists. Vasco Pratolini's description of the "pogrom of the prostitutes" in his novel *Cronache di poveri amanti* (1947) is perhaps the best-known account of the all-out crusade by the Fascist police, but there were many accounts from real life as well. One young woman who didn't want to identify her name or place of origin recounted being brought to an unfamiliar café by a boy who had asked her out on a date, and "that evening the police came to that café, and asked me for my documents, but that place had a dubious reputation and they believed that I was one of the regulars. They brought me to the police station, and from there began my darkest story." Refusing to listen to her explanations, the police took away her identity documents and gave her instead the *libretto*, the booklet that registered her as a prostitute and in which the results of her required examinations for sexually transmitted diseases would be listed. The first vaginal examination, a harrowing and shameful experience for an inexperienced girl, was performed and recorded before her release. Now registered as a prostitute, she was committing a crime by not entering and residing in a state-regulated brothel: she had no choice but to become the prostitute they had mistaken her for. Although this girl did not blame her "date," such men commonly received a commission for recruitment from the madam of the brothel, also ironically known as a "house of tolerance," to which the girl was brought.[3]

This testimonial was reprinted by Senator Merlin as part of her campaign to sway public opinion in favor of abolishing state-regulated brothels, and it was guaranteed to strike anyone as barbaric and unfair that the state was effectively kidnapping girls and turning them into sex slaves. Nearly every part of the political spectrum of the postwar reconstruction period in Italy, and in fact internationally, agreed that the time for regulation was past. Yet Merlin's proposal did not become law for ten years, and the actual law of 1958 was in some ways very different from her original draft. What Merlin framed as a liberating reform became a protective, moralizing law which upheld the isolation and second-class citizen status of prostitutes. While her original bill identified men as criminals who seduced and exploited women cast as victims, the final law construed women as the criminals who were the proper focus of police and state scrutiny. The Legge Merlin's contorted journeys through Parliament illuminate a set of complicated interactions between the parties of the Left, the Christian Democrats, and the postwar women's movement which ended, despite the successful passage of a version of the law, not so much in affirmation of women's rights but rather in compromise and unforeseen consequences.

Still it is misleading to assert that Merlin would have been a liberator but for the guardians of moral conservatism who repressed her radical reform.[4] Moral disapproval of the state's involvement in prostitution, as a facet of the moral purity adopted even more stringently by the PCI and PSI than by the DC, was common to every faction in the mainstream parties already in 1948. At the same time, public belief that prostitution was an eternal feature of society, a necessity for the functioning of Latin virility, and should be made as safe as possible by the state was never seriously affected by any of these parties' campaigns over the law. The public never gave up its nostalgia for the *civiltà erotica* (erotic culture) passed from generation to generation in the brothels. Whether or not the public identified the brothels with Fascism, they had undeniably become a part of people's self-understanding and sexual identities in such a way that neither Merlin's emancipatory pleas nor the Christian Democrats' moral crusade could sway the people's belief in their essential functionality.[5] The abolition-regulation debate illustrates the sophisticated analyses of women's citizenship made by the women of the first forty-five, the tensions between reformist visions and the pragmatic nature of everyday government, and the essential continuity from Fascist and even pre-Fascist culture present in Italian society, even as over the course of the 1950s that culture began to tear wide open.

In the aftermath of Fascism and the Cold War bid to become part of the family of democratic nations, many of the aspects of Italy's "backwardness" gained more urgency for redress, as political leaders were anxious to prove to the international community what a modern and democratic nation Italy was becoming. Distancing the state from prostitution became a political aspiration as well as a moral one. It held particular urgency for the women of the Lost Wave since they were at pains to present women as the natural leaders of Italy's rebirth as a democracy. Women's dignity as citizens was extended, in the debates about prostitution as in the debates about maternity, beyond the false boundary of public and private, into the question of dignity and respect in sexual politics.

A glance at the international status of regulation reveals that it was already moribund before World War II in much of Europe and nearly everywhere after the war. Between 1890 and 1914, at the height of the first abolitionist campaigns, Norway, Denmark, Finland, Spain, Bulgaria, and Holland all closed state-regulated brothels. England had repealed its Contagious Diseases Act in 1886. Czechoslovakia and Poland followed suit in 1922, Switzerland in 1926, Hungary in 1928. Germany had had a patchwork system from region to region until the National Socialist regime came to power, after which prostitution was labeled asocial. Prostitutes were among the first victims of sterilization and of concentration camps, although there were also party-controlled brothels where they were kept in relative safety from arrest. In 1946 all forms of regulation were abolished. In the same year Marthe Richard won her abolitionist campaign against regulated brothels in France.[6]

That this was not merely a succession of individual national decisions was made clear by the UN charter and the Declaration of Human Rights. Signed by all member nations, including Italy, these documents declared all forms of prostitution to be exploitative and pledged no government involvement except for prevention of the phenomena of prostitution and of trafficking in women. Senator Boggiano Pico of the DC complained, "It is unfortunately well-known that our country lagged behind every civilized nation," and Deputy Lombardi was angry that Spain and Portugal were actually ahead of Italy in this matter, that Italy "remained alone in Europe with this sad prize."[7] The women members of Parliament, too, quickly sensed this and worked to link the issue of legalized prostitution to their vision of women's rights.

Merlin and her colleagues insisted that their parliamentary struggle was a matter of guaranteeing equal civil rights to all citizens of Italy, as the Constitution stipulated in Article 3. Yet prostitutes were not considered by any of the concerned legislators, doctors, police officers, nuns, or journalists to be members of society, indistinguishable from other women. Prostitutes were a targeted population for either charity or police control, oppressed women to be redeemed and rehabilitated, or criminals to be suppressed. Even the activists of UDI and CIF in this campaign saw themselves as social workers and champions of the less fortunate, in the tradition of pre-suffrage feminist movements who practiced social work as political activism.[8] The women of the Lost Wave wanted to save their less fortunate sisters by helping them to "change their lives," by rehabilitating these troubling marginal examples of femininity into of the respectable womanliness society deemed worthy of full citizenship.[9]

Angelina Merlin was born in Pozzonovo di Padova, a small town about thirty miles southwest of Venice, in October 1887, to a respectable bourgeois family. Her father was secretary of the city council and an enthusiastic proponent of the family tradition of patriotism and civic service. There were many military honors in the family legacy, and her two brothers both volunteered to fight in World War I as soon as Italy entered the conflict; sadly, they were also both killed. Despite a family culture more dedicated to civic morality than religious piety, she completed her preparatory studies for university with the Canossian nuns, since the high school in their area was only for boys.[10] Upon receiving her teaching certificate she began teaching middle school in Padova. In 1919 she became a member of the Socialist party and remained in the PSI when the communists left to form their own party in 1921. "Of Marx I only knew the name and a few notions from philosophy textbooks; I only knew that the party worked to realize an ideal of justice that was the same as mine. None of the rest mattered to me."[11] After delivering a passionate and sentimental speech commemorating Rosa Luxemburg, she was approached by Dante Gallani, a local doctor and socialist member of Parliament some eight years her senior, who congratulated her but advised that she must become more theoretical and less emotional and advised her to read Marx. Gallani later admitted the comment was a pretext; he was inspired to approach her by the beauty of her voice, "capable of transfixing the masses."[12] But Lina took the attention to heart, deepening her understanding of Marxism and becoming closer to Gallani, even though she remained convinced that socialism's best virtue was honesty rather than theory.

The party named her secretary of their electoral committee in 1924. Among her activities at this time was providing Socialist Deputy Giacomo Matteoti documentation of the Fascist atrocities in her area. Matteoti denounced the tactics of Mussolini and the Fascist Party in two famous speeches from the floor of the Chamber, and published a book called *The Fascists Exposed* that used Merlin's data. Following Matteoti's assassination in June of 1924, Merlin was increasingly in danger. Her refusal to become a member of the Fascist party when membership was required of all public school teachers made it impossible for her to keep a job. In 1926, after five arrests by the Fascists in the space of twenty-four months and an attempted escape to clandestinity in Milan, she was caught and condemned to five years in Sardinia in *confino*, the internal exile instituted by Mussolini to punish political dissidents. Upon her release, she joined the Resistance and quickly distinguished herself in various leadership positions, achieving a level of power that casts doubt on her assertions that she was a naïve idealist.[13]

Merlin returned to Milan, where she reencountered Gallani, and they married. He was a widower with two sons from his first marriage, she adopted her orphaned niece Elena Marinucci, and together they tried to enjoy family life even as they struggled against the regime. After Gallani's death in 1936, Lina remained single for the rest of her life, dedicating herself to activism and sharing an intense familial bond with Elena. After the fall of Mussolini and the disorganized announcement of Italy's armistice with the Allies on September 8, 1943, she returned to her school and organized a resistance cell, putting teachers and students to work helping her to produce PSI news reports and propaganda, and posting the janitors as guards to warn of the surprise visits of Nazi and Fascist officials.[14] During the Resistance and Liberation, the National Liberation Committees (CLN) were the source of military and political organization for all partisans and included representatives from all the antifascist parties. While the country was virtually split in half by Nazi occupation, Merlin was a member of the CLNAI (*Comitato Liberazione Nazionale Alta Italia*), which served as the de facto government of occupied Italy. She was further named the Socialist party representative on the steering committee of the *Gruppi di difesa della donna* (Groups of Women's Defense, GDD). On the day after Milan's liberation, Merlin's leadership was acknowledged as she was made vice commissariat for education in Lombardy.

Unlike Teresa Noce, Merlin never rebelled against doing "women's work" within the party, seeming to accept it as a natural focus and instead attempting an original approach and rethinking of the "woman question."

Like Noce, however, she refused to give up her participation in "general politics," knitting together a unique career of diverse experiences and activism with a sophisticated and idiosyncratic feminist analysis. She shared with many of her cohort of "veterans" in the parties of the Left a tireless and passionate defense of women's rights, but her understanding of women's dignity made her hold herself and others to a strict moral code. Unlike the second-wave feminists who would make it one of their first mass rallying issues, she stood consistently against divorce even as it was legalized in 1970 and approved by referendum in 1974, arguing that it would make it too easy for men to abandon women.[15] Her refusal to back down over the ten years of the campaign to abolish the state brothels owed a great deal not only to the ideas of constitutional rights feminism but also to her personal belief in the morality of defending "those girls" and her determination not to appear intimidated or degraded by the ugliness of the maneuvers against her. Modeling the behavior of the emancipated woman she hoped to lead others toward, she stood firm and admitted no weakness or doubt.

As she worked to help reconstruction, Merlin participated in the founding of UDI and helped to issue a statement in April 1946 for the referendum of June 2: UDI was an association "FOR the rebirth of our country; FOR the defense of the family; FOR the interests of women workers; FOR the social and political elevation of women; FOR the salvation of peace." The program points listed under the "social and political elevation of women" were: the fight against prostitution (not, notably, against regulation), the fight against illiteracy, the creation of "institutions that permit the cultural elevation of women," legal reform, and "full participation of women in the administrative and political life of the country."[16] Merlin continued to gain power and influence within her party and in national politics. Elected to the regional government of Lombardy in 1945, she was then elected to the Constituent Assembly in 1946, and to the Senate of the first legislature in 1948. In all of these venues she petitioned for progressive and egalitarian treatment of women as citizens.

Nearing the age of sixty, but uncomfortable remaining in Rome, which she characterized as full of careerists and con artists, she took on the responsibility of traveling nationally for the party, putting the PSI organization back together and encouraging the formation of local women's chapters of UDI.[17] Nevertheless when the time came for the Constituent Assembly's Committee of 75 to debate the formulation of Article 3, she was present to fight a spirited and successful battle for the inclusion of the words "of sex" in the list of unacceptable reasons for discrimination against the equality of all citizens, thus enabling the movement of constitutional rights feminism. Merlin served as Senator in the first two legislatures, one of only four women in the upper house, and then as a deputy during the third legislature. Although she is remembered as a nonconfrontational, gracious figure, her ideas and her tenacity were startlingly unconventional. Perhaps her famously ingratiating voice smoothed over this contradiction in her colleagues' perceptions.

In June 1948, as the Senate came to order, Merlin was already a leader of national stature and fresh from a historical victory in the creation of the new constitution. So on what political issue, her party and her fellow activists wondered, would she choose to unleash her power? Almost immediately she answered with her first proposal and confounded everyone by campaigning to close the state brothels and restore their residents to full citizenship, which "bourgeois feminists" had fought for for decades. This apparently idiosyncratic choice was perfectly logical to Merlin: Article 3 would be immediately put to the test, and constitutional implementation would begin with a success that would condition the entire fight for women's rights. Regulation of sex was also brought to the fore as an acute wartime problem, given the presence of occupying and liberating armies all over Europe. There was the propagandistic image of grateful girls rewarding Allied soldiers, but also a growing demand for the services of professional prostitutes, as well as a huge black market exchange of sexual favors for provisions. The ambivalence of occupation was further expressed in a wave of rapes and rape accusations—that these two categories were not entirely overlapping is suggested by the numerically implausible prevalence of accusations and convictions of soldiers of color for rape.[18] Thus not only a recomposition of families and the respectable gender order but also the need to discipline sex itself had become international political priorities when Merlin first proposed her reform. The UN Convention duly addressed the issue, and Marthe Richard in France had already won her legislation's passage in 1946. Closer to home, prostitution and citizenship rights were linked in the original decree granting women's suffrage. Its Article 3 stipulated that women "indicated in article 354 of the public safety law"—that is, prostitutes outside of the brothel system—could not be enrolled on electoral lists. So prostitutes in the *case chiuse* could vote, but "dangerous women" were still being identified and controlled by the new state—hardly the affirmation of mass participatory democracy the suffrage was meant to be. This part of the decree was abrogated in 1947 with the ratification of the Constitution so that all women were eligible to vote in the first national parliamentary elections; but it was a first sign that democratic states, no less than Fascist ones, would continue to categorize and restrict the rights of women who did not conform to accepted sexual norms of respectability.[19]

Those concerned with prostitution tended to advocate abolition or regulation. Generally abolitionists did not discriminate between public health and morality. While regulationists felt pragmatically that prostitution was an inevitable and even necessary evil to be made as undamaging as possible, abolitionists felt that the regulationist state was trying to make "vice safe for the sinner."[20] Neither of these viewpoints constitutes an acceptance of prostitution as merely a free economic exchange, a point on the spectrum of acceptable private sexuality, or a free negotiation of gender roles. Both assume the state has the right and duty to be arbiter of sexual behaviors and that tying together sex and commerce carries the taint of sin, or at least crime. The histories of feminism and abolitionist demands were intertwined from the start. Josephine Butler in Britain, and Anna Maria Mozzoni in Italy, who founded the *Lega promotrice degli interessi femminili* (League to Promote the Interests of Women) in 1881, had been important exponents of this issue at the turn of the century, exciting public sentiment with their melodramatic stories of women kidnapped and exploited in filth and poverty, and young girls enticed into sin and sold into bondage in far-off lands.[21] In the course of the Merlin law's journey through Parliament, however, an imminent sea change in sexual mores, encouraged by the coming of the economic miracle and mass consumer culture, became ever clearer. The old regulation/abolition understandings of prostitution, and the definitions of masculinity and femininity it implied, were increasingly out of step with new debates over sex and sex work. The length and vehemence of the debates over Merlin's bill are evidence of change as much as they are reiterations of long-held and traditional viewpoints.

Merlin's first proposal to the Senate, of August 1948, is a vision of abolitionist goals in line with her emancipationist and feminist heritage. Its title—"On the abolition of the regulation of prostitution and the fight against exploitation of the prostitution of others"—defines its aim quite well.[22] It consists of four sections: 1) the abolition of brothels, the prohibition of any form of registration, and the prohibition of trafficking and recruitment; 2) the protection of public morale and human dignity, outlawing public solicitation and procuring; 3) the protection of public health against venereal disease; 4) provisions for ex-prostitutes and for the dissolution of the *polizia del costume* (the vice squad). Article 1 states that all currently state-authorized brothels, as well as all houses of prostitution, defined as any private place where two or more women habitually practice prostitution, must close within forty-eight hours of the law's passage. Article 2 prohibits all forms, direct or indirect, of registration of prostitutes or women suspected of prostitution as well as the provision of any special identification documents to such women. Articles 3 through 5 make it a crime to own, manage or direct any house of prostitution; to recruit or traffic in persons for the purpose of prostitution; to form associations for the purpose of furthering either of these activities; or to live off of another's earnings from prostitution. It doubles the sentences for any of these crimes when committed against a minor and/or a family member, or when committed against two or more women. In the second section, Article 6 prohibits any solicitation, advertising, procurement, or "invitation to lewdness" (*invito al libertinaggio*) in a public place, including being "scandalous" or following anyone in the street. It also, however, stipulates that when such actions are interrupted by the police, if the person in question is in possession of regular documents, then she cannot be arrested or brought to the police station. Articles 7 through 10 provide that minors who are found to live on their earnings from prostitution may be admitted to state institutions for care, and that no woman, foreign, resident, or minor, can be forced to submit to a medical examination or blood test, nor be harassed in any way by the police. The third section, Articles 11 through 17, to be inserted in the penal code, prevents doctors from discriminating against anyone infected with a venereal disease and protects their anonymity. At the same time it provides that any person who is found to be infected and refuses to undergo treatment or cure for the disease can be arrested and fined, and requires anyone working in certain industries, entering school, or getting married to present certified proof of a negative blood test for syphilis. The protective attitude of the proposal toward the private citizen is reiterated at the end, however: "No coercion, moral or material, direct or indirect, may be exercised on the ill, without distinction of sex and social category, to the end of inducing them to accept hospital admittance or to remain there, when they manifest the will to be released." Finally, Articles 18 through 23 provide for other possible problems, such as establishing that all property contracts made by brothel owners are declared null and may not be renewed, and that all debts prostitutes may have contracted to owners are annulled. Two articles especially reveal Merlin's attitude toward prostitution: Article 18 abolishes the *polizia del costume* and states that it must be replaced immediately with a special female police corps with the task of "prevention of juvenile delinquency and of prostitution," and that in the interim women from the Red Cross would be responsible for these cases. Article 19 creates, in all province capitals, institutions to provide "instruction for professional qualification" for ex-prostitutes over the age of twenty-one to enter "at their request."

The law, then, was meant to keep prostitution legal, but to criminalize those who exploited the prostitute, in the form of pimps and brothel owners or in the form of police and doctors, and to give all women opportunities and aid to leave the profession. Especially notable are the prevalent use of the word "woman" when referring to prostitutes (overlooking male prostitution), the strict timetable of the provisions, and the specification of job training for ex-prostitutes at the state's expense. Although the moral condemnation of prostitution is already implicit, the main purpose of the law is clearly this "fight against exploitation." It assumes that the men surrounding them in the business coerce prostitutes, and that freeing women from this criminal underworld will offer them protection. It also shows how feminists like Merlin believed that if prostitutes were simply approached with sympathy rather than harassment by the police and the medical community, they would voluntarily change their ways.

Within this lay two unspoken assumptions. First was the wish that all prostitution, not merely regulated prostitution, would end. If women simply had better options for employment, they would discontinue prostitution. The second motive is the isolation of prostitutes from public visibility: a prostitute may not live with any other prostitutes, nor may she support a partner, even her own husband, on her earnings. She may not solicit in public or advertise her services, but she also cannot have anyone who procures clients for her. The proposal reflects what most abolitionists and feminists had always argued: prostitution should be ended, but it should be through social and moral campaigning, not by legislation or police systems that abused prostitutes. Social and moral reform would target criminal men and hold them to a single moral standard, while at the same time defending and rehabilitating victimized women.

Merlin introduced this proposal to the First Permanent Commission of the Senate on August 6, 1948. Her first report had two main themes: first was the antifascist need to end the arbitrary power of the police, to restore privacy and personal liberty to the private citizen. Second was the equality of the sexes and the reassertion of the dignity and conscience of women and of their rights. She accused men of irresponsibility and hypocrisy, saying that the goal of regulation was not to guard the population's health, but "for men in general, to procure for themselves comfort and safety in their vice, to hold at their discretion every and any woman with the menace of police inquisition, to reaffirm, in spite of public declarations and constitutional principles, masculine privilege and the inequality of the sexes."[23] Merlin asserted with this first proposal that sexuality and family were not the themes at stake in this issue. She concentrated on the liberating, emancipatory nature of the law for women, asserting that all women are potentially discriminated against by regulation and that the system is one that favors men and their interests at women's expense.

Despite Merlin's initial attempt to frame her proposal outside of those terms, reactions were immediate and focused on the threat to conventions about masculine virility. Regulation may have been sexual discrimination, but many women actively supported it. Merlin recounted in her memoirs the example of the wealthy matron who asked her: "But then where I am supposed to send my sons?" Merlin responded that she should arrange with her other women friends to exchange their daughters for their sons, since after all every prostitute is somebody's daughter.[24] Another time she answered the same question with an acknowledgement of new sexual mores in the younger generation: "Boys and girls of the same age will learn together."[25] Notwithstanding the critique of both hypocrisy and class interests in her responses, it was clear even to Merlin that as many women as men found the *case chiuse* convenient and unobjectionable. And both Merlin and her opponents took for granted that the end of prostitution and the challenging of masculine privilege to it were intimately linked with the advance and success of the emancipated woman citizen. Merlin was underestimating how valued this particular masculine privilege was to most Italians.

From the Napoleonic Wars, during the Risorgimento, after Unification, during Fascism, and right up into the first republic after World War II, the Italian state and prostitution had an intimate relationship. State regulation of prostitution, registration and required medical examinations of prostitutes, and state-run brothels were the rule whether the state was liberal or fascist. Discipline of dangerous women was one major theme of regulationist rhetoric; the other was quarantine of contaminated and contaminating women. This theme stemmed from one dreaded disease and its hold on the nineteenth-century imagination: syphilis. Although syphilis never killed as many people as did tuberculosis, its difficulty to diagnose and its painful and dangerous treatment by mercury assured its power as a metaphor for fear of contagion.[26] The contaminating sickness of the prostitute is her moral corruption and deviance, but syphilis is their concrete physical proof, and through bodily contact both are transmitted. In the fight against syphilis, regulation becomes a quarantine of the "sick" away from the healthy body of society, a prophylactic shield for the rest of the population. Prostitutes were an obvious target for disease regulation not only because they were morally suspect and likely carriers, but also mainly because they were believed to be, in the age of Cesare Lombroso, a different physiological type from "normal" women.

There were two methods of registration: voluntary and forced. A prostitute could either present herself at the Health Office and get a *libretto*, a "little book" with her personal information and the dates of her medical examinations, or the police could pick up any woman they suspected and arrest her. If she were believed to be a prostitute but had no *libretto*, she would be given a vaginal exam to check for venereal disease and the result would be registered before she was released; once registered, no matter the result of the exam, she was legally a proven prostitute. Thus, the state was the first and definitive penetrator of the "fallen" woman, the speculum the "penis of the State," and state-mandated visits were not for disease prevention, but acts of forced submission.[27] Registered prostitutes underwent biweekly medical exams, were restricted from many parts of the city, and had a curfew of ten o'clock. Food, gaming, and drink were forbidden in brothels, so as to discourage patrons from spending long amounts of time or becoming over-exuberant while there. These measures reflected both the idea of quarantine and that of discipline, as regulation was supposed to free prostitution from its criminal ties. Article 17 of the 1860 Regolamento Cavour defined prostitutes as "all women who notoriously practice prostitution," while a brothel was a place "where prostitution is habitually exercised." The police were left to label women as they chose. Grounds for suspicion were normally that the woman was found unaccompanied on the street and/or that she was homeless or unemployed. [28]

Despite these measures, regulation did not manage to truly control prostitution in Italy. In 1870 there were 8,302 registered prostitutes; in 1881, 10,422; from 1900 to1910 there were between 5,500 and 6,500. This was never more than. 04% of the population, although in cities both the absolute numbers and the percentage were higher. But even at the height of the *case chiuse*'s numbers, in 1881, those 10,422 women represented only 64% of all registered prostitutes, and the number of clandestine prostitutes was rising as well.[29] Especially in the worsening economic climate after the 1890s, a woman often practiced prostitution in a very fluid manner, not entering a brothel and remaining there, but exchanging full-time work for prostitution at certain periods in her life, and mixing legitimate employment and part-time prostitution at others, in order to supplement her own and her family's earnings. As hard as the police tried, it was simply impossible to identify and register every woman who prostituted. Not only did she not look different from the "normal" population, she was no different.

With Fascism came the desire to control the entire national population more closely, and the system became more repressive almost immediately upon Mussolini's rise to power. Again the formulation of a new state and the codification and control of female sexuality went hand in hand. Extreme nationalism and, later, racism made healthy bodies and "moral regeneration" political ideals.[30] Again, prostitutes were an especially easy category of the "dangerous classes" to target. In 1923, 1929, 1931, and 1940 Mussolini issued regulationist decrees. The 1923 regulation required that all prostitutes, even *isolate* (registered women practicing outside the brothel system), carry the *libretto* with all exams listed at all times, transforming it into a kind of internal passport. The 1931 law defined a brothel as a place where even one person "habitually exercises" prostitution and set standards so that the state would control and receive the taxes from all possible prostitution.[31] In addition, in 1926 new Public Security codes were issued, which also addressed the need for a crackdown on illicit sexuality in public spaces. It was at this time that unregistered prostitutes—presumably many women who had committed no other crime than to be insufficiently protected by respectable men—were brought forcibly to brothels by the *polizia di costume* conducting mass raids throughout Italy's urban centers.

Fascist propaganda also trumpeted the ideal of the "New Woman" and the dangers of the decadent, American-style "crisis woman," saying that birth control caused neurasthenia, urinary tract infections, and peritonitis; that lipstick caused lip cancer, and that kissing bred disease.[32] Collaborating with the medical community and the Catholic Church, the Fascist regime told women that sexual contact led to illness and abnormality of the body, thus sharpening the divide between "normal" women and "deviant" prostitutes. More formally, in 1929 the penal code revision by Rocco included in articles 545–555 of Title X provisions that transformed the "knowing transmission of a venereal disease" into a crime "against the race."[33] Perhaps at no other moment had regulation of prostitution in Italy represented such a drastic denial of the prostitute's membership in society, nor such an adamant insistence on her fundamental difference.

After the fall of Fascism and the end of World War II, France served as the model and perhaps most pressing incentive for Italy's abolitionists. There Marthe Richard, a city councillor of Paris and member of the National Assembly, demanded an abolitionist law that came to bear her name. Like Merlin, Richard had been a leader in the Resistance and at war's end enjoyed considerable popularity as one of few female politicians. But the law created by a government commission between her December 1945 demand and its passage in April 1946 was more accurately considered a prohibitionist law in that it continued to criminalize the entire context in which prostitution took place, though not the act itself. The 1946 Richard law made prostitution in itself legal but made brothels, solicitation, procuring, and advertising sexual services illegal. Involuntary registration and forced examination were also outlawed. All existing registers were to be destroyed. In France, the political circumstances favoring abolition were comparable to those in Italy. In light of the Vichy government's repressive regulationist system and brothel-keepers infamous for colluding with German occupying forces, postwar sentiment was strongly against all things tainted with fascism. Abolition was presented as part of the campaign for antifascist purification, helping in France to pass the law overwhelmingly and nearly without debate. Second, the medical profession now favored universal sanitary measures to control disease rather than quarantine of targeted populations. Politically, the electoral success of the Popular Front parties and of the *Mouvement Républicain populaire*, of centrist and Catholic inspiration, favored progressive social reform. Finally, a renewed pronatalist discourse combined with traditional familist moralism argued that sexuality should be harnessed only in the pursuit of national repopulation.[34]

Public belief in the usefulness and service of the brothels, however, along with the old arguments in favor of regulation (though weakened in the era of penicillin), and the ambivalence in feminist and abolitionist circles towards prostitution itself, had remained unchanged. Rather than a unifying banner behind which the women's movement rallied voters to its cause, abolition was a proposal surprisingly unsupported by much of public opinion. As in Italy, the proposal to abolish public brothels met with immediate criticism from a wide swathe of the French population.

Concern with public opinion was also a political effect of antifascism and aspirations for the new republic, as well as an echo of American-inspired sociology. Pierpaolo Luzzatto Fegiz, a professor and statistician in Milan, founded the *Istituto DOXA*, a privately funded research corporation, in 1946. Inspired by the American model of George Gallup and desirous of "a daily collaboration between the government and the people," the institute, in addition to performing market research for private companies, sponsored nationwide opinion polls designed to gather information on a variety of issues, from food consumption and fashion preferences to newspaper readership and political sympathies. A 1949 poll conducted by DOXA revealed that 80% of respondents believed prostitution would not diminish upon abolition of the *case chiuse*, that 87% thought that there would be a rise in illegal prostitution and in diseases, and that almost 86% felt the *case chiuse* were still "the lesser evil."[35]

When asked "Are you in favor or against the closing by law of the tolerance houses?" 24% of people answered, "I don't know." Of the rest, five out of seven people declared themselves against the closure. Of the men questioned, the proportion was 68% in favor of the continuation of regulation, 9% against, and 23% unsure. Of the women, 43% percent simply answered "Don't know," but 48% were in favor of the *case chiuse*. Like men, only 9% of women declared that the houses should be closed.[36]

Medical experts tended to favor regulation, offering as scientific evidence the "physical and psychic health of the Latin male," and the control of prostitution as an important "safety valve" for the "irrepressible physiological demands of young men." It was occasionally mentioned that even illicit sex was preferable to the alternatives: sodomy and masturbation.[37] The Latin libido, one doctor went so far as to argue, finds its proper environment in the Catholic family with controlled prostitution as an occasional outlet, unlike the Anglo-Saxon model, where regulation had been abolished for a long time but where a different "sexual morality" reigned: "divorce."[38]

The truth for many Italians was that the *case chiuse* were seen not merely as a "lesser evil" but actually as a positive site for male socializing and for erotic education for men. Even the generation of men who frequented the houses during the Fascist regime found much to defend about their experiences there. As novelist and artist Dino Buzzati later put it, "Think of it! At any hour of the day or night, and at a reasonable price, without any complications or risk, without wasting time, to be able to have... a very young girl, of extraordinary beauty... and superior bravura, who [otherwise] would require long and tormented approach maneuvers and the spending of a great deal of money."[39] This is clearly an idealized view of prostitutes as uniformly young, gorgeous, sexual athletes; but the sense of entitlement to sexual access to women implied in the resentful complaint that it is far too much trouble to get a girl on one's own is notable.

Buzzati's was an unconventional and idiosyncratic voice, but in this case he seemed to speak for many people. Men like him relied upon the state as a supplier of approved sex; they saw regulation not as a necessary evil, but a wonderful benefit of citizenship in the Italian state. Buzzati went further in this patriotism, characterizing the *case chiuse* as the transmitters of "*civiltà erotica,* which . . . was passed down, by words and by example, from generation to generation, nourishing an often refined art, which I now fear has been lost forever." He accused Merlin of "destroying an immense capital of culture, never again recuperated."[40] Author and actor Giancarlo Fusco felt solidarity with the prostitutes at his favorite brothel in Via Pomino in Genova, calling them the "*operaie della seduzione*" (the working class of seduction). As a poor student he passed time with his fellow students, other customers, and the girls in the waiting room just for company and conversation, studying there, keeping warm in the winter, and becoming a favorite of the madam.[41] He even went so far as to characterize the houses of tolerance as sites that aided antifascism, giving men a place apart, untouched by the demands of the regime on men in public, yet more social than the private home: "There where tolerance was practiced (*dove si tollerava*), the mind rediscovered itself in free encounter, it opened itself to hope, in a certain sense even to rebellion."[42] In short, the public brothels were important sites of the production and passing down of masculinity in Italy, places of patriarchal identity and certainty. Their management by the state lent legitimacy to this structure of gender definition and hierarchy. By 1958 the mass media had popularized the idea that modernization, Americanization, and consumption in Italy were leading to the triumph of the masculinized woman and the end of men. *L'Europeo* that November would run two different series of articles and caricatures affirming that "*la donna conquista il potere*" (women have conquered power), and "*il sesso forte depone le armi*" (the stronger sex lays down its weapons). The legge Merlin became a lightning rod for such fears, symbolizing women's takeover and destruction of every last space of masculine refuge.[43]

While men would find a way to transition into the world of mass consumption, with new masculine and virile identities assured through the right products and the image of the father and successful entrepreneur, the abolitionist campaign would remain a top-down attempt at social reform.[44] As late as 1973, a study of women in Italy found that only a minority of those interviewed considered the legge Merlin a positive reform, while the majority opined that it had only served to increase private and uncontrolled prostitution in the streets.[45]

After Merlin's first presentation in the Senate and before the DC had officially responded, Merlin's strategy was seen as an "able political move," provocative because it stole the initiative from the DC "in a field in which it could not declare itself agnostic."[46] Merlin had guessed that this would be true. In her autobiography she wrote that there was never a "true and proper political coalition" on the issue, but that it was "logical" that neither the DC nor the socialists and communists could oppose it, "since, in spite of the divergent ideologies, they had to be consistent with their own doctrines: of equality before God the former, of emancipation from every form of slavery the latter."[47]

Merlin had consciously chosen an issue for "the first social law of Italy" that would force both the Right and the Left to come together, but she had not perhaps fully prepared herself for the power the DC would immediately bring to bear. Continuing the pattern set during deliberations over Noce's maternity leave proposal, six months later seventeen DC party members presented a bill in the Chamber of Deputies titled "Closing of locales of prostitution." To reach a compromise on the evident conflict between legislative projects, the Merlin project would be pursued in the Senate, and the Christian Democrat senator Antonio Boggiano Pico would become Merlin's collaborator.[48] His revisions are conspicuous, and in letters to his son during this period he explicitly claimed authorship and even the original impetus for the proposal.[49]

Antonio Boggiano Pico was a famous representative of the social and political arm of the Catholic Church. Born in 1873 to a venerable and devout Piedmontese family, by 1915 he had distinguished himself sufficiently that the Pope called him to the executive committee of Catholic Action. In 1918 he helped found the PPI or *Partito Popolare Italiano*, which marked the first moment of Catholic participation in national Italian politics. Boggiano Pico refused to join Mussolini's government and was one of about 150 members of Parliament who withdrew to protest the murder of Giacomo Matteotti in 1924. He spent the remainder of the regime in apolitical university posts. As a senator of the new republic and later president of the Senate's foreign affairs committee and representative to the UN, he had a great deal of prestige and influence both domestically and abroad.[50]

When Boggiano Pico first became involved in the Merlin proposal, he wrote to his son that it was a "good moralizing campaign" and that he had already been thinking about such an effort for a long time, but that he felt it was politically advantageous that it emerged from "the other shore," sustained by "a socialist woman senator" and by Senator Terracini, who was "Jewish and a communist."[51] The proposal would need many modifications in committee, he had written in October 1948, and by the time of his December 12, 1949 letter he said he had been "very involved" and was actually "the true and proper author of the text" brought before the whole assembly. He remarked that there might still be other changes to the law, but that the first article which closed the brothels was the only "fundamental" one and that it had been approved in the "text formulated by myself."[52] He clearly deprioritized the protection of women from involuntary medical examinations and the provision of alternatives in the legitimate job market. His rhetoric emphasized marriage, not work or politics, as the ultimate site of fulfillment and happiness for women.

A revised text of the proposal was presented to the Senate on October 12, 1949. This time, Merlin's speech reflected a new focus: the moral elevation of the Italian state.[53] Merlin still argued that regulation violated the principles of the law and was openly unconstitutional, and she repeated that her moral judgment was concerned with ending male hypocrisy. Prostitution was not a crime, she contended, for if it were, both participants would be condemned. She also argued that if a man's first sexual experience is one where he learns only brutality and contempt, he will then treat all women in his life with these qualities; his wife will only be his slave "and that is not the least cause of the ruin of the institution of the family, which is the base of our ethical social relationships."[54] Prostitutes can only provide "brutality and contempt" in their relations; good women, women who are wives and mothers, cannot be treated the same way prostitutes are treated. The emphasis had shifted from women's equality to the necessity to safeguard the family and to the willing condemnation of prostitutes as "brutal" women who exist outside familial structures. Merlin's abandonment of her earlier call to end discrimination against all women sounds an ominous note.

Boggiano Pico orchestrated this change of emphasis during committee deliberation and in fact gave the impression that he had never intended to let Merlin's arguments persist. He explicitly worked to redirect abolition from its feminist source into a Catholic campaign of moralization which he linked with a need to fight pornography, immoral cinema, and "miseducation of our youth."[55] UDI had issued a document in June 1948 criticizing the "Vatican- government" alliance that continually sabotaged all social work and welfare proposals from "democratic origins."[56] This was a clear example of that "sabotage." Yet Merlin continued to be the nominal leader of the campaign. She neither stepped down nor, apparently, was she asked to do so. She must have agreed to support the new format and thought that it was still a worthwhile reform. Both the parties of the Left and the militants of UDI, sensitive to critiques of immorality and destruction of the family, were especially careful to proclaim themselves as the guardians of peace and safety for that fundamental social institution. The programmatic "defense of the family," the need to protect and nurture it now more than ever, was ubiquitous across the political spectrum.

Boggiano Pico's substantially revised text expressed this more disciplinary and repressive attitude. He removed the entire third section from the bill, so that population-wide detection and treatment of venereal disease was no longer offered as the alternative to ending regulation. The distinction between state-authorized brothel and house of prostitution and the definition of house of prostitution were gone, replaced by "brothel as defined by the... 1931 Public Security decree," which had defined houses of prostitution as those where even one woman practiced. These "brothels" were given four months to close, as opposed to the forty-eight hours in the Merlin bill, effectively prohibiting all prostitution but allowing the state to gather more taxes from these women in the meanwhile. Instead of a passage in Article 3 prohibiting the ownership or gestation of such an establishment, there was now a list of public establishments whose owners and managers would be held accountable for "habitually tolerating the presence of one or more persons" who practice prostitution: including hotels, *pensioni*, drink stands, recreation circles, dance halls, theaters, and any locales "attached or dependent" to them. Another new addition to Article 3 was a provision stating that it was illegal to "*favorire*" or "*agevolare*," roughly to facilitate, the prostitution of others.[57] Article 6 now stated that a person previously convicted of any of these crimes was banned from holding public office for two to twenty years from the end of their sentence. Article 8, which stated that the institutions to be established for ex-prostitutes would be directed toward the "guidance, assistance, and reeducation" of the women, did not explicitly make participation optional, and it added that they were for women who "intend to return to an honest life." Article 10 stated that minors who were practicing prostitution would preferably be returned to their families; only if their families refused to care for them could they enter a state home. Article 12 no longer abolished the *polizia del costume*, but simply said that a female corps would be constituted by a separate law. Finally, Article 15 now stated that debts contracted between prostitutes and owners were illicit, but that "contrary proof is admissible." Women leaving the houses could still be forced to remain financially in service of the former owners.

Amidst the general change of tone, the use of the word "woman" is made more specific. It is replaced by "persons" in all the criminalizing articles of the bill but left intact in the provisions referring to repayment, reeducation, rehabilitation, and repatriation. This focus on women is no longer emancipatory nor even protective, but disciplinary. Although Merlin's own proposal was far from free of moralizing influences, it gave the women it affected far more alternatives after leaving a brothel. The new bill made prostitution as difficult and isolated as possible, and at the same time curtailed the provision of aid and alternative employment. No longer victims of criminally exploitative men, prostitutes were recast as criminals themselves.[58]

This was the bill introduced to the public. At no time was the original proposal the focus of public discussion. It is difficult to say if it would have made a difference, since the public distrusted the entire enterprise. In addition, during the six-month gap between Merlin's original proposal and report and the revised project with the DC contribution, public attention was focused on the possibility of communist revolution. Palmiro Togliatti, the charismatic head of the PCI, was shot by an assassin in July, triggering an immense furor, sensationalist press coverage, and spontaneous strikes in every industrial center. This fueled the image of a Marxist army awaiting only their leader's signal to overthrow the murderous capitalist order. Togliatti recovered and hurriedly calmed his party. The PCI, and indeed the entire left, sought to reassure the Italian people that it wanted only peace.[59] As the PCI and the PSI rushed to soothe ruffled feathers, their support for Merlin was withdrawn to some extent, in favor of concentrating on safer issues.[60] The DC was quick to seize on the Left's moment of hesitancy, as communists were ousted from cabinet positions and increasingly marginalized in the legislature. Abolition became a Christian Democratic issue. Even if she had wanted to advance a feminist discussion of abolition, Merlin never had more than that six-month window before the competing agendas of both her own party and the DC shut it down.

The DOXA polls revealed that in one category, people who regularly read the newspapers, regardless of political orientation, an even higher percentage of respondents was against abolition of the houses. The pollsters concluded that this demonstrated that "the cultured classes are more concerned with the negative consequences" of abolition.[61] Yet this correlation may merely reflect that nearly the entire press portrayed abolition as a dangerous and libertine course of action, and Merlin herself as a sexually obsessed free-love radical. Even the *New York Times* referred to her as a "widow" and a "freethinker," instead of as "Senator," while *Newsweek* called the eventual passage of the law a "Spinster Victory" and referred to her throughout the article as "Miss Merlin." Antonio Fusco described a political cartoon of Merlin dressed as an ancient Roman matron, presumably in imitation of Cornelia, who famously referred to her children as her most valuable jewels. In the cartoon another woman, adorned with gems and jewelry, looks on as Merlin shows her a spirochete and a gonococcal sphere (the germs that symbolized the contagion of sexually transmitted diseases) and says proudly, "These are my jewels!" This cartoon thus simultaneously criticizes Merlin for being a mother and not being a mother, lampooning her perversion of the maternal role by devoting her nurturing and sacrifice to diseased, dirty prostitutes rather than children of her own. It also links this criticism to the classical Roman ideal of humble, self-sacrificing motherhood, thus implying that Merlin is unpatriotic, unItalian. Even her supporters tended to weaken her image as a political leader or rights activist, referring to her as "the mother of prostitutes, the apostle of 'those girls.'" A cartoon published in a progressive journal the same week as the Roman matron cartoon showed Merlin breaking the chains of a "white slave" who thanks her for her freedom.[62]

But Merlin herself never completely gave up the democratic and emancipatory tone of the first proposal, as revealed in a published volume of letters she received from prostitutes. In its 1955 introduction, she proclaimed: "Regulation . . . is one of the most patent and clamorous cases of the situation in which men want to see woman confined, but also one against which denunciation and revolt come most immediately and spontaneously. . . . [Abolition] is an important means to awaken (*conquistare*) the Italian woman's consciousness of the necessity of her emancipation, the element which conditions, in notable measure, the possibility for democratizing the life of our country and . . . to put an end to the exploitation of the many by the few."[63]

The letters written by prostitutes and sent to Merlin were collected and published by *Avanti!*, the socialist party newspaper, and clearly meant as an antidote to the otherwise negative publicity the proposal received. They are the only instance of prostitutes' direct voices in the debate. While detailing the day-to-day conditions in the houses and the restrictions and difficulties of daily life for registered prostitutes even after they left the house network, they were not devoid of rhetoric or political savvy. Merlin and her coauthor, journalist Carla Barberis, took care to publish letters both for and against abolition, but in no letters does a woman characterize the nature of her work or her entry into the profession as voluntary. Whether this is due to Merlin's editing or to self-editing is impossible to say, but the voluntary-involuntary distinction was not a part of this debate; it was in the best interests of any woman, politician or prostitute, to establish her own morality as legitimate if she wished to have her voice heard.

Having established this legitimacy, most of these women's comments still convey pride and the rejection of abolition as charity, preferring to concentrate on the issues of social justice in their stories. They ask to be treated like any other woman, to be able to reenter normal society. "It is often said . . . that we are not obligated to enter into the life. It's not true: we are worse than obligated. . . . It is always others who obligate us, who force us to receive thirty to thirty-five men a day . . . We want to return to being women like any other, and to be assured of an honest job and not a handout."[64] Another woman had similar wishes, but doubted the ability of the state to fulfill them: "I admire and am almost happy about your project; but thinking of the perhaps short time that I have left to exploit my years in this abject work, after which I won't be able to feed my children, makes me feel almost bitter. Will the government give us jobs? Or will we be disrespected and isolated then as we are today?"[65] Yet another woman doubted a law would ever be passed, since everybody, from the government on down to the chambermaids in the brothels, profited from their work: "[the women] have to cover all expenses themselves of disinfectants, doctors, food for everyone, gifts to the madams, to the directors, tips to the personnel." Still another denounced those in power for how they "disrespectfully and insultingly, at the same time convinced of their ability to keep anyone down with their power, instead of administering this most delicate matter with human justice, continue to profit from it." Another wrote: "I understand the government will no longer profit from those millions from taxes. But let it legalize some other trade, not the flesh of its own women."[66] In these letters the theme of moral shame, that of the government and that of exploiting men, is very strong and surely what Merlin meant to highlight. From the prostitutes' own voices comes a further theme that the Lost Wave failed to stress: sex work is work. And these women expect to work, one job or another. None says she wishes to marry and have children and be a housewife. What Noce and the women's associations could emphasize about mothers, that their labor should be valued as work by the society at large, Merlin could not even mention. Prostitutes saw themselves as working women, but the supporters of abolition could not equate sexual freedom with political freedom. That was simply not an available strategy for the women of the Lost Wave, who sought mass consensus by claiming to help restore the respectable sexual order of Italy.

The published letters added emotion to the debate, but they could not refocus its themes once Boggiano Pico began working with Merlin. The coalition which formed around abolition had in fact guaranteed the law's passage by 1955, even if it would take three more years until the Chamber of Deputies took its final vote. That same coalition had recovered from any loss it may have suffered from Merlin's seizure of the initiative in 1948 and had turned the issues firmly away from a feminist and emancipationist agenda and toward the guardianship of the family. UDI could not counter effectively; although her exploits were recorded in the minutes of the UDI Congress, the association produced little echo of Merlin's struggle in Parliament after 1952, the end of the first legislature. When Merlin was reelected to the Senate and managed to resubmit the project in 1953 for the beginning of the second legislature, her support came from CIF, not UDI.[67]

After 1955, the die was cast. In Parliament, two projects about to become law, as well as the final revision of the Merlin proposal, set the parameters for the final legal status of prostitution in Italy. The crystallization of the situation also set the precedent for the process of social reform and public debate for many years to come.

The two projects were both passed in 1956: one, the virtual copy of section 3 from Merlin's original 1948 proposal, concerned provisions for public health and venereal disease; it required proof in the form of a medical identification card that applicants to many job categories and anyone deemed at risk had to show to demonstrate they had tested negative for syphilis and other contagious diseases.[68] That is, the *libretto* was restored, as prostitutes are nearly by definition "at risk." The second law was a revision of the Fascist public order laws from the Rocco Code of 1930; it became the tool by which the police would justify their continued harassment and recording of prostitutes, which continues to effectively label prostitutes as criminals. This law, n.1423 of December 27, 1956, provided that police could exercise control over people deemed dangerous to safety and particularly those who habitually practice activities "contrary to public morals and common decency." This has been interpreted since the abolition of the *case chiuse* to apply to street prostitution. The chief of police can officially warn a street prostitute to "change her life." Once she has been warned, if she is practicing outside her native city of residence she can be kept under special surveillance, lose her driver's license, be arrested and held in jail, and be given a *foglio di via*, a forced repatriation order to her town of legal residence.[69] A woman confronted in a routine stop by the police would theoretically have to show her proof of medical examination, her driver's license, her state ID, and her *foglio di via*. Should she fail to produce the proper combination of these she would be jailed and released only once properly documented and relocated. The prostitute thus finds herself in a strange historical eddy where the waters of regulationism, fascism, and democracy all swirl together to maintain an internal passport system directed specifically at her.[70] Even more demonstrative of this connection between identity papers, prostitution, and state control is the fact that when dealing with the growing population of transgender and transsexual prostitutes, arresting police often charge the accused with identity fraud: by dressing as a female but carrying identity papers assigning a male gender, the prostitute has committed a crime against the state. This system also fails to take into account the large numbers of prostitutes today who are not citizens or legal residents of Italy, but migrants, many of whom have been trafficked.

Most surprisingly, the police and public health authorities retained their copies of *libretti*, and in some cases even continued to issue new ones, despite the fact that Merlin's law had ordered them destroyed. This strange afterlife of the *libretti*, combined with the use of the *foglio di via* as a sort of internal passport limiting the movement of identified prostitutes, implies that the gendered discrimination they made possible under Fascism was also necessary to the construction of a democratic Italy. The *libretto* is one of many ways that states, even ones nominally committed to gender equality, have maintained sexual difference and its hierarchies of power so that women's experience of citizenship's rights and obligations remains unequal.

Setting aside the legacies of law n.1423, in January of 1955 the Senate finally approved and passed on to the Chamber of Deputies the text of the Merlin proposal that would become law. Discussion there began in April of 1956. There were two notable changes from the draft already created by Boggiano Pico's collaboration in 1949: first, rather than four months, the brothels were given six months after the law's passage to close. Second, the abolition of the *polizia del costume* and the establishment of the female corps would no longer be legislated, but would take place "gradually and within the given limits" and would be enacted by presidential decree upon the recommendation of the Ministry of the Interior.[71] This has never taken place.[72] The provision, at the expense of the state, of transitional housing and job training to prostitutes leaving the brothels was also a fraught enterprise. At first the agency charged with helping the women, the C.I.D.D. or *Comitato italiano di difesa morale e sociale della donna* (Italian Committee for the Moral and Social Defense of Women), could not even make contact with them, since most prostitutes so thoroughly distrusted the state that they were certain these treatment centers were meant to re-entrap them.[73] Instead, the groups charged with protecting and helping to rehabilitate prostitutes have historically cooperated with the police to identify their clients by visiting the jails each morning, whereupon the police hand over women arrested the night before.[74] In this way even intervention on behalf of these women's rights was facilitated by the police's retention of the power to track and detain them. This constituted more of a continued denial of their autonomy and agency than a liberation.

There was a great deal of sound and fury in the Chamber of Deputies between April 1956 and January 1958 about abolition, but in the end it signified nothing. The bill they received was the law they approved. The only opponents of the legge Merlin were the ex-fascist MSI and the Monarchists, marginal parties that represented nostalgia for the past. They presumably also represented an important gap in the consensus-building power of the antifascist coalition, if not in number of votes, certainly on social matters. Members of the police and medical communities who were seriously alarmed at the support for the legge Merlin anxiously provided professional analyses and quantitative evaluations of the phenomena of female deviance and sexual contagion. Further proof of this lack of consensus was the second DOXA poll, carried out in 1959. Repeating the 1949 questions about the public's view of abolition and regulation, the pollsters received the same answers: the majority of public opinion, male and female, still favored the *case chiuse*.[75] As the writer Pietro Bianchi made clear, most men of a certain generation continued to look upon the *case chiuse* with affection and nostalgia: "It had its own importance, the fact that we all knew the houses were under the control of the administration; the state, which gave us our schools, also gave us our brothels."[76] Another author commented, "I still cannot succeed in seeing any reason for which the state cannot and should not... be the intermediary of love. At bottom it is an issue of service to a high public interest."[77] Although the women of the Lost Wave succeeded in producing a constitution that guaranteed women's equality, and although the first forty-five passed many laws that aided women's achievements in politics and paid work, Merlin simply could not sustain the constitutional rights discourse when it came to sexual custom. This was not because it was seen as strictly private and no business of the state, but precisely because it was one of the factors of Italians' loyalty to the state. Italians, like the authors quoted here, saw both schools and brothels as training grounds for Italian citizenship and were not willing to alter the version of masculine identity either inculcated. Teresa Noce seems to have been right when she said that nothing would truly change if only women changed: men too had to become different citizens, more focused on the duties than the privileges of citizenship. And sexual privilege has been a trait Italian men have appeared unwilling to relinquish.

One big difference between the sexual politics of then and now, however, is that in 1958 respectability demanded that politicians would not express loyalty to the brothels in public, much less go on record as opposing this law and risk being tarred as immoral or, more dangerously, pro-fascist. The tone of speeches on the day of the law's approval, January 28, 1958, is best represented by Beniamino de Maria of the DC: "It does not become civilized men to be daily audience to the exploitation of poor unhappy creatures by base, abominable individuals," he said. He argued that a democratic Parliament could not call itself such unless it "returned dignity to women who have lost it, thrown into vice, into procuring, into exploitation." Society and the state "owe protection" to their women, he said; they cannot permit that "woman reaches this depth [of vice], the creature of which the poets make angels, to whom Christianity brings the honors of divine maternity."[78] From Merlin's hope that the law would help to make women equal emerged one rooted in keeping women in their place: subordinate, but idealized. The stereotype of the *mamma* was duly summoned to reinforce the DC victory.

The final vote was 385 in favor, 115 against. As Merlin had long predicted, the majority parties had no possibility of dissenting. Neither at that moment nor later did Merlin publicly comment on the difference between her proposal and the law that bore her name, even though at least two, sometimes three, drafts are printed in the appendices of the books she authored, suggesting that she was well aware of the difference of intent that emerges through their reading. Notwithstanding the appearance of solidarity on the political stage, the attacks on the law continued even after its passage. Petitions were circulated trying to create the requisite 500,000 votes for a recall, and student demonstrations were organized. Twenty-five magistrates in Torino signed a document proposing the abrogation of the law and introducing jail time for prostitutes. At the same time, Merlin herself had to hold a press conference at the Venice Film Festival screening of Antonio Pietrangeli's *Adua e le compagne* (1960), in which four unemployed prostitutes attempt to open a restaurant in Rome but end up succumbing to the landlord's demand that they also run a brothel upstairs.[79]

The furor over the legge Merlin was clearly over ideas more than reality. The law freed only 2,705 prostitutes, since the brothels had been dying out in the wake of postwar social changes anyway. "Instead of the law on closed houses, it should have been called the law of the empty houses!" jokes Roberta Tatafiore, a present-day scholar of sex work. "The market had already moved on. It had been ten years since the Ministry of the Interior had approved a new license."[80] But proposals to amend the law were quick to reactivate the whole debate: in 1959, 1961, and 1963 new bills made their way through Parliament, each one intended to revise the Merlin law's articles forbidding registration and required medical visits. Although none of these laws passed, the women's associations saw the threat as real and from 1960 formed commissions to lobby against all forms of documentation for prostitutes in a campaign against "neo-regulationism." The CIDD's assembly minutes of 1960 and 1961 show them reactivating feminist cooperation on the issue. In 1965 a group of senators launched yet another attack, presenting a government-sponsored bill they called "Reform of the legge Merlin" but which in effect reinstated state registration and medical *libretto* requirements for prostitutes. CIF and UDI mounted immediate and massive letter-writing campaigns urging legislators to vote against the bill, but it passed the Senate and made it to full assembly discussion in the Chamber of Deputies before being tabled.[81] The issue has never gone away: three more bills entered committee between 2007 and 2010, while Silvio Berlusconi and his infamous minister for equal opportunity, the former TV model Mara Carfagna, supported the reintroduction of the brothel system. In 2013 municipal governments cooperated to gather signatures to put a referendum proposal on the next ballot calling for "the partial abrogation of the legge Merlin," which would reopen regulated brothels as a measure against "public disorder." While the law has withstood these attacks, positive attitudes toward the *case chiuse* and negative judgment of the legge Merlin do not appear to have substantially changed in public opinion.[82]

The law continued to define Merlin's public persona and her legacy. In 1964 she was still answering critics with articles and letters to the editor defending abolition and reminding readers that the law merely implemented principles long established in the Constitution and the UN Convention.[83] Yet Merlin's career was prolific and varied away from the spotlight of the prostitution problem, as she continued to develop the constitutional rights feminism she had spearheaded from the beginning. Already in 1953, in the midst of the battle for her eponymous law, she began another decade-long battle for a law forbidding the firing of married women workers, thereby closing the loophole from the legge Noce.[84] In the course of her three legislative tenures, the indefatigable Merlin proposed twenty-five separate laws, five of which passed, served on the special commission to investigate the Mafia, and was elected secretary of the Senate Presidential Office.[85]

In 1961 she broke with the PSI after open polemics about her candidacy for the next election. The leaders felt she was too old and too controversial and would lose votes for the whole party. She wrote an open letter denouncing them, for the first time in her long career openly breaking party discipline. She subsequently resigned and later moved to Padova, where her niece Elena helped her prepare her memoirs. Lina enjoyed a quiet retirement, finally given respite from her notoriety, until her death on August 10, 1979 at the age of ninety-two.[86] Elena finished editing the autobiography and it was published in 1989, helping to usher in a wave of testimonials from the Lost Wave generation that continues to this day.

Most present-day commentators on the law see it as essentially a failure, owing to the inability of Merlin, and by extension the whole feminist movement in Italy, to be sufficiently autonomous and radical in the attempt at reform. Some present the changes in Merlin's project as an illustration of feminism's betrayal by the religious conservatives in the DC. Merlin intended her project to be entirely emancipatory and to open up a new kind of discourse on women's rights, but she was not strong enough to resist the moralizing, charity-driven instincts of the Christian Democrat-dominated parliament.[87] But the postwar feminists were not themselves free from ongoing tensions between radical subversion and acceptance of reigning gender norms. Such tensions were particularly fraught on this issue, and Merlin spent all the political capital she had accrued in a lifetime of activism trying to resolve them.

The passage of the legge Merlin after a century of state-decreed regulation does reflect, in the end, the success of political and national renewal attempted by the antifascist postwar governments. Merlin and the rest of the first forty-five did succeed in advancing another step on the road to constitutional implementation, and women's rights had been at least abstractly reaffirmed. But as with so many of the laws affecting women's equality, its limits, qualifications, and compromises point to a postwar political culture that was far from ready to relinquish an older vision of sexual identities and gender roles, or give up institutional control or masculine privilege as regarded women's rights or their bodies. The legge Merlin, perhaps more that any other law inspired by constitutional rights feminism, highlights the complicated interrelations between the public and the private, civic laws and private behaviors, and the economics of desire and morality whose burdens women, as individuals and as citizens, carry with them when they join the battle for equality.

5

Both the Rights and the Duties of Citizenship

The Cocco Law for Access to All Public Careers

Just after Clare Boothe Luce's appointment as United States ambassador to Italy in 1953, the Italian weekly news journal *L'Europeo* organized a reception in Rome to present her to an entirely female group of guests. Catholic, conservative, and cozy with Eisenhower, she was married to Henry R. Luce, the publisher of *Time* magazine. She had also achieved fame in her own right as a playwright. Italians were quite unsure what to make of Clare Boothe Luce, or her arrival in another charged election season with thinly veiled offers of huge numbers of lucrative American offshore military procurements (OSPs) in the event of a DC win against the communists. But the guests at this particular reception were most fascinated by the novelty of a woman diplomat, a career still closed to women in Italy. Among those invited to speak were Angela Maria Cingolani, by this time the Undersecretary for Artisanry at the Ministry of Industry and Commerce; Anna Garofalo, a well-known political journalist; Nina Ruffini, a member of the Liberal Party and president of the National Council of Italian Women; Josette Lupinacci, president of the National League of Italian Women, the Roman Soroptimist club, and an honorary judge in Juvenile Court; Teresita Sandeschi Scelba, a doctor and president of the Italian Women's Alliance; and Mary Tibaldi Chiesa, one of the "first forty-five" from the Republican party and the first woman to have argued in the Chamber of Deputies for women's right to join the diplomatic corps.[1] Although it was a glittering affair and a splendid affirmation of the re-blossoming of the women's movement, guests were acutely aware that Clare Boothe Luce alone among all these accomplished women could represent her country and its citizens abroad.

This gathering took place a full ten years before all careers in public service were legally opened to women in Italy. The woman who wrote the law that finally proclaimed women's full juridical personhood, a young Christian Democrat from Sardinia named Maria Cocco, was still far from the political spotlight.

In 1953, opportunities opened and closed to women were a strange patchwork. Women could vote for and be elected to any political office, but they could not sit on a jury. They could serve as any minister or under-secretary in the government, but could not join those same ministries as entry-level functionaries. They could bring suit and argue as lawyers in the courts, but could not become the judge in that courtroom. They could represent Italy to the world as president of the Republic, but could not join the diplomatic corps. And they could debate and declare war in the Parliament, but were unable to enter a military academy, perform military service, or even join the forest rangers.

In short, a woman could not perform all the services her country asked of its people and so her citizenship, proclaimed to be in all ways equal to men's by the Constitution's third article, was in reality legally incomplete. By the beginning of the third legislature in 1958, women had acquired many of the rights and privileges of citizenship. Yet few of the duties of citizenship were required of them, notably the fundamental obligations to provide fair trials to one's peers by doing jury service and to help protect the republic's safety by taking up arms.

In 1963, a law and its flanking campaigns whose primary purpose was to guarantee women's right to enter the judiciary would end up involving the entire spectrum of citizens' obligations. Women questioned whether the rights of citizenship could properly exist without its duties and whether the traditional exclusion of women from these services, usually understood to be substituted by their "service" and their need for protection as mothers, was a privilege or an instance of discrimination. These women demanded that their duties be required of them; to be a true and equal citizen, they said, a woman must not be excused or excluded; she must serve. But as the third legislature of 1958–1963 began, women's political engagement at the national level had not sustained momentum. Women's numbers in Parliament had dropped again, to a mere 28 of 839 total members, or 3%. The Lost Wave's mission of service as the bulwark of mass democracy was beginning to ebb, but not before its women fought one more landmark battle.

Maria Cocco was born in 1916 in Domus Novas, a small town on the island of Sardinia. She was the oldest of five children of a mother who, despite only having an elementary school education, effectively managed a busy household; and a father who served as a town administrator and local judge without ever becoming compromised with the Fascist regime. Cocco recalled, "He had been an officer from 1914–1918 with the machine-gunners and he was proud of reminding us of his service; I never saw him in a fascist uniform," she said. Cocco studied classics at the university in Cagliari, 40 km from Domus Novas, and lived at home while she did so. Although the long daily commute by train was a hardship, she credits her family with fostering her confidence so she could begin exploring the outside world: "Even though we lived modestly, the tranquil well-being at home gave me a foundation of honesty as I chose, decided, judged." Her childhood, like those of the "Resistance recruits," was lived almost entirely under Fascism, but the regime did not seem to impact daily life in her close-knit and intensely Catholic family. She spent a great deal of time involved in Catholic Action activities, enrolling in its "social formation" courses, and helping organize the regional students' groups of the AC.[2] At university, she was in a select minority of female students (women made up between 15 and 20% of all university graduates in these years, and even fewer outside the faculties of languages and literature[3]).

In January 1941, at the age of 25, Cocco went to Rome for about a month to do some research for her senior thesis. While there she experienced the regime and the popular rejection of it up close. "In the shops, in the Catholic institute that hosted me, in the air I noticed that there lingered a superficial acquiescence; but I quickly gathered the suffering of people going hungry and I often heard people joking that they preferred butter (instead of guns!)," she said. Despite her growing political consciousness, she did not participate in the Resistance, instead returning home and devoting her time to finishing her studies and service in AC. "I'm an island girl," she protested, noting Sardinia's geographic and cultural separation from the mainland. Cocco took great pride in her Sardinian identity and used it to navigate the pressures of Rome as a student and later, as a member of parliament, playing on both her exceptionalism and her group identity as it suited her.

In 1944 she returned to Rome to prepare for the teachers' certification exam and to continue her own research in Rome's archives. There she met and began collaborating with Maria Federici, the famous DC veteran of the Constituent Assembly and original president of CIF. Cocco continued to work with Federici until 1948, during which time she joined CIF and the DC and read many of Federici's preparatory documents for her arguments in the Constituent Assembly, including those pertinent to article 51, which Federici wished to guarantee women's access to all careers and specifically their right to become magistrates. When Cocco returned to Cagliari, it was as Sardinia's regional representative to CIF's national council and with a clear dedication to public service. Throughout the period of postwar reconstruction she led Sardinia's CIF in building after-school programs and summer camps for needy children, founded and won accreditation for Sardinia's School for Social Work, and helped create courses on pedagogy for mothers and civic education for all women. As the Cold War took hold, Cocco's vocation in Catholic social action took on an additional political aspect: "The motive of CIF's creation was the education of women in democracy. My political identity—as I define it today, and exactly as it was then—was the simple duty made clear by the watershed of the communist/democracy divide." Perhaps an effect of her isolation from the more leftist-friendly culture of the Resistance, Cocco's anticommunism was a faithful echo of hardline Vatican rhetoric, and she never changed her stance.

By the time Cocco was elected to the Parliament's third legislature from 1958 to 1963, her political identity could be described as firmly Catholic, anticommunist, and aimed at using legislation to improve conditions in her own region for women and children, those most affected by the continued poverty and isolation of what was, geographically and metaphorically, a marginal part of the nation. She characterized the first decade of women's activity in the Republican legislatures as being focused on general consciousness raising about women's condition in regards to defense of working mothers and women's right to equal work opportunities and equal pay. With her participation in the second decade of Parliament, she would succeed in passing legislation to encourage women's contributions to public service at all levels. Rejecting the common complaint of women who were activists in both the associations and the parties about the burdens of "double militancy," she claimed to feel fortunate to be both a parliamentarian who could change the law to reflect social justice and a regional leader of CIF who would observe and participate in the improvement of women's lives because of those legislative changes.[4] She also learned from the women around her that the parliamentary area of the women's movement was concerned not just with the language of universality and social justice already so important to her, but with the strategies for translating that language, found in the Constitution and the UN Declaration of Human Rights, into legislation. But she did not experience the level of cooperation between women members from different parties characteristic of the earlier years. Instead she found that the gap between majority and opposition had hardened. While her party did explore reaching out to the Socialists in these years, this increased the isolation of the Communists, who remained colleagues but little more. The elections of May 1958, which saw Cocco's entry into Parliament, continued the essential stability of Italian electoral politics since the start of the Republic. No party gained or lost more than three percentage points. But among the women the slide had become marked; from the original high of 45, there had only been 37 women in the second legislature, of which Merlin had been the only woman senator, and now there were only 28 women left. The PCI had hemorrhaged members in the face of the Soviet upheavals of 1956—some 400,000 members left between 1955 and 1957, mostly young and many of them women, especially those women who belonged to UDI and began to insist on that association's autonomy.[5] In general the decrease in numbers reflected the retirement of veterans like Noce and Merlin without their replacement by younger women. As the economic miracle took hold, the social revolution beginning in Italy demanded a political response. Until 1962, governments were formed by the DC in weak centrist coalitions; after 1962 and a debate within the party, Amintore Fanfani and Aldo Moro led an "opening to the left" as the party finally turned its back on the ex- and neo-fascists of the MSI, and the Monarchists, and invited the socialists to join the government.

With the ascension of Kennedy in the United States and Pope John XXIII in the Vatican, Italy began experiencing new movement from previously stalemated Cold War positions, from which Maria Cocco and her fellow women activists were able to benefit.[6]

Cocco directed her efforts at two main issues. First, given her sense of responsibility to her regional constituency, she spent a great deal of her time supporting aid bills and committees to investigate economic plans for Italy's depressed regions. Second, she participated in her fellow women party members' projects for women's rights, such as the pension for housewives. She was appointed to both the committees for Labor and Public Welfare and for Justice, allowing her to pursue this double advocacy. But when writing about her motivations and her accomplishments, Cocco never noted a divide in her work; she always emphasized her philosophy of "making laws that simplify" and finding the "underlying human value" in any debate to avoid opposition and conflict in its solution. "I called upon constitutional values, basic principles, which cannot be disobeyed or ignored," she said. "Confronted with those principles Parliament couldn't say no."[7]

Cocco sought to address the problem that, although the Constitution guaranteed women's equality as citizens, there were many examples of functions from which women were barred. One important obstacle was the system of state examinations, which women were not allowed to sit for. In 1946 women had obtained both active and passive suffrage, the right to be both electors and elected; making them eligible for any elected office in the land, up to the presidency. Since the legislative and executive branches of government in a parliamentary system are linked, women could also be appointed to any job in the government and its ministries. In the judiciary and in any job in the civil service that required sitting for state examinations, however, women were completely locked out. These tests are used to award civil service jobs, including in the diplomatic corps, the magistracy, and the police, to those who earn the highest scores throughout the country. While this meritocratic system may have offered more equal opportunities to young men from marginal class or regional backgrounds, it excluded women completely.

An additional obstacle to women's entry into these professions was rooted in Italy's legal history. A civil law country, Italy had two functional groups of lawyers: the prosecutor (*procuratore*), who was responsible for adherence to formal proceedings, and the advocate (*avvocato*), who did the pleading. This division played an important role in women's entry into the profession, as well as in the autonomy and political function of the profession as a whole. Advocate lawyers (*avvocati*) are private and hired by clients, and are not employees of the state. Apart from requiring the law degree and certification to practice, the state does not regulate the profession. But all duties considered to be public and functions that pertain to the state are performed by magistrates, who serve as both judges and prosecutors, and the preparation, training, and promotion process for both positions is supervised by the same body. There are two career trajectories within the magistracy: the role of investigator and public prosecutor (*procuratore*), and the role of judge (*giudice*). Upon gaining judicial robes, or as the Italians call it, *toga*, a magistrate may switch back and forth between the two roles. A 1919 law allowed women to be *avvocati* but otherwise reaffirmed strict traditional hierarchies by proclaiming the control of the judiciary over the legal system, and of the male sex over public offices. Since women could not perform any duties that the state, centralizing its power, claimed as its own purview, between 1919 and 1963 the feminization and the marginalization of the lawyering profession by the national state were simultaneous, although it retained its autonomy from government politics. The judiciary maintained its higher status and was a bastion of masculine hierarchy but it lost its autonomy to the state.[8]

Similar sexual inequalities regarding government work are embedded in several articles of the Constitution, particularly 51 and 97–98. Article 51 of the Constitution states, "All citizens of either sex are eligible for public office and for elected positions on equal terms, according to the conditions established by law." Articles 97 and 98 establish that civil servants are employed through competitive examinations, that they may not simultaneously hold any other paid position, and that they must be politically neutral. Each of these articles occasioned debate during the Constituent Assembly as to whether there should be explicit language regarding women's rights, guaranteeing their equality or limiting it. There was heavy debate on a proposed addition to the end of Article 51, "and conforming to their aptitude." This was successfully rejected by the women constituents and those of their male colleagues who supported them, but the qualifying phrase "according to the conditions established by law" stayed, and provided the main defense of those who wished to justify the restriction of the magistracy.

Maria Federici had warned that precisely such a thing would happen when she argued against any qualifier in the article on May 22, 1947, saying, "It is strange that women, who pay taxes and bear all the same burdens of society, shouldn't be able to advance their careers in equal conditions with men." A woman ought to be able to choose how she pursued her career, "according to her own spontaneous desires, guided by education and by other elements including those with spiritual value, rather than by reason of a profoundly insulting injustice."[9] Federici argued that the only qualifying language should concern merit and preparation; anything else would be clearly discriminatory against women. To those who argued that the phrase "according to the conditions established by law" would not concern the magistracy, only the police and military, she again answered that no limiting language should be necessary at all. While it might be difficult to find a woman capable of leading the armed forces, it had recently proven equally as difficult to find a man capable of doing it. If an example was necessary of how to be a good military leader, she said, let Joan of Arc serve for everyone.[10] Naming this female religious martyr, Federici was also implicitly reminding her audience of the heroic sacrifice many women had performed in the Resistance; such acts justified recognizing women as founders of the new nation and awarding them equal rights in even those traditionally masculine duties of citizenship as military service.

As the Constituent Assembly debated the shaping of the judicial system in November 1947, the question of women judges came up again: should the Constitution explicitly accept or deny women's entry into the magistracy? The right was openly against women's participation. Giovanni Leone, a DC deputy who had been elected secretary of the Committee of 75's subcommittee on the judiciary, argued that although the women around him in the Assembly were doing a good job, they should be happy with that achievement and satisfied with limitations on their participation. Women might help to make the Constitution and the laws, but menstruation and menopause prevented them from attaining the serenity necessary for a judge.[11] Overall the arguments were a trio of venerable cliches: first, that women are more sentimental than reasonable, while judges have to be more reasonable than sentimental; second, that women are physically incapable of staying focused for the long and complex hours of argumentation and consideration required; and third, that women have physiological limits because of menstruation, child bearing, and menopause that impede their performance and must be guarded from any overwork or strain in order to protect the health of their reproductive systems and progeny.[12] Each of these arguments betrayed male jurists' near panic at the idea of women disrupting the rhythms and habits of the judicial chambers, that last redoubt of patriarchal authority and masculine collegiality.

Maria Maddalena Rossi and Teresa Mattei had proposed an amendment to read, "Women have access to all the orders and ranks of the magistracy," but after this kind of debate it was defeated, by a vote of 153 to 120. Heeding Maria Federici's prediction, the next day all the women constituents united to pass an order of business affirming that Article 51 did guarantee women's right to enter the magistracy, but this motion had little effect.[13] Once the qualification "according to the limits of the law" became part of the constitutional text, it was interpreted to mean that the 1919 law remained in force.

The law, number 1176, known as the Sacchi Law, had actually been a victory of the first wave feminist movement in Italy, profiting from its alliance with the Radical Party, then one of the few parties to include universal suffrage in its platform. At the end of World War I, in recognition of the immense changes in women's employment patterns and participation in civil society during the war, women achieved the vote in numerous countries, including Britain (only women over thirty), the United States, Austria, and Germany. A law extending the franchise to all women was debated and approved in the Italian Chamber of Deputies in 1919, but the bill died when the Liberal government fell into the crisis occasioned by Gabriele D'Annunzio's occupation of Fiume. Just days before, however, the passage of the Sacchi Law had fulfilled a different aim of the women's movement, asserting women's right to enter the free professions and civil posts, and abolishing the requirement of spousal approval (*autorizzazione maritale*). Sponsored by Ettore Sacchi, a leader of the Radical Party, this law was commonly known as women's "demobilization reward."[14] The law excluded those professions which "imply jurisdictional power, the exercise of political rights, or any authority over the military."[15] In this way the demobilization prize recognized women's performance in the emergency of wartime but also encouraged the reassertion of prewar gender roles. The law, in its time a victory for feminists and the democratic radical faction of the Liberal state, did not inspire allegiance in Maria Cocco, both because of her commitment to full citizenship for women, and, perhaps, due to the general Catholic hostility to the explicitly secular Liberal state. The constitutional legitimacy given to the Sacchi Law by Article 51's qualifying phrase meant that well into Cocco's political career the issue remained unresolved.

As the 1960s began a series of auspicious events encouraged Cocco to consider presenting a law to finally guarantee women's access to all careers, public and private, with a particular focus on the problem of women's exclusion from the judiciary. First, the passage of other reforms opened the judicial system and the judicial profession in particular to a wider swath of society. Italy's judicial system had been, since the modern era, under the influence of the Napoleonic model, with its strict hierarchy and bureaucratic nature. The Fascist regime had only reinforced this tendency, establishing many special tribunals controlled directly by the government to address political crimes, and encouraging judges to become, at worst, servants of the Fascist agenda and, at best, apolitical. The Constitution of the Republic thus sought to make the judiciary a completely independent body and shield it from all government or party influence. It established the Higher Council of the Judiciary (*Consiglio superiore della magistratura*), which finally began to operate in 1959, and which makes all decisions on the promotion process and status of judges and public prosecutors. Notably, the Higher Council's policy regarding promotion is primarily determined by seniority. Virtually every magistrate would reach the highest rank after twenty-eight years of service.[16]

Already in 1960 and 1961 Cocco could discern in the commencement of the Higher Council's activities an important change in the judiciary that served her purpose specifically. The judiciary was becoming more independent and more standardized, opening itself to the reforms and aspirations of antifascist republican ideology. This meant that all applicants for the magistrates' exam would face new examination standards and so women would not have the same obstacles in "catching up" to their male fellow competitors. Once magistrates were in, seniority would guarantee promotion so that discriminatory practices against female magistrates would be difficult to maintain.

But the fundamental problem in the courts was resolved only by intervention from outside. Throughout the early years of the Republic, law experts argued about how the project of constitutional implementation should be pursued. The core of the problem was whether the Constitution was programmatic or prescriptive; that is, did the Constitution set forth principles as ideals to be slowly attained through ever evolving legislative reform; or was it itself immediately enforceable law that automatically invalidated any contradictory laws on the books the moment it took effect on January 1, 1948? If the former, the legislative and executive branches had more power than the judiciary and could act as a conservative brake on the progressive agenda of the Constituent Assembly; if the latter, the courts had untouchable power and, if there was a strong presence of so-called "activist" judges, might be a quite radical force in society. For women's constitutionalist rights strategy to continue to work in the Parliament and in the courts themselves, it was imperative that the Constitution be considered prescriptive; only then would they be able to continue to insist that it was constitutional law, not feminism, that drove their proposals and required consent across all party and ideological lines. The Noce and Merlin laws had been less affected by this indecision, since their battles had not involved or been prompted by court cases. Both benefited from the natural inclination of legislators a decade closer to the Constituent Assembly not to question the Constitution's authority.

Because of the reluctance of the Allied occupation and early postwar governments to conduct widespread purges, the judiciary was mostly staffed by longtime Fascist appointees who were unlikely to usher in radical change. In the early 1950s the lower courts had reflected this ambivalence; three separate court decisions from 1952 to 1953 stated that Articles 37 and 51 of the Constitution were only programmatic and therefore not for immediate application, rejecting suits from women who claimed they were unconstitutionally discriminated against at work and in the judicial system. But as time went on some possibilities opened up. In 1955 and

1958 the same courts issued sentences in which they characterized those same articles as "for immediate attention, of clear prescriptive character."[17] The Constitution established a Constitutional Court to deal with these questions, but it took until 1956 for the Court to come to order. That year in its historic first sentence, the Court affirmed that it had jurisdiction over all laws in force in the Republic, and that all laws, including those from the Fascist era and before, must conform to the principles of the Constitution and must be annulled if they did not. This decision legitimated the Lost Wave strategy of implementation or *adeguamento* and encouraged Maria Cocco to revisit the question of women in the judiciary. It also made possible other reforms that had languished without constitutional implementation, such as the institution of regional governments and the introduction of the right to hold referenda.[18]

Cocco was also propelled by other events. Although Maria Cocco generally maintains that she thought of the law that bears her name on her own, she had plenty of outside inspiration. During the first legislature of 1948–1953, Erisia Gennai Tonietti (battle name Sisto), a DC deputy from the ranks of Catholic Action, had proposed a law admitting women to the Court of Assize.[19] A criminal court dealing with very serious crimes, it has a panel of judges, two of whom are career judges and six of whom are lay judges, and randomly selected private citizens between the ages of thirty and sixty-five, who enjoy full political and civil rights, show good moral conduct, and possess requisite education certificates. They are in substance jurors, and women's exclusion from this role was a limit on their full citizenship.

The bill did not pass, and at the start of the second legislature the PCI took a turn at the effort. A group of communist deputies led by the lawyer Emilio Rosini proposed the cancellation of the Fascist judiciary code of 1941, which forbade the entry of women into the judiciary. The bill made it out of committee but was not approved by the full Assembly. During the debates on these matters it became clear that the majority of men felt that Article 51 of the Constitution, with its qualification deferring to other legislation on women's status in the public careers, was not an affirmation of women's equal right to enter all professions but instead invited male legislators to consider the particular situations for which women might or might not be suitable. An exemplary quote from the sponsoring speech in the bill's presentation reads: "...in harmony with Article 51...which states that 'All citizens of either sex may fill public offices and elective offices in equal conditions, according to the conditions established by the law' that is by the legislator who keeps in mind the particular aptitudes and adaptability of women to the tasks and functions inherent in certain offices and positions."[20]

At the beginning of the second legislature in December of 1953, the DC picked up Gennai Tonietti's proposal again and submitted a bill for the "Admission of women to the office of lay judge in the Courts of Assize and the Appeal Courts of Assize, and to the office of private component of the Juvenile Tribunals and the Juvenile Appeals Court." On December 27, 1956, law number 1441 passed, known as the Moro Law after the Minister of Justice Aldo Moro, whose office sponsored the bill in the Senate. The law limited the number of women lay judges on the Court of Assize to a maximum of three out of six and specified that a Juvenile Tribunal should be composed of two magistrates and two private citizens, only one of whom could be a woman, and both of whom should be experts in social work, biology, psychiatry, criminal anthropology, pedagogy, or psychology and over thirty years old.[21]

The Moro Law did not address the ability of women to become magistrates, but it at least made clear that women's citizenship rights did extend to the judicial branch. Women citizens' right to be judged by a jury truly composed of their peers when they have been accused of a crime was finally recognized, as was their obligation to serve on juries. Jury service for women clarifies that women as citizens are not to be considered exempt from either rights or duties by virtue of any privilege of sex or duty to family, which had previously preceded and preempted the claims of the state.[22] Rather, the relationship of any individual citizen to the state is defined by his or her constitutional rights and obligations, and nothing else.

Taking that endorsement of constitutional implementation to heart, the women's associations made a concentrated effort for the next few years to force the passage of and then compliance with the law. From 1951 to 1957 CIF organized a mass drive to register as many women as possible on the council lists for lay judges to the Court of Assize. Before the Moro Law's passage, Josette Lupinacci used this registration drive in a tactic known as *ricorso*, or "recourse [to trial]." Knowing that the women's applications to serve would be denied, CIF and its allies in the Union of Women Jurists, an association for women with degrees in law and the social sciences (and eventually for women practicing law and magistrates), could take advantage of the fifteen days mandated to appeal jury service denials and take their arguments to trial. UDI also participated in the campaign, especially in Rome, where the Court of Appeals of Rome had rejected a petition from the mayor's office to accept the three hundred women's names submitted for the court lists in 1952.[23] In addition, UDI's focus in this period on the battle for pay equity served to reinforce and draw attention to the need for women's equality of professional access, on both a national and a continental scale.[24] But the women of CIF energized and sustained the national campaign for lay judges in court, in the legislature, and in the court of public opinion. Their use of "recourse" to trial was a pioneering step; it was not common in Italy to use court cases to fight discrimination and reinterpret or strike down unfair laws, mostly because judges were more conservative than the Parliament. But once feminist movements had begun to imitate each others' strategies and Italian women introduced the use of *ricorso*, it became more popular as a grassroots tool to fight against discrimination in many different categories.[25]

Lupinacci won her case. Once the law passed, the registration drive was on in earnest, giving women their first experience in fulfilling these duties of citizenship. From the beginning of 1957 *Cronache*, CIF's internal publication, reprinted copies of the registration card with advice on how to fill it out correctly and published repeated reminders of the upcoming deadline. While the process for picking panels was meant to be random, the registration cards were differentiated between men's and women's applications in order to comply more easily with the three-woman limit.[26] It would take until 1978 for the limit of three places for women jurors to be removed.[27]

Another bill that helped to set a precedent for Maria Cocco was proposed by Maria Badaloni, a member of the first forty-five from the DC's "veteran" generation, to delete the part of the Communal and Provincial Code that barred women from being appointed to the position of town clerk (*segretario comunale*). She argued that this policy was in conflict with Article 51 of the Constitution. The Chamber of Deputies agreed, but the bill was blocked in the Senate, where it was argued that the position required nearly unlimited hours, consisted of problems unsuitable for women to deal with, and couldn't be filled by substitutes who wouldn't be up to date with all situations needing immediate attention. Thus it was a poor match for women with family and household obligations.[28] These objections highlight again the dilemma the Lost Wave faced: even when they presented their claims as reforms only to the public sphere and did their best to appear to preserve and protect women's normative roles as family nurturers, male leaders defended their own territory by pointing out the ways that public and private coincided. As women brought up each specific point of discrimination, men defended the cultural rather than legal motives for discrimination and argued for its continuation.

In January 1957 the Supreme Administrative Court (*Consiglio di Stato*) issued a sentence that upheld women's exclusion from the examinations for judicial auditors (*uditore giudiziario*), the trainee position for magistrates. One of the judges, Vezio Crisafulli, explained in his comment to the decision that for many men, even those who were not prejudiced, "the idea of being judged by a woman provokes a sense of discomfort," a discomfort he admitted to sharing.[29] The women members of Parliament consoled themselves that perhaps they were at least conducting work of "sensitization."[30]

The process of sensitization was also moving forward on the front of women's equal salary for equal work and the pronouncements of the courts that the constitution did have prescriptive power. In 1955 two cases in Milan were decided in favor of female complainants that they had been demoted or discriminated against for requesting equal pay to men doing the same jobs. In both cases judges ruled that Article 37 of the Constitution had been violated.[31]

In its ongoing campaign, the Union of Women Jurists made the themes of both its own congress in 1955 and of a national conference in April 1957 "The Constitution and the admissibility of women to public office," with the intent to further publicize the Moro Law and the need to do more.[32] CIF and UDI, along with numerous other women's associations, participated in the conference. Maria Sofia Lanza, the president of the Union of Women Jurists, reported extensively on the congress for CIF's journal, *Cronache*:

> Of incandescent interest was the issue of women's access to the magistracy and in general to all public offices, without quotas or limits on advancement.... The famous and much discussed article 51 of the Constitution, which explicitly recognizes the right of citizens to enter all public and elected offices, cannot in its aside "according to the requirements of the law" limit this right; containing in itself such a profound contradiction, it would be without doubt a suicidal norm. What is more, we are certain that the article must be considered abrogative of the previous laws which contradict it and therefore of immediate application.... It was pointed out that in the current state of the law's interpretation, it is theoretically possible that a woman be elected to the highest post of Head of State and therefore acquire, in such a role, the power to preside over the Superior Council of the Magistracy, even though she could not even be admitted to sit the examination for trainee magistrates. Many other absurdities could be listed, but I will limit myself to observing that a woman could be named Consul, responsible for preserving the interests of an entire foreign nation's citizens here in Italy, while a woman with the same qualifications cannot defend her own fellow Italian citizens' interests abroad at any level. It is to be hoped that all these absurd and anachronistic residues disappear from our legislation: only when the affirmation of women's complete juridical personhood is recognized will the fundamental principles of logic and justice be safe and respected.[33]

With such passionate support, events began to move quickly indeed. From 1956 to 1958, Maria Cocco contributed to the campaign to fulfill the Moro Law by serving as a lay judge in the Appeals Court as an expert in pedagogy. Seeing in the Moro Law a path to the "mental maturation" of men's opinion on women's emancipation, she became convinced that further legislative reform would be more effective than association campaigns alone. She thus began her election campaign and was elected to the Chamber of Deputies in the third legislature in 1958. In the meantime several "recourse" cases were brought by women barred from the various competitive examinations, or *concorsi*, that function as gatekeepers to the professions and civil service. In January 1958 the Ministry of Justice published an announcement for a *concorso* for one hundred places for legal auditors that explicitly listed one of the prerequisities for sitting the exam being male. The Committee for the Defense of Women's Rights defended three women who took recourse to the State Council and asked that the case be transmitted to the Constitutional Court to get the announcement and the policy that produced it ruled unconstitutional, arguing that they violated Articles 3, 37, and 51. The plaintiffs were Edda Sorti, Giovanna Berti, and Luciana Camastri, each possessing a degree in jurisprudence and all other qualifications to sit for the exam. Among the lawyers arguing the case was Ada Piciotto, president of the Federation of Italian Women Jurists.[34] The Ministry of Justice argued that the suit was inadmissible and the question of constitutionality was unfounded. On May 8, 1958 the State Council agreed with the Ministry of Justice, saying that since the women had not actually participated in the *concorso* they had no right to ask for admission to the Magistracy, since only those who have taken the exam and been rejected have the right to appeal using recourse. The Council thus ignored the fact that the women's complaint was that they had been excluded from even taking the *concorso* because of sex and avoided taking any stand on the issue itself or sending the case to the Constitutional Court.[35]

Although the State Council had not seen the legal merit in challenging the Ministry of Justice's policy, a huge turning point came in a case that was less directly about the Magistracy itself. In May 1960, the Constitutional Court upheld a decision by the State Council that the Ministry of the Interior could not bar Dr. Rosa Oliva from the state examination for an entry-level position in the Ministry of Interior's administration.[36] The Ministry of the Interior argued that law number 1176 of 1919, the Sacchi Law, in particular its Article 7, required the exclusion of women. The Court recognized that the spirit of that article's phrase "according to the conditions established by law" did not permit legislators to exclude women, since citizens' equality in regards to employment regardless of sex was explicitly established elsewhere in the Constitution. In its sentence of May 18, 1960, number 33, the Court declared Article 7 of the Sacchi Law illegitimate: "Sexual difference considered in and of itself cannot ever be cause for legislative discrimination. It cannot mean, that is, a different treatment of one sex or the other before the law. Any norm which does so violates a fundamental principle of the Constitution, that in article 3, of which article 51 is only a specification, but also a confirmation." [37] The 1919 law and its ensuing 1920 regulatory code had been the basis for excluding women from almost every type of *concorso*, so not only the Ministry of the Interior but all government offices had to strike any rules based on them. This landmark decision effectively and conclusively removed the fig leaf of "women's aptitude and adaptability" from discrimination, at least from the legislative standpoint, and it removed the last block to women's full citizenship, the Sacchi Law's contention that only men could demonstrate or enjoy full legal personhood.

In 1961, as the third legislature reached its midpoint, Maria Cocco herself won a last victory in preparation for her law, at the time in limbo between its first presentation and the beginning of debate. She introduced an amendment to a bill under debate in the Committee on Justice, on which she sat, which represented the first of the coming ten years' worth of major reforms to personnel policies in the Ministry of Justice. Seeing an opportunity, she inserted language making the positions of Court Clerk (*cancelliere*) and Court Secretary (*segretarie giudiziarie*) open to women. The law passed as amended.[38] Cocco was ready to cement the gains made for women in the judiciary; women would be present in the courtroom not only as plaintiffs and witnesses, but also as jurors, functionaries, and even judges on the bench.

The bill Maria Cocco presented on August 5, 1960 was co-signed by eighteen other deputies, all DC members. Eight of them were women, one of whom was Erisia Gennai Tonietti, author of the first attempt to admit women to juries. The text of the bill was very short, consisting of only two articles. It stated:

> Art. 1. Women may be employed in all public positions with the State, with public agencies, and state-controlled bodies, in any role, career, and category, without limitations of their responsibilities or the development of their careers.
>
> The enrollment of women in the Armed Forces and in special corps is regulated by specific laws.

> Art. 2. The law of July 17 1919, n. 1176, the successive regulation approved by decree n. 39 on January 4, 1920, and all other provisions incompatible with this law are abrogated.[39]

Accompanying the presentation of the bill was a report by Cocco which argued first and foremost that the Constitution's Articles 3 and 51 were prescriptive, that is, they were for immediate application, and that the 1919 law and any resulting discriminatory regulation should therefore not still be in force. Cocco argued that women had clearly demonstrated their capacity in the executive and legislative branches of the state and this made the contrast with the judicial branch, from which women were absent, all too apparently unnecessary. She mentioned the law of 1956 and the recent Constitutional Court sentence that had set the precedents for overcoming any restrictions on women's careers in public offices. All that remained was to officially dismantle the law of 1919. The tone of her report was at once celebratory and conciliatory: "In fact—as in the spirit and the letter of the Constitution—any sense of the presumed incapacity of women to fully exercise their political rights and powers has been fully overcome," she said. Yet she hastened to reassure her colleagues that women were not claiming their equal status in the public professions in a spirit of revenge nor in order to dominate men. "The Italian woman has been rapidly maturing a consciousness of civic honor and humanism which does her great credit, and which she wants to put to the service of her community; and the pressure she exerts to be allowed to do so... isn't determined by a will to dominate... [but] in the sense of the most civilized challenge... in order to improve the entire level of merit among competitors and colleagues."[40] Cocco also pointed out how the first article of the new law would not force the thorny question of women in the armed forces, as it contains its own qualifying phrase referring to "specific laws" to regulate that aspect. The irony of the usefulness of the phrase "regulated by special laws" in effectively forbidding an area of activity to women for years to come was not lost on Cocco: she followed this reminder with the remark that in truth she didn't think any restrictions at all were opportune in the law, given the trouble they had caused in 1919 and 1948. She specifically noted that back in 1920 Minister of Justice Mortara had seen no reason to include specific restrictions in his regulation following the 1919 law, thinking it a given that women would be inserted in all local government posts according to the law's affirmation of their rights, and had been overruled. How could she, then, nowhere near such status, have been expected to withstand similar overruling?

Consistent with Cocco's combination of modesty of expression and underlying intensity of purpose, the conciliatory tone masked some pointed considerations. The acceptance Cocco and her coauthors expected for this bill had been hard won and should by rights have been moot long before. The Constituent Assembly debates clearly showed the framers' intent that Article 51 should guarantee women's equal access to the professions, but over the last twelve and more years legislators had to take one baby step after another to implement that intent. Cocco allowed that the "ironclad... masculine resistance" to women's entry into each new level of equality had always been "chivalrous" in intent, but made it clear that such chivalry was no longer necessary, if it had ever been so. Cocco's comments were restrained given her exertions and those of so many other women, especially since the law's passage in committee and in assembly would not be easy or uncontested, if the Noce and Merlin laws were any guides.

After nearly two years of bureaucratic holdups the bill was sent to the Committee of Constitutional Affairs, which sat in *sede legislativa*, meaning that its vote would be decisive and the bill would not go to the full assembly. The delays had apparently been due to the need to reconcile several proposals. Maria Alessi, Laura Diaz, and Maria Maddalena Rossi all had submitted proposals relating to various aspects of guaranteeing women entry to the state examinations and specific grades of administrative employment, including to the examinations for personnel in the national penal system. There was also a government *disegno* from Amintore Fanfani allowing women to enter the diplomatic corps.[41] Eventually it was decided that Cocco's bill subsumed all of these and in November 1962 the committee entered her *proposta* into its record and commenced debate.[42]

On November 28 Alfonso Tesauro, a DC deputy who had been named sponsor (*relatore*) for the bill, introduced Cocco's proposal in a decidedly ambivalent way, declaring himself and his party in favor of it but adding that amendments were likely in order to clear up the exact intentions of the law. He said that the 1919 law had already basically been abrogated by the Constitutional Court ruling of 1960 but that this law would serve the purpose of officially cancelling it and specifying the new norms. In sum, the law was a perfect example of successful implementation of the Constitution. Tesuaro used the word "*attuare*" rather than the women's preferred "*adeguamento*," but in using a close synonym it was clear he was giving credit to their long-term strategy. Five other committee members intervened in the ensuing discussion, including Cocco herself, agreeing that amendments might be necessary but specifying that any text must make it clear to future legislators that they were not to exclude citizens from the magistracy or any public post, understood in the most comprehensive sense, on the basis of sex. These deputies understood Tesuaro to mean that any amendments would be specific, positive mentions of posts women must be allowed to compete for, most importantly the magistracy, so that legislators and lower courts could never again "interpret" the law to allow women's exclusion. But the amendment he actually proposed had the opposite motive: to suppress the second phrase of Article 1 and substitute the following negatives:

> Women may not enter any posts in the Armed Forces, in the civilian careers of the Ministry of Defense which concern military personnel or operations, or those positions which in time of war are subject to military control, nor to the careers of public safety officers or railway officers.
>
> Women's participation in judiciary offices and their access to careers in the rehabilitation and penal systems is regulated respectively by the judiciary code and by specific laws.

Deputy Roberto Lucifredi and Senator Giuseppe Medici, both DC members and undersecretary and minister, respectively, of the Ministry for the Reform of Public Administration in the Fanfani government, cooperated to move this amendment. They explained that although they supported women's entry into the judiciary, they found the original language of Cocco's proposal too comprehensive and feared that it opened all careers to women, even those which were obviously unsuitable for women, foremost among them the military.

Cocco argued that there was no need to specify exclusion in the law's text. There was a scarcity of qualified people taking the state examinations for magistrates and a number of other positions, and it was important to have as good a selection from as large a pool of candidates as possible. One could trust that women would be self-selecting, applying only for those positions they were already prepared to fill, and it was reasonable to expect that women, just like men, would not enter those jobs whose rigorous physical requirements they did not meet. The committee voted down the amendment.

The bill was not, however, to survive with its original wording intact. The committee, as forewarned by Tesauro, did change Cocco's wording of the original first article so that instead of saying, "Women may be employed in all public positions with the State, with public agencies, and state-controlled bodies, in any role, career, and category, without limitations of their responsibilities or the development of their careers," it read "Women may be employed in all *offices, professions and public posts, including the Magistracy,* in any role, career, and category, without limitations of their responsibilities or the development of their careers, *according to the conditions established by law*" (emphasis added). The next sentence read, as before, "The enrollment of women in the Armed Forces and in special corps is regulated by specific laws"; and Article 2 remained unchanged. They duly changed the title of the bill as well, so that the law became "Admission of women to public offices and the professions" (*Ammissione della donna ai pubblici uffici ed alle professioni*).[43] This bill was approved by unanimous vote, 25 out of 25, the same day it was introduced and sent to the Senate for approval.

Overall, the original intent of the proposal was largely unchanged by the new text. Certainly this was far less tinkering than either Noce or Merlin had had to accept. This can be ascribed to several factors. Cocco was able to benefit from years of experience and several precedents that had paved the way for women's right to equal opportunity in employment to be approved by the entire spectrum of the members of Parliament. In that sense, women had come a long way since the Constituent Assembly in 1946–1947. She was also a member of the Christian Democratic party, the ruling party, and unlike Noce and Merlin, representatives of the opposition, she could count on the government ministers to back the bill and not meddle too much. Indeed, although she does not say this, it is clear that the party had given prior approval to the idea of such a law, since DC members had already proposed similar laws in the previous two legislatures. Finally, the weight of the 1960 Constitutional Court decision was such that, despite some men's continued feeling that "it would be hard for judges to think objectively" when "women were nearby," the old cliches no longer held the same power.[44]

But what had Cocco intended by the original language, and did the new text have any significance apart from the deputies' stated desire to explicitly resolve the question of women in the judiciary? Cocco's text was indeed less legally explicit language, but this may not have been due to her inexperience as a legislator; as a recognized expert often consulted by regional officials and courts, she was familiar with the legal niceties surrounding the women jurors campaign as well as the rest of the history of her law's precedents. As she herself stated in her sponsoring report and all of her interventions in committee, she believed that it was best to put as few restrictions on women's employment as possible and that to add qualifying statements regarding "regulation by specific laws" had already been the downfall of more than one attempt to clear the way for women. As Cocco was no doubt aware, other women activists were already beginning to prepare a campaign for a law that would guarantee universal application of the equal pay for equal work principle; she would want her law to aid that effort and be as far-reaching as possible. So the addition of the last phrase to Article 1 about specific laws' requirements must have seemed like a setback. But the other change was advantageous. While Cocco's guarantee focused on the state, the new language implied a larger range. By stating that all *public* employment must be open to women, while at the same time specifying that the magistracy was a primary focus for enforcement, the law both solved the historic problem of barring women from the judiciary and opened the possibility that any woman prevented from applying for a position or sitting an examination could use the law as recourse. The new title further opened this possibility. While the original title had a certain triumphant ring by announcing that the law admits women to public office and *to the professions*, the new one alerted women who may get degrees and sit for public exams in law or the other traditionally "free" professions that even if they apply for private jobs they are protected as members of their professions.

Evidently Cocco was aware, however, that Minister Medici might still harbor some reservations, for she resurrected Teresa Noce's tactic and led a delegation of women from all the parties to visit him in his offices and request that he encourage the Senate to quickly take up the bill and approve it so that it might become law before the end of the third legislature. Tullia Carettoni, a PCI member, participated in this delegation and remembers that Medici, visibly taken aback by the appearance of so many women at his door, stalled for time, inviting them all to sit, offering sweets and refreshments and all the niceties. Finally he sat down and came to the point: when he imagined the ermine that hung on the shoulders of the magistrate's *toga,* he said, he couldn't see ermine around a woman in any other form than as a *signora*'s elegant dress coat. He sighed. Maria Cocco got up, shook his hand, thanked him for his time, and told him the bill would pass without him. The rest of the women left without another word. The bill, Carettoni adds, was debated and passed within the next month. She tells this story to illustrate the underlying courage and independent spirit of Maria Cocco, who was young, modest, and so committed to her religious principles that it might have seemed she was merely a naive pawn in her party's designs. There is yet another angle to this story; although no women from the left had their names on the bill's list of authors when it was presented in 1960, three years later they cooperated against a male member of Cocco's own party.[45] Just as Carettoni is at pains to generously portray Cocco in a complimentary light, so too Cocco the determined anticommunist had gladly made use of her leftist colleagues when such an important women's milestone was on the line. Both women's narratives testify to the survival of the Lost Wave members' collective passion animating their fight for women's rights. Further, they illustrate the ongoing maneuvers the women of the Lost Wave undertook as the circumstances of the Cold War changed political opportunities and alliances in Italy. CIF's leaders could take advantage of new Vatican attitudes that more openly favored women workers and women's political activism as announced in John XXIII's speech to CIF members in 1960 and especially in his 1963 encyclical *Pacem in terris.* They exploited—and encouraged—the mood of reform and autonomy among Catholics that accompanied the work of Vatican II to take more explicitly feminist stances. UDI, by contrast, needed to work hard to bolster cooperation among women on the left as the Socialists turned toward the DC in the strategy of "opening to the left." The year 1963 marked the UDI delegation's dramatic exit from the Women's International Democratic Federation meeting in Moscow in protest against the pressure to conform to Soviet directives. Cocco, and the campaign for her law, benefited from a moment in which both organizations chose to prioritize women's issues in order to rise above party conflicts and maximize the potential for unity among women during a moment of thawing in the Western European theater of the Cold War.[46]

As Cocco had promised, the Senate approved the bill in its Committee on Constitutional Affairs on January 30, 1963, also unanimously, and the law was published on February 9, 1963 as law number 66. The newly elected national president of CIF, Alda Miceli, celebrated Cocco's achievement as the crowning victory of a long and arduous battle that the entire world of women's associationism had been fighting for years. Yet she predicted more trouble to come, noting that despite the unanimous votes of approval, there had been comments on the floor from some men complaining that soon the hearth fires would go out all over Italy, as the "angels of the house" (*angeli della casa*) would be flying away.[47]

It's difficult to say what has happened to the hearth fires, but while the first women to present themselves for the *concorso* for the magistracy made the news, by 1997 women routinely made up 50% of those sitting for the exam, and by 2002 60% of top scorers on not only the magistrates' but all state exams were women, a percentage that has remained stable since.[48] Today in Italy around half of all judges are female; worldwide the figure is close to one quarter. While this feminization may explain or be explained by the relatively low salary levels for magistrates, it has brought about structural reform in the entire judicial system, lessening hierarchical and political influence on personnel. And as a corollary, after 1963 both the legal and the judicial professions were feminized and perhaps lowered in status (a possible confirmation of this is the relatively low salary of judges in Italy compared to other countries), but reformed in their structures and returned to nearly complete autonomy. In this arena as in others, the constitutional rights strategy created a large influx of women into the public sphere, leading to a "feminization" of democracy, with the effect of broadening the mass participation of all citizens in their own civil and state institutions. In other words, in the judicial branch as in the legislative and executive ones, the activism of the Lost Wave helped to ensure Italy's future as a democratic state.[49]

However, the phrase in Cocco's law that qualified women's eligibility for the armed forces, like such phrases in other laws, remained unfulfilled for years, effectively barring women from the military judicial system, the military and police academies, and even the Forest Service.[50] Italy was the last NATO member to continue to exclude women from the armed forces, but also the only country where the opening of the military came about due to the grassroots campaigning of women volunteers themselves. After years of letter-writing campaigns and demonstrations, in 1981 law number 121 admitted women into the *polizia di stato,* the civil national police force (as opposed to the *carabinieri,* the military national police force). And in 1994 a government *disegno* admitted women into the *guardia di finanza,* the financial and customs police, also a militarized force.[51] In 1992 the Army selected thirty girls to participate in an experimental "recruitment simulation" and live in the barracks for thirty-six hours in the exact same conditions as male recruits. About half of those participants formed the Association of Aspiring Women Soldiers, or ANADOS (*Associazone Nazionale Aspiranti Donne Soldato*), the organization generally given credit for the groundswell of positive public opinion and support from high-ranking military officials that culminated in the passage of law number 380 of 1999, mandating the entrance of women into all voluntary positions in the armed forces (it doesn't include women in the obligatory eighteen-month national military service) and requiring complete compliance with national equal opportunity policy. The number of applicants to the next *concorso* for the military academies doubled, and women represented around 30% of new entrants in most branches.[52] This has not led to complete equality of women serving in the military, but it does represent the final fulfillment of the Constitutional guarantee in Article 51 that the Cocco Law sought to implement. At last, the law contains no limiting qualifications. While she did not do it alone, Cocco's independence from her party's male naysayers and her firm belief that the strategy of implementation would work again were crucial to the passage of the 1963 law that bears her name.

Maria Cocco continued her career and her fight for women's equality. From 1960 to 1962 she was appointed Undersecretary of Industry and Commerce in the cabinet of Prime Minister Amintore Fanfani's third government, and from June to November 1968 she served as Undersecretary of Health in the second Leone government, the very same Giovanni Leone who had argued in 1947 that women should not and could not become judges. In 1990 she was still active, giving testimony before the Parliament's special committee on parity for its investigation of European women's working conditions.[53] Now retired from politics, she retains her interest in her community and in women's rights from her home in Cagliari in Sardinia. She never married or had children but insists it was worth it, for the greater freedom she enjoyed and the comfort of her circle of Catholic solidarity. Although she sought and attained entry to power-wielding groups with strongly patriarchal cultures—Sardinia's university elite, Catholic Action, the Christian Democratic party, Parliament, and the judiciary—over the course of her life, within them she moved independently. A modest woman, she displayed enormous reserves of courage and resilience (she called it hardheadedness), while occasionally flashing a satiric humor.

Between this pattern and her father's example of public service without bringing home political problems it cannot be a coincidence that upon her election to Parliament she proposed two laws dealing with women's access to careers in public service. But overall, her family, her volunteerism with AC, and her studies in Greek literature nurtured in her a lifetime identification with the values of humanism. Even her later activism on behalf of women struck her as inspired by a fundamental belief in social justice for all people rather than by any feminist sensibility.

Despite the recurrence in her life of the sense of being alone in the crowd, she turned that sense of isolation into the positive value of liberty. Religious conviction, an independent profession, political power, and having no domestic obligations are all, like citizenship, both privileges and burdens. But what really stands out about Maria Cocco is that she was the last of a generation that accepted the isolation brought on by autonomy for women, that cohort some children of the economic miracle nicknamed the "dragons of emancipation." The achievement of women's entry into the magistracy was in many ways the crowning and the killing of that generation's vision of women's citizenship, for Cocco completed the picture of women's citizenship at the same time that it was becoming more complicated. The passage of the law and the end of the third republican legislature mark the end of one era of women's rights activism and the beginning of another, for Cocco's arguments, like those of Noce and Merlin, relied on the Constitution and socio-institutional guarantees of equality. In years to come women activists would largely abandon the constitutional argument in favor of other strategies. Constitutional issues would become more marginal as a new generation of women activists, products of the economic miracle and the immense cultural shift of the 1960s, refused to stand for parliamentary office and joined the youth movement and the second wave feminist movement, which were focused instead on the political significance of one's private identity. Such individualism and refusal of civic involvement remained alienating to Cocco. While her religiosity prevented her from sharing their support for abortion and divorce rights for women and for gay rights, issues she and her generation thought unspeakable in public, she could not help but to admire their bravery and independence.

Maria Cocco was unlike Teresa Noce or Lina Merlin in terms of her political sympathies, her age, her Resistance experience, and her status as part of the sprawling Catholic and DC hegemony in postwar Italy. She was not gregarious and confessional like Noce; she did not enchant crowds as did Merlin. But like them, and most importantly for the molding of women's citizenship in Italy, she had a passion for politics, a base in the solidarity of social justice, and a courage and persistence in her identity as a woman and an activist.

Conclusion

The Legacy of the Lost Wave and Constitutional Rights Feminism

In 1948 Lina Merlin, flush from her success passing Article 3 in the Constituent Assembly, first presented her law to abolish regulation of prostitution with egalitarian verve and optimism. It was simple: state brothels' very existence denied women equal citizenship rights; that was now unconstitutional, therefore already illegal. The work seemed already finished. At almost the very same moment Teresa Noce, with even greater emancipatory zeal, presented the first draft of her law to protect working mothers. Not only equal citizens as women, but as workers in a republic founded on labor, working mothers undeniably deserved those special protections she had personally worked to ensure the Constitution guaranteed. It would pass immediately, she believed. Nearly a decade later, with undampened enthusiasm, Maria Cocco attacked another obvious injustice: women could hold the highest elected office in the land but could not ascend the lowest rung in the justice system. Implementation of the constitution necessitated the passage of her law, and as a Christian Democrat she even had the backing of the government. No member of Parliament could do anything but support the bill, she was sure.

And yet each of these women and her law faced obstacle after obstacle, from procedural slowdowns to party machine maneuvering, from surprise amendments to perceived betrayals from sister legislators, from governmental hidden agendas to unapologetic unreconstructed sexism. While this to some extent merely illustrates the revision and compromise that are always part of the legislative process, especially in the infamously fragmented and overlegislating Italian system of proportional party representation and government inertia, the cumulative impact is, frankly, demoralizing. Despite Italy's progressive Constitution and passionately activist women's movement, the optimism of Noce, Merlin, and Cocco was in no way predictive of the true outcome of the postwar refoundation of the state. Just as neither reconstruction's Resistance rhetoric nor the economic miracle could successfully mask or completely heal the damage wrought on civil society by Fascism, war, and deprivation, nor could a dazzling cohort of newly legitimated women activists instantaneously revolutionize the politics or culture of women's subordination, a regime with a history far longer than Fascism.

Still, the Lost Wave's legacy of activism in associations and legislation through constitutional rights feminism clearly did secure a new kind of mass democracy in the Italian Republic, one that both male and female citizens have benefited from and built upon in subsequent generations. By the 1960s the relation of the citizen to the state in Western Europe had nearly inverted from the interwar model of subjects who should sacrifice for and serve their nation, largely through military service; the new model was a state that served its citizens through "a dense tissue of social benefits and economic strategies."[1] The legislative process might have been slow and full of compromise, but by the time the laws passed they were not only supported by parliamentary women across party lines but had also reached something like unanimity or at least a sense of inevitability in the Parliament as a whole, with public opinion additionally having had time to mature and reach consensus. Across fifteen years and three legislatures, there was in fact a notable capacity to reach political and legislative objectives for women. If a law were not passed before the deadlines of committee and session, in the next legislature it would be picked up again, either by the same woman or by another, even if she were not a member of the same party. This cooperation and persistence is evidence that women acted as a political interest group apart from the party system to solve real and urgent problems.[2] As Nilde Iotti remembered in 1995:

> Our strength, the same which powered the feminist movement, was that we were able to find the path of unity, even during the

> Constitutional debates. And it was we women, from within our single groups, who conducted the battles which led to unanimity in full assembly. It was our unity that guided us forward, whether in our political struggles or in the major social achievements of these last decades.[3]

The women of the postwar movement also felt that it was discriminatory and marginalizing to see early childhood development, poverty, housing, education, and equal rights at work as only women's issues. These were matters of social justice and part of the women's movement's task was to sensitize everyone to them. PCI deputy Nadia Spano explained, "It would be absurd to seek in our work at that time any discourse like today's on the public and the private, a discourse we couldn't even conceive of, taken as we were by the urgency and gravity of the situation."[4] And yet it would be wrong to assume, as did many young neofeminists of the 1970s and 1980s, that Nadia Spano and her peers had no sense of the demands of the private, the body, the underlying subordination that laws could not adequately address. The Lost Wave was one of several historical feminist movements, a "wave" to be reconciled to the rest of feminist history. But this reconciliation has not come easily.

In 2002 and 2003 I was living in Rome, seeking out members of the Lost Wave before their entire generation passed away. I had the good fortune to find several women who were generous with their time and patient with a young foreigner's interest in their stories. One afternoon I found myself graciously welcomed in the front parlor of eighty-six-year-old Luciana Viviani, PCI deputy in the Chamber from 1948 to1968. I set my tape recorder on the table between us and described my research project to this longtime working-class militant. I proposed my idea of "constitutional rights feminism," asking if she thought it accurately captured the strategy of female parlamentarians in the postwar period. She confirmed that it was a good description but was reluctant to talk about her intentions and activism in those years. Instead she protested that she had been unsophisticated, especially in feminist thought, merely driven by a sense of common justice. Certainly, she repeatedly emphasized, at the time she and her colleagues had understood nothing of the feminist discourse of "the body"; they had not reached the consciousness that "the personal was political"; and she still wasn't qualified to truly speak as a feminist.

After many more questions, I returned to my desk with a sense that I had bungled the interview. How had I failed to ask the questions that would have led Viviani to open up and describe her sense of women's rights, her thinking back then in the time she was a "Resistance recruit"? Why had she thought I only wanted to hear about the neofeminism of the 1970s and 1980s? I must not have explained myself well enough. But as I secured further appointments with former members of Parliament Giglia Tedesco, Tullia Carettoni, Maria Cocco, and others, I knew that it was not a lack of language skills or improperly articulated questions that repeatedly led me up against this stumbling block. In the time since then I understood I made a beginner's mistake, but it wasn't in how I talked, it was in how I listened. Going back over these women's responses and learning more from other scholars and historians in Italy, I realized that I had to consider yet another long-term historical development that had affected how the history of the Lost Wave was interpreted: second-wave feminism, or "neofeminism" as it is called in Italy, and its members' founding of women's studies in Italy.

In the 1970s and 1980s, the girls of the "*prima generazione*," the first generation to grow up entirely within the new material circumstances of the economic miracle, rediscovered and refounded feminism as a mass movement.[5] Disillusioned by the sexism rampant in the youth movement of 1968, in which many had participated but found themselves marginalized as mere "*angeli dei ciclostili*," copy girls handing out mimeographs instead of speakers and leaders helping set the agenda, young radical women gravitated to the separatism of a feminism that rejected mainstream and mixed-sex arenas of action. The preferred space of the second wave was a loose network of "*piccoli gruppi*," women's-only consciousness-raising groups where women shared their most personal and emotional struggles and tried to discover and rebuild a feminine identity uncontaminated by patriarchal thinking or structures. These women were dismissive and indeed harshly critical of the "dragons of emancipation." The neofeminists charged that by chasing party politics and national office the dragons were helping replicate the very oppressive structures that marginalized women. By proving themselves capable on the same ground as men they had helped to erase women's difference and authentic identity. These younger women, brought to activism through youth revolt, and without any direct experience of the circumstances of Fascism, war, and privation that had formed their parents' outlook, were not coincidentally involved in a politics that was also a daughters' coming-of-age rejection of their mothers.

While constitutionalist rights feminism could be easily condemned as insufficiently critical of cultural norms, its laws and their accompanying public campaigns actually did a great deal of cultural work in creating debate and questioning old assumptions about women's work, responsibilities, and identities.[6] This, together with the revolutionary effects of the economic miracle, made neofeminism possible by raising a new generation of girls for whom the available feminine models simply weren't adequate and who were equipped with the ambition, self-confidence, and autonomy to critique, dismantle, and reject them. The women of the Lost Wave to some extent tried to prevent this rupture. In 1968 *Noi donne,* the magazine published by UDI, featured their "women of the year," among whom was a generic militant university student, described as "young, beautiful—of a beauty that confers political passion and ideals—decisive, hard to frighten, impossible to stop... She doesn't have a name, or better, she has the name of thousands of girls, students or workers, who in the course of the last year have been magnificent protagonists of one of the many struggles that shook the world, from the factories to the universities, in offices, and in the squares."[7] Yet such overtures from UDI and other postwar era associations didn't really take. Since the new social movements of the 1960s and 1970s were generally more radical than the mass parties and the women's associations, preferring political activism and protest outside of formal institutions, the new generation of feminists rejected the Lost Wave for having accepted too many compromises with the patriarchal forms of family and government. They preferred rebellion and protest over any search for mass consensus. The "*prima generazione*" failed to follow their mothers into politics or the associations and so lost the chance for direct transmission of that memory. More importantly they lived in a world whose material conditions and life expectations had radically changed.

From the mid-1950s to the early 1960s reconstruction tapered off and the economy recovered and then began to grow at a very fast pace. Italy experienced a time of intense and profound economic, social, and cultural change referred to as the economic miracle. This corresponds to the "*trente glorieuse*" and the "*desarollo*" of France and Spain and was characterized by large migrations from rural areas to cities and from the South to the North, the growth of consumption and of consumer goods, the importance of mass popular culture, and rising levels of education and employment. All these processes associated with modernization left a very deep mark in a very short time, economically as well as symbolically. Gender roles were also heavily involved, especially in the extension of consumerist identities, as women were often the primary consumer for their family and the first to confront and master the new world of consumer durables in the home and new literacy and numeracy demands of marketing outside it. Like Lost Wave feminism, these processes also presented a feminine identity endowed with new forms of autonomy, blurred traditional boundaries between the public and private spheres (and those of production, reproduction, and consumption), constituted a transition to a mass society, and were characterized by conflicts between change coming "from below" and "top down" attempts at control and politicization. The Cold War in Italy was fought as much through competing popular culture and consumer regimes as by arms and ideologies. The identity of consumer joined other identities in the rights of citizenship. The growing welfare state and spreading consumption together seemed to lessen and erase previous forms of social inequality, especially of class but also of gender, that had visibly marked Italian society before the boom. The boom caught both the traditional left and right unprepared and critical, unable to appreciate that the working classes and younger generation were learning to expect higher living standards and consumer luxuries.[8] Trends in consumption generally lagged behind rises in income, but eventually exposure to consumerist lifestyles and modern domestic spaces did homogenize Italian expectations and behaviors in ways that cut across left-right Cold War divides as well as softened regional and class divisions. While the feminism of the Lost Wave attempted to channel the resulting feminization of the social body into increased public participation and politicization, the "citizen-consumer" model tended to reinforce privatization and depoliticization as characteristics of the new prosperity. Women's household labor and consumption "amortized" the disruptive changes of the postwar years and facilitated the reach of the welfare state into families.[9] Thus gender roles were put into a state of flux and contestation throughout the very period in which the women's movement tried, by fixing the constitutional guarantees of equality in law, to heal and restabilize the gender order.

In her study of the girls of the *prima generazione* Piccone Stella argues that due to all this flux in gender roles and material life, there were no role models available to this generation. Since the women of the Lost Wave were at that very moment working so hard to create these models and the legal and civil bases for their consolidation, it is a serious concern that they did not seem to provide leadership and mentoring for the generation just coming of age. She contends that the postwar ideals of parity began to come into conflict with the neofeminist championing of women's specificity at precisely this point. The authors of UDI's institutional history follow a similar argument when they describe the tragic solitude in which the "dragons of emancipation" dealt with their own personal lives as women:

> The anxieties, needs, and desires of women's bodies and of feminine sexuality had no legitimacy and the drama of sexuality as it was often lived did not even enter into communication. Every woman in those years confronted in solitude such problems as how to avoid pregnancy or where to get a clandestine abortion. Thus the "dragons" hid from themselves and from others their "difference" and carried the entire weight of it themselves, never calling on men to pay the price.[10]

The demands of the emancipationist model were such, they argue, that none of the women leaders with public identities felt they could compromise the claim that women could operate as capably as men in the public and political spheres by admitting that they faced those obstacles because they were women. Therefore they never helped the next generation of women to liberate themselves, because they never shared these experiences, but merely dumped the obligations of emancipation on them. Women, they taught by their example, should as a matter of course find that equilibrium by which it is possible to have a profession, be a good wife and mother, and also make a contribution to political and civil life. So each of these women and each of their daughters fought her own demons in a solitary prison of anguish and silence.

The problem with this line of argument is that the Lost Wave culture did not deny the difference of women. Even if they did not use a vocabulary of "difference," "desire," and "the body," they nonetheless argued for the recognition of women's special needs to be reflected in the law in a non-punitive, non-discriminatory way. Indeed, in their campaigns for maternity leave, child care, and salary parity they emphasized the fatigue, difficulty, and exploitation of women who simultaneously worked and cared for their families. But desire, seduction, and pleasure in the public images of women, especially as they were being popularly recast in such new roles as flight attendant, tour guide, hostess, and beautician, were simply not part of the Lost Wave's formation or its agenda. The collective hope of the generation preceding the economic miracle was that getting out of the miseries of the war and out from under the strictures of the economy of reconstruction would lead directly to a recomposed, dignified, harmonious life. Imagine the disillusionment of this generation to find that eliminating want from their children's lives, reunifying families, and reactivating normal rhythms had not guaranteed the conquest of stable values or the elimination of social problems. The Lost Wave had imagined a very specific future throughout the privations and fear of the war and Resistance, and they encouraged the next generation to imagine translating a similar heroism and commitment into a time of peace and prosperity. Their feminine ideal was to find some kind of "harmonious equilibrium," and despite their own dissatisfactions with female roles in the culture they continued to believe it worth striving for this balance. Instead, Italians coming of age in the 1950s and 1960s, with movie stars and motorinos, were trying on autonomy, transgression, and rebellion.

Scholars from the *prima generazione* and the neofeminist movement were the founders of women's studies as a legitimate scholarly field, with its own scientific literature, its own theory and methodology, and its own departments and degree-granting programs in academic institutions. But it was perhaps an unfortunate side effect of this generation's research interests and personal preferences that, when they wrote the first histories of feminism in Italy, when they began to teach the geneaology of feminist thought in their classrooms, they either ignored or bitterly criticized the postwar women's movement and the phenomenon of associationism in their narratives. In addition, their formative political years had come during an easing of Cold War tensions. As Italy joined NATO, its identity became more integrated into the coalescing European Union, and such watershed moments as the signing of the Helsinki Accords in 1975 recognized the stability of the East-West border in Europe and made nuclear warfare less thinkable. The United States no longer saw Italy as a revolutionary battleground and focused its interventions elsewhere. Although the DC remained the hegemonic mass party, the socialists fully entered mainstream politics and its corruptions, and the communists further distanced themselves from the Soviet Union, theorizing the possibility of a more reform-oriented and indigenous Eurocommunism. The narratives of women's history in Italy created by *prima generazione* scholars did not concede much causal force to Cold War politics, having not experienced it as consequential themselves, and therefore missed the ways that Italian women had been such frontline agents in bolstering the legitimacy of the Italian state. Thus did those women become a "lost" wave, missing from popular memory and from historical accounts.[11]

As I became aware of this aspect of memory politics in Italian society, I returned with some new questions and this time I heard new stories. Many of the women of the Lost Wave, especially those who, like Luciana Viviani, had been heavily involved in UDI, had been so traumatized by the criticisms and accusations leveled at them by second-wave feminists that they learned, in order to be accepted and, as it were, rehabilitated into the women's movement, to censor all talk of themselves as having contributed to women's rights or mass democracy in the time before their "conversions." The high point of this crisis came in 1982 when UDI, trying to gesture towards the autonomy vaunted by the consciousness-raising group model, voted to dissolve itself as a national organization with any formal connections to the political parties and immerse itself in neofeminism's multiplicity of small groups as simply one women's "movement" among many.[12]

This trauma has eased, and there has recently been a new outpouring of scholarly work on the postwar era in general and the women's movement in particular. This, in turn, has encouraged a number of new interviews, oral histories, and autobiographies from the protagonists themselves, ready to reexamine their stories in a new light. So it was with some excitement that I attended a talk given at UDI's (resurrected) national headquarters in Rome by Marisa Ombra, a PCI militant and "Resistance recruit," to an audience of local high school girls about her experience in the partisan brigades. She described her experiences and interpretations of that time and was surprised and gratified by how much the students seemed to already know about women in the Resistance and how many questions they were eager to ask. One young woman with several tattoos and earlobe-stretching plugs asked Ombra how, on the run and in the midst of so many men, she had managed her menstruation. Ombra responded that she didn't really remember and that in any case she never thought it was a problem or had any complications. She later told me she disliked those kinds of questions, didn't think they showed that the students were hearing the most important points she was trying to make, and was unhappy that they had become more frequent. I sympathize with both those women. The student was expressing the most concrete issue of gender difference she experiences in her life, trying to relate the concept of political resistance to her own context. Meanwhile, Ombra had finally found an audience to whom to relate her experiences but still felt misunderstood amidst this gendered question of "the body." This anecdote is a reminder to honor both approaches, listening to what the Lost Wave wanted to say as well as asking about what is not said, what is buried, and what has changed.

In reexamining this episode, the true historical mystery is how Italy's initial burst of women in Parliament managed to sustain numbers and productivity for so long. When the decline began, it was led by male party leaders' abandonment of their postwar courting of female voters with female candidates, in a more relaxed phase of the Cold War when they felt they had regained their masculine legitimacy to lead. It was reinforced by the youth rebellion against parliamentary politics and other symbols of the aged, sterile, and oppressive institutions of "old Europe." After 1968 the women's movement was divided along political lines, perhaps more so than in many other countries. Women activists, feminist or not, were radicalized and often belonged to extraparliamentary groups.[13] So party leaders stopped looking for women candidates, and women candidates stopped presenting themselves. From over 250 women candidates in the early elections the number dropped to barely 150 in 1975.[14] These numbers did not rise again until 1987, and even with various laws and a constitutional amendment attempting to establish quotas in 1993 and 1995, the numbers of women in the Italian Parliament did not approach parity, with women holding 97 seats out of a total of 950 in both chambers in the resulting twelfth legislature of 1994–1996 (a percentage of 10.2%). So far the only quotas to have survived appeal are those of the leftist parties which voluntarily impose them; the laws were declared unconstitutional, ironically with respect to Article 51 itself, which in this instance the court interpreted as forbidding any distinction as to sex with regards to the exercise of political rights, active or passive.[15] Since the era of Berlusconi and the 2008 economic crisis, the challenges to Italy's democratic legitimacy and mass political participation have become manifold. Nonetheless the narrative of decline in women's political representation was not definitive: the legislature elected in 2013 under the prime ministership of Democratic Party leader Enrico Letta included substantially more women. Voters elected 197 women of 630 deputies in the Chamber, and 92 female senators out of 317 in the upper house. Women in the Chamber rose from 21% in the previous legislature to 32%, and in the Senate from 19% to 29%. These are the highest numbers in the history of the republic.

For many years the constitutional rights strategy continued to produce new laws for women's rights. In 1955 the socialist Bianca Bianchi successfully sponsored law number 1064, erasing the label "N.N.," which designated "paternity unknown," from passports and identification papers. All children in Italy thus became "legitimate." In 1963, the Noce Law had its last loophole closed when employers were prohibited from requiring their women employees to resign if they married (the "matrimony clause" or *clausola di nubilato*); in 1968 two sentences from the Constitutional Court nullified the 1942 law differentiating between male and female adultery; in 1970 civil divorce was legalized (later confirmed by referendum in 1974); and Italy's second major referendum legalized abortion in 1978. Beginning in 1975 the family code was reformed so that husbands no longer had the right of *patria potestà;* previously the courts had held that Article 37 of the Constitution allowed a husband to stop his wife from working outside the home if he felt it impeded her responsibilities of taking care of him and their children, that she had to take his last name, respect his choice of residence, his right to open her mail, and even his right to discipline her and their children. In 1977 a law was passed that required equal pay for equal work after years of attempting to enforce the 1956 Constitutional Court ruling that Article 37 was prescriptive and required immediate remediation of all salaries.[16] Although women members of Parliament virtually disappeared from the legislatures between 1968 and 1987, women's true experience of democracy and political office expanded dramatically in local government and school administrations, cementing their presence in institutions at the local level rather than the national one.[17]

The women of the Lost Wave envisioned female political activism as leading toward the achievement of "active citizenship," a concept of democracy as always expanding and characterized by direct and constant grassroots intervention in institutions and the government, and which imagines that recently marginal groups can take on prime agency without negotiating the mediating forces of former elites.[18] They did not reinvent the sexual order in Italy, but they did contribute both to improving women's citizenship and legitimating Italy as a democracy. The strategy they chose of crafting women's rights laws to implement the Constitution may appear to have little in common with other forms of feminist protest. Yet as writer and second-wave feminist Laura Lilli ruefully admitted, "Certainly between a law and its application in real life we must bridge a gulf. But without the law we cannot even begin."[19] The women of the Lost Wave were correct in their analysis that women's political equality is also a crucial barometer of successful democracy. Inasmuch as Italian women—and feminists anywhere—still strive to be the bulwark of democracy, that wave is not lost.

APPENDICES

Appendix 1

RELEVANT CONSTITUTIONAL ARTICLES

Article 1

Italy is a democratic republic founded on labor.

Sovereignty belongs to the people, who exercise it according to the forms and limits of the constitution.

Article 2

The republic recognizes and guarantees the inviolable human rights of man, be it as an individual or in the social groups where he expresses his personality, and it ensures the performance of the unalterable duty to political, economic, and social solidarity.

Article 3

All citizens have equal social status and are equal before the law, without regard to their sex, race, language, religion, political opinions, and personal or social conditions.

It is the duty of the republic to remove all economic and social obstacles that, by limiting the freedom and equality of citizens, prevent full individual development and the effective participation of all workers in the political, economic, and social organization of the country.

Article 4

The republic recognizes the right of all citizens to work and promotes conditions to fulfill this right.

According to capability and choice, every citizen has the duty to undertake an activity or a function that will contribute to the material and moral progress of society.

Article 29

The family is recognized by the republic as a natural association founded on marriage.

Marriage entails moral and legal equality of the spouses within legally defined limits to protect the unity of the family.

Article 31

The republic furthers family formation and the fulfillment of related tasks by means of economic and other provisions with special regard to large families.

The republic protects maternity, infancy, and youth; it supports and encourages institutions needed for this purpose.

Article 37

Working women are entitled to equal rights and, for comparable jobs, equal pay as men. Working conditions must be such as to allow women to fulfill their essential family duties and ensure an adequate protection of mothers and children.

The law defines a minimal age for paid labor.

The republic establishes special measures protecting juvenile labor and guarantees equal pay for comparable work.

Article 51

All citizens of either sex are eligible for public office and for elective positions under equal conditions, according to the rules established by law. [Amendment of February 20, 2003: To this end, the republic adopts specific measures in order to promote equal opportunities for men and women.]

Appendix 2

PRINCIPAL LAWS OF CONSTITUTIONAL RIGHTS FEMINISM

Legge 26 agosto 1950, n. 860: "Tutela fisica ed economica delle lavoratrici madri." The Noce Law, for the physical and economic protection of working mothers.

Legge 31 ottobre 1955, n. 1064: "Disposizioni relative alle generalità in estratti, atti e documenti e modificazioni all'ordinamento dello stato civile." Bianca Bianchi, Maria Pia Dal Canton, Lina Merlin, collaborators. The law removes all notations as to paternity or legitimacy on identification papers.

Legge 27 dicembre 1956, n. 1441: "Partecipazione delle donne all'amminstrazione della giustizia nelle Corti di assise e nei Tribunali per i minorenni." Women are allowed to become jurors in two courts, the Assize and Juvenile.

Legge 20 febbraio 1958, n. 75: "Abolizione della regolamentazione della prostituzione e lotta contro lo sfruttamento della prostituzione altrui." The Merlin Law, abolishing regulated prostitution.

Legge 2 aprile 1958, n. 339: "Per la tutela del rapporto di lavoro domestico." For the rights of home workers.

Legge 7 dicembre 1959, n. 1083: "Costituzione di un Corpo di polizia femminile." Maria Pia dal Canton, creation of the female task force envisioned by the Merlin Law.

Parità salariale 1960: A national labor accord promoted by the women's movement ends the separate calculation schedules for determining men's and women's pay scales.

Legge 29 novembre 1961, n. 1325: "Modificazioni alla legge 26 aprile 1934, n. 653, sulla tutela del lavoro delle donne e dei fanciulli." Updates to the Noce Law, enforcing a national childcare system.

Legge 9 gennaio 1963, n. 7: "Divieto di licenziamento della lavoratrici per causa di matrimonio." Merlin and others, correcting the loophole in the Noce Law so that employers may not require women to resign when marrying.

Legge 9 febbraio 1963, n. 66: "Ammissione della donne ai pubblici uffici ed alle professioni." The Cocco Law, making women eligible for all public careers.

Appendix 3

WOMEN OF THE FIRST LEGISLATURES

Assemblea Costituente

22 Women out of 586 Members

1) Bastianello Celeste
2) Bei Adele
3) Bianchi Bianca
4) Bianchini Laura
5) Conci Elisabetta
6) Delli Castelli Filomena
7) De Unterrichter Maria
8) Federici Maria
9) Gallico Spano Nadia
10) Gotelli Angela
11) Guidi Cingolani Angela Maria
12) Jotti Leonilde
13) Mattei Teresa
14) Merlin Angela
15) Minella Angela
16) Montagnani Togliatti Rita
17) Nicotra Maria
18) Noce Longo Teresa
19) Penna Buscemi Ottavia
20) Pollastrini Elettra
21) Rossi Maria Maddalena
22) Titomanlio Vittoria

Note: I report twenty-one women in the main text since Ottavia Penna left and was substituted by Angela Gotelli.

First Legislature, 1948–1953
Camera dei Deputati: 41 Women out of 574 Members

Bianchi Bianca	Catania	P.S.U.
Bianchini Laura	Brescia	D.C.
Bontade Margherita	Palermo	D.C.
Borellini Gina	Parma	P.C.I.
Chiesa Tibaldi Mary	Pisa	P.R.I.
Chini Coccoli Irene	Brescia	P.C.I.
Cinciari Rodano M. Luisa	Roma	P.C.I.
Conci Elsa Elisabetta	Trento	D.C.
Coppi Ilia	Siena	P.C.I.
Dal Canton Maria Pia	Venezia	D.C.
Delli Castelli Filomena	L'Aquila	D.C.
Diaz Laura	Pisa	P.C.I.
Fazio Longo Rosa	C.U.N.	P.S.I.
Federici Agamben Maria	Perugia	D.C.
Floreanini Della Porta Gisella	Torino	P.C.I.
Gallico Spano Nadia	Cagliari	P.C.I.
Gallo Elisabetta	Cuneo	P.C.I.
Gennai Tonietti Erisa	Milano	D.C.
Giannini Olga	C.U.N.	P.M.I.
Giuntoli Grazia	Bari	D.C.
Gotelli Angela	Genova	D.C.
Guidi Cingolani Angela Maria	Roma	D.C.
Jervolino de Unterrichter Maria	C.U.N.	D.C.
Iotti Leonilde	Parma	P.C.I.
Lombardi Colombi Pia	Roma	D.C.
Marcellino Colombi Nella	Bologna	P.C.I.
Martini Fanoli Gina	Milano	P.C.I.

Minella Angiola	Genova	P.C.I.
Natali Ada	Ancona	P.C.I.
Nenni Giuliana	Bologna	P.S.I.
Nicotra Maria	Catania	D.C.
Noce Teresa	Parma	P.C.I.
Pollastrini Elettra	Perugia	P.C.I.
Pucci Maria	Ancona	D.C.
Ravera Camilla	Torino	P.C.I.
Re Giuseppina	Milano	P.C.I.
Rossi Maria Maddalena	Verona	P.C.I.
Titomanlio Vittoria	Napoli	D.C.
Valandro Gigliola	Verona	D.C.
Vecchio Vaia Stella	Mantova	P.C.I.
Viviani Luciana	Napoli	P.C.I.

Senato: 4 out of 342

Bei Ciufoli Adele	Marche	P.C.I.
Merlin Angelina	Veneto	P.S.I.
Montagnana Rita	Emilia-Rom	P.C.I.
Palumbo Giuseppina	Sicilia	P.S.I.

Second Legislature, 1953–1958
Camera dei Deputati: 36 out of 590 Members

Badaloni Maria	Roma	D.C.
Bei Ciufoli Adele	Ancona	P.C.I.
Bianchi Cieco Maria	Bari	P.N.M.
Borellini Gina	Parma	P.C.I.
Capponi Bentivegna Carla	Roma	P.C.I.
Cecchini Lina	Parma	D.C.
Cinciari Rodano M. Luisa	Roma	P.C.I.

Conci Elsa Elisabetta	Trento	D.C.
Dal Canton Maria Pia	Venezia	D.C.
De Lauro Matera Anna	Bari	P.S.I.
Delli Castelli Filomena	L'Aquila	D.C.
Del Vecchio Guelfi Ada	Bari	P.C.I.
D'Este Ida	Venezia	D.C.
Diaz Laura	Pisa	P.C.I.
Fittaioli Luciana	Perugia	P.C.I.
Floreanini Della Porta Gisella Torino	P.C.I.	
Gallico Spano Nadia	Cagliari	P.C.I.
Gatti Caporaso Elena	Pisa	P.S.I.
Gennai Tonietti Erisa	Milano	D.C.
Gotelli Angela	Genova	D.C.
Grasso Nicolosi Anna	Palermo	P.C.I.
Jervolino de Unterrichter Maria	C.U.N.	D.C.
Iotti Leonilde	Parma	P.C.I.
Marchionni Zanchi Renata	Firenze	P.C.I.
Matarazzo Ida	Benevento	P.N.M.
Mezza Maria Vittoria	Parma	P.S.I.
Molè Elsa	Catanzaro	P.S.I.
Nenni Giuliana	Bologna	P.S.I.
Noce Teresa	Parma	P.C.I.
Pollastrini Elettra	Perugia	P.C.I.
Ravera Camilla	Torino	P.C.I.
Rossi Maria Maddalena	Verona	P.C.I.
Titomanlio Vittoria	Napoli	D.C.
Valandro Gigliola	Verona	D.C.
Viviani Luciana	Napoli	P.C.I.

Senato: 1 of 243

Merlin Angelina	Veneto	P.S.I.

Third Legislature, 1958–1963
Camera dei Deputati: 22 Women out of 590 Members

Badaloni Maria	Roma	D.C.
Bei Ciufoli Adele	Ancona	P.C.I.
Bontade Margherita	Palermo	D.C.
Borellini Gina	Parma	P.C.I.
Cinciari Rodano M. Luisa	Roma	P.C.I.
Cocco Maria	Cagliari	D.C.
Conci Elsa Elisabetta	Trento-Bolzano	D.C.
Dal Canton Maria Pia	Venezia-Treviso	D.C.
De Lauro Matera Anna	Bari-Foggia	P.S.I.
Diaz Laura	Pisa	P.C.I.
Gennai Tonietti Erisa	Milano-Pavia	D.C.
Gotelli Angela	Genova	D.C.
Grasso Nicolosi Anna	Palermo	P.C.I.
Jervolino de Unterrichter Maria	Benevento	D.C.
Iotti Leonilde	Parma	P.C.I.
Merlin Angelina	Verona	P.S.I.
Minella Angiola	Genova	P.C.I.
Re Giuseppina	Cosenza	P.C.I.
Rossi Maria Maddalena	Siena	P.C.I.
Savio Emanuela	Torino	D.C.
Titomanlio Vittoria	Napoli-Caserta	D.C.
Viviani Luciana	Napoli-Caserta	P.C.I.

Senato: 3 out of 249

Gallotti Balboni Luisa	Emilia Rom.	P.C.I.
Nenni Giuliana	Emilia Rom.	P.S.I.
Palumbo Giuseppina	Sicilia	P.S.I.

NOTES

Introduction

1. *Atti Parlamentari.* Consulta Nazionale, Assemblea Plenaria, VI. Seduta di 1 ottobre 1945, 121.
2. This is an admittedly superficial summary of the narrative running through a number of very serious works of scholarship analyzing gender politics during the world war and interwar years in Europe. Collectively they have shown how militarization and national mobilization in the unprecedented experience of total war, depression and inflation, and the ideological rivalry of the interwar years were linked to a profound sense of crisis in and reordering of gender. The Nazi and Fascist states pursued gender policies that supported their racial and military projects. Even the Allied "liberation" ending World War II has been shown, in Mary Louise Roberts' work, to be founded in large part on a sexual narrative that led soldiers, particularly American GIs, to see liberation as a "sexual romance" with the devastated and vulnerable women of the defeated nations—but one that included brothels, streetwalkers, venereal disease, and rape. Kathleen Canning offers a thorough review of the scholarship in *Gender History in Practice*, especially 42–59; signal works include Higonnet, Jenson, Michel, and Weitz, eds., *Behind the Lines: Gender and the Two World Wars* (New Haven: Yale University Press, 1987); Karen Hagemann and Stefanie Schüler-Springorum, eds., *Home/Front: The Military, War, and Gender in Twentieth Century Germany* (Oxford: Berg, 2002); Susan Kingsley Kent, *Making Peace: The Reconstruction of Gender in Interwar Britain* (Princeton, NJ: Princeton University Press, 1993); Mary Louise Roberts, *Civilization Without Sexes: Reconstructing Gender in Postwar France, 1917–1927* (Chicago: University of Chicago Press, 1994); idem, *What Soldiers Do: Sex and the American GI in World War II France* (Chicago: University of Chicago Press, 2013); Klaus Theweleit, *Male Fantasies*, vol. I, *Women, Floods, Bodies, History* (Minneapolis: University of Minnesota Press, 1987); Victoria de Grazia, *How Fascism Ruled Women: Italy 1922–1945* (Berkeley: University of California Press, 1992); Claudia Koonz, *Mothers in the Fatherland: Women, Family Life, and Nazi Ideology, 1919–1945* (New York: St. Martin's Press, 1986); Miranda Pollard, *Reign of Virtue: Mobilizing Gender in*

Vichy France (Chicago: University of Chicago Press, 1998); Sonya O Rose, *Which People's War? National Identity and Citizenship in Wartime Britain, 1939–1945* (Oxford: Oxford University Press, 2003).

3. Important works on this topic in Italy in the relevant period include Victoria de Grazia, *How Fascism Ruled Women: Italy, 1922–1945* (Berkeley: University of California Press, 1992); Anna Bravo and Anna Maria Bruzzone, *In guerra senza armi. Storie di donne. 1940–1945* (Rome: Laterza, 1995); Mafai, *L'apprendistato della politica*; idem, *Pane nero. Donne e vita quotidiana nella seconda guerra mondiale* (Milan: Arnaldo Mondadori, 1987); Robin Pickering Iazzi, *Politics of the Visible: Writing Women, Culture, and Fascism* (Minneapolis: University of Minnesota Press, 1995); Giovanni de Luna, *Donne in oggetto. L'antifascismo nella società italiana 1922–1939* (Torino: Bollati Boringhieri, 1995).
4. Canning makes a similar observation about Weimar Germany and citizenship in Canning, *Gender History in Practice*, 163.
5. A prime example of this idea that the local hardly matters, accompanied by a triumphalist account of the United States "winning" the Cold War, is in John Lewis Gaddis, *We Now Know: Rethinking the Cold War* (New York: Oxford University Press, 1997).
6. See Giovagnoli, *Il partito italiano*, 38. David Ellwood has been quite sensitive to this issue; see David W. Ellwood, *The Shock of America. Europe and the Challenge of the Century* (Oxford: Oxford University Press, 2012); though Ellwood credits Volker Berghahn with being among the "first to suggest that Europeans tried to take over from America's models just what was useful to them and nothing more " (8–9). See Berghahn, "Conceptualizing the American Impact on Germany: West German Society and the Problem of Americanization," paper presented at the German Historical Institute conference in Washington, DC (March 1999), http://www.ghi-dc.org/conpotweb/westernpapers/berghahn.pdf. The special issue *Cold War History* devoted to radio broadcasting also reflects this current, "argu[ing] against the idea of an American—and British—unchallenged leadership in the cultural Cold War." L. Risso, "Introduction: Radio Wars: Broadcasting in the Cold War," *Cold War History* 13 no. 2 (2013): [145–152, quote 150]; Simona Tobia, "Did the RAI Buy It? The Role and Limits of American Broadcasting in Italy in the Cold War," *Cold War History* 13, no. 2 (2013): 171–91. Also see Formigoni, "La rifondazione;" Brogi, *A Question of Self-Esteem*; idem, *Italia e L'Egemonia nel Mediterraneo*; Tosi, *Politica ed economia nelle relazioni internazionali*; Rossi, "Una democrazia a rischio;" Del Pero, *L'alleato scomodo*; Lundestad, "Empire By Invitation"; idem, *No End to Alliance*; idem, *The United States and Western Europe*; Lundestad and Westad, *Beyond the Cold War*; Westad, *Reviewing the Cold War*.
7. *"Baluardo principale per impedire ogni rigurgito di totalitarismo,"* writes Simona Lunadei: women's political activism was "an essential action of making the social, political." Simona Lunadei, "Donne e governo della Capitale (1946–2001)," Una democrazia incompiuta: Donne e politica in Italia dall'Ottocento ai nostrum giorni, Nadia Maria Filippini and Anna Scattigno, eds., (Milan: FrancoAngeli, 2007), 250.
8. Simonetta Piccone Stella, *La prima generazione. Ragazzi e ragazze nel miracolo economic italiano* (Milano: FrancoAngeli, 1993); Paul Ginsborg, *A History*

of Contemporary Italy: Society and Politics 1943–1988 (London: Penguin, 1990); idem, *Italy and its Discontents, 1980–2001* (London: Penguin Books, 2001); Victoria de Grazia, *Irresistible Empire: America's Advance Through Twentieth-Century Europe* (Cambridge: Belknap, 2005); John Foot, *Modern Italy* (New York: Palgrave Macmillan, 2003); idem, "The Family and the 'Economic Miracle': Social Transformation, Work, Leisure and Development at Bovisa and Comasina (Milan), 1959–1970," Contemporary European History 4, no. 3 (1995): 315–38; Patrick McCarthy, ed., *Italy Since 1945* (Oxford: Oxford University Press, 2000).

9. In Italy: Gaiotti de Biase, "Impact of Women's Activity;" Penny Morris, ed., *Women in Italy, 1946–1960* (New York: Palgrave Macmillan, 2006); Gabrielli, *Il Club delle virtuose*; idem, *Vivere da protagoniste. Donne tra politica, cultura e controllo sociale* (Rome: Carocci, 2001); Sandro Bellassai, *Morale comunista: pubblico e privato nella rappresentazione del PCI: 1947–1956* (Rome: Carocci, 2000); idem, *La mascolinità contemporanea* (Rome: Carocci, 2004); idem, *La legge del desiderio: il progetto Merlin e l'Italia degli anni Cinquanta* (Rome: Carocci, 2006). Elsewhere: Elizabeth Heineman, *What Difference Does a Husband Make? Women and Marital Status in Nazi and Postwar Germany* (Berkeley: University of California Press, 2003); Tim Mason, "Women in Germany, 1925–1940: Family, Welfare and Work," in Nazism, Fascism and the Working Class: Essays by Tim Mason, ed. Jane Caplan (Cambridge and New York: Cambridge University Press, 1995); Robert Moeller, *Protecting Motherhood: Women and the Family in the politics of Postwar Germany* (Berkeley: University of California Press, 1993); Seth Koven and Sonya Michel, eds., *Mothers of a New World: Maternalist Politics and the Origins of Welfare States* (New York: Routledge, 1993); Gisela Bock and Pat Thane, eds., *Maternity and Gender Policies: Women and the Rise of European Welfare States, 1880s–1950s* (New York: Routledge, 1991).
10. Kathleen Canning, *Gender History in Practice: Historical Perspectives on Bodies, Class, and Citizenship* (Ithaca, NY: Cornell University Press, 2006), 4–5. Sonya O. Rose, *What Is Gender History?* (Cambridge, UK: Polity Press, 2010) is a useful introduction to the field. A recent historiographical reconsideration of practices in gender history that emphasizes their multiplicity and disciplinary border crossings is Donna R. Gabaccia and Mary Jo Maynes, "Introduction: Gender History Across Epistemologies," in Gender History Across Epistemologies (Chichester, UK: Wiley-Blackwell, 2013), originally published as special issue of *Gender and History* 24, no. 3 (2013): 1–19. The two works that served as the original foundation for my understanding of gender are Joan Wallach Scott, "Gender: A Useful Category of Historical Analysis," American Historical Review 91, no. 5 (1986): 1053–75, and Denise Riley, *Am I That Name? Feminism and the Category of "Women" in History* (Minneapolis: University of Minnesota Press, 1988). Anna Rossi-Doria is the authority on this topic in Italian; see especially her *Diventare cittadine. Il voto alle donne in Italia* (Florence: Giunti Gruppo Editoriale, 1996); and idem, *Dare forma al silenzio. Scritti di storia politica delle donne* (Rome: Viella, 2007). Broader European and world history treatments are A. Timm and J. Sanborn, *Gender, Sex, and the Shaping of Modern Europe: A History from the French Revolution to the Present Day* (New York: Berg, 2007); S. Dudink,

K. Hagemann, and J. Tosh, eds., *Masculinities in Politics and War: Gendering Modern History* (Manchester: Manchester University Press, 2004).

11. To highlight two more foundational texts, Carole Pateman, *The Sexual Contract* (Stanford, CA: Stanford University Press, 1988); and Iris Marion Young, *Justice and the Politics of Difference* (Princeton, NJ: Princeton University Press, 1990). See also H. J. Kim-Puri, "Conceptualizing Gender-Sexuality-State-Nation: An Introduction," *Gender & Society* 19, no. 2 (April 2005): 137–59.
12. On citizenship as practice and status, see Ruth Lister, *Citizenship: Feminist Perspectives* (New York: New York University Press, 2003). On the importance of obligations or duties as well as rights or privileges Linda Kerber, see *No Constitutional Right to Be Ladies: Women and the Obligations of Citizenship* (New York: Hill and Wang, 1998); and idem, "Presidential Address: The Stateless as the Citizen's Other: A View from the United States," *The American Historical Review* (February 2007). Other important conceptualizations of citizenship as gendered are Kathleen Canning and Sonya O. Rose, "Gender, Citizenships, and Subjectivity: Some Historical and Theoretical Observations," in *Gender, Citizenship, and Subjectivities,* eds. Canning and Rose, (London: Blackwell, 2002) 1–17; Joan Scott, *Paritè! Sexual Equality and the Crisis of French Universalism* (Chicago: University of Chicago Press, 2005); Nitza Berkovitch, *From Motherhood to Citizenship: Women's Rights and International Organizations* (Baltimore: Johns Hopkins University Press, 1999); Nira Yuval-Davis and Pnina Werbner, eds., *Women, Citizenship and Difference* (London: Zed Books, 1999); Nancy Cott, *Public Vows: A History of Marriage and the Nation* (Cambridge: Harvard UP, 2000); Candice Lewis Bredbenner, *A Nationality of Her Own: Women, Marriage and the Law of Citizenship* (Berkeley: University of California Press,1998). For examples of the debates about citizenship as a concept and category of historical analysis, an excellent starting point are the essays in Gershon Shafir, ed., *The Citizenship Debates: A Reader* (Minneapolis: University of Minnesota Press, 1998).
13. Canning, *Gender History as Practice,* 218.
14. The penal code, known as the *Codice Rocco,* was passed in 1930. Although substantial sections of it have undergone revision especially as the result of feminists' activism, it remains the penal code still in force in Italy today.
15. For a more in-depth analysis of this instrumentalist view of the appeal of human rights in the postwar period, see Andrew Moravcsik, "The Origins of Human Rights Regimes: Democratic Delegation in Postwar Europe," International Organization 54 no. 2 (Spring 2000): 217–52.
16. The decree granting women the right to vote was *Decreto legislativo luogotenenziale* n. 23 del 1 febbraio 1945, "Estensione alle donne del diritto di voto," passed by the Bonomi government. As Anna Rossi-Doria shows, some women in Italy did participate in activism to agitate for suffrage, and the postwar reappearance of these first wave feminists argues for some continuity in Italy's women's movements. Anna Rossi-Doria, *Diventare cittadine. Il voto alle donne in Italia* (Florence: Giunti Gruppo Editoriale, 1996), 20–6; Paola Gaiotti de Biase, "The Impact of Women's Political and Social Activity in Postwar Italy," in *The Formation of the Italian Republic,* eds. Frank Coppa and Margherita Repetto-Alaia (New York: Peter Lang, 1993), 221.
17. Gaiotti de Biase, "Impact of Women's Political and Social Activity," 222.

18. Gaiotti de Biase, "Impact of Women's Political and Social Activity," 229; Miriam Mafai, *L'apprendistato della politica. Le donne italiane nel dopoguerra* (Rome: Editori Riuniti, 1979), 66–67. The most famous of Togliatti's expositions of the link between women's emancipation and democracy was made to the first women's conference of his party in June 1945: see Palmiro Togliatti, "L'emancipazione della donna," reproduced in *Donne Comuniste. Antologia di scritti e discorsi*, ed. Graziella Falconi (Rome: Claudio Salemi, 1989), 52–80.
19. While recognizing this issue of difficult periodization, Tony Judt's *Postwar* nevertheless accepts 1945 as a watershed moment in his masterful account of postwar European history. It is more productively questioned in Claire Duchen and Irene Bandhauer-Schoffmann, "Introduction," *When the War Was Over: Women, War, and Peace in Europe, 1940–1956* (London: Continuum International Publishing, 2010), 1–12. Claudio Pavone has done groundbreaking work on the continuity of the Italian state and legal system, see Claudio Pavone, *Alle origini della repubblica. Scritti su fascismo, antifascismo e continuità dello stato* (Torino, Bollati Boringhieri, 1995). Demoralized by years of Berlusconi and the economic crisis since 2008, recent historiography seems to be focusing on a narrative of Italy's failure to ever successfully change or reform political and economic institutions in the postwar: Mariuccia Salvati, "Behind the Cold War: Rethinking the Left, the State and Civil Society in Italy (1940s–1970s)," *Journal of Modern Italian Studies* 8 no. 4 (2003): 556–77. International aspects of recovery after 1945 have been problematized in Mark Mazower, Jessica Reinisch, and David Feldman, eds., "Post-War Reconstruction of Europe: International Perspectives, 1945–1949," *Past and Present* supplement 6 (2011), particularly Mark Mazower, "Reconstruction: The Historiographical Issues," 17–28.
20. For an excellent general history in English, see P. Willson, *Women in Twentieth-Century Italy* (London: Palgrave Macmillan, 2010).
21. Judt, 338n12, points out that Italy remained an anomaly in this sense long into the years of the "economic miracle;" in 1957 less than 2% of Italian households had refrigerators; as late as 1971 95% of all food was purchased from small, specialized merchants as opposed to in a single trip to the supermarket.
22. Willson, 118.
23. Exemplary of Pius XII's approach to "the women question" are two speeches given by the pope on October 29, 1951, and November 26, 1951: *Moral Questions Affecting Married Life: Addresses given to the Italian Catholic Union of Midwives 29 October 1951, and 26 November 1951 to the National Congress of the Family Front and the Association of Large Families*, National Catholic Welfare Conference, Washington, D.C. In both he asserted the need to "win[] married people over to a service of motherhood" and upheld the correctness of the most famous papal pronouncement on the sanctity of motherhood and the resulting necessity of forbidding birth control and abortion, Pius XI's *Casti connubi* encyclical of 1930. For further information on his controversial papacy see Zuccotti Cornwell, text of the speech to midwives available at Catholicculture.org, http://www.catholicculture.org/culture/library/view.cfm?id=3462&CFID=103675889&CFTOKEN=26566144. See also Lucetta Scaraffia, "'Christianity Has Liberated Her and Placed Her Alongside Man in the Family': From 1850 to 1988 (mulieris Dignitatem)," in *Women and Faith: Catholic Religious Life in Italy from Late Antiquity to the Present*, ed. Lucetta Scaraffia and Gabriella

Zarri (Cambridge: Harvard University Press, 1999), 249–80 (original in Italian, 1994).

24. S. Lanaro, *Storia dell'Italia repubblicana. L'economia, la politica, la cultura, la società dal dopoguerra agli anni '90* (Venice: Marsilio, 1992); G. Crainz, *Storia del miracolo italiano. Culture, identità, trasformazioni fra anni Cinquanta e Sessanta* (Rome: Donzelli, 1996).
25. Ellwood, 330, 359.
26. See Tambor, "Red Saints," for the detailed articulation of this argument. Mire Koikare has also written about the "trope of heterosexual romance" between American citizens (figured as masculine) and the occupied Japanese (figured as feminine, often literally focused on making women into democratic citizens) in the Cold War in a book with important comparative value: Koikare, *Pedagogy of Democracy: Feminism and the Cold War in the U.S. Occupation of Japan* (Philadelphia: Temple University Press, 2008), 3 ff.
27. Dagmar Herzog, "Desperately Seeking Normality: Sex and Marriage in the Wake of War," in *Life After Death: Approaches to a Cultural and Social History of Europe during the 1940s and 1950s*, Richard Bessel and Dirk Schumann, eds. (Cambridge: Cambridge University Press, 2003), 161–192; idem, *Sex after Fascism: Memory and Morality in Twentieth-Century Germany* (Princeton, NJ: Princeton University Press, 2005).
28. Cynthia Enloe, *The Morning After: Sexual Politics at the End of the Cold War* (Berkeley and Los Angeles, California: University of California Press, 1993); John Foot, "The Family and the 'Economic Miracle': Social Transformation, Work, Leisure and Development at Bovisa and Comasina (Milan), 1959–1970," *Contemporary European History* 4, no. 3 (1995): 315–38. Moeller, *Protecting Motherhood*; Canning, *Gender History in Practice*, 56–59.
29. Guido Crainz, *Storia del miracolo italiano* (Donzelli, 2005); Victoria de Grazia, *Irresistible Empire: America's Advance Through Twentieth-Century Europe* (Cambridge: Belknap, 2005).
30. Gabrielli, *Il club delle virtuose. Udi e Cif nelle Marche dall'antifascismo alla guerra fredda* (Ancona: Il lavoro editoriale, 2000).
31. As Canning has written, "One significant outcome of critical feminist thinking on citizenship and its spatial location in civil societies and public spheres is the critical analysis and ultimate rejection of the presumed opposition between private and public spheres which was at the core of both liberal and republican traditions of political thought." Canning, *Gender History in Practice*, 17. Leonore Davidoff has been a leader in this respect: Leonore Davidoff, "Gender and the 'Great Divide': Public and Private in British Gender History," *Journal of Women's History* 15, no. 1 (Spring 2003): 11–27; idem, "Regarding Some 'Old Husbands' Tales': Public and Private in Feminist History," in *Worlds Between: Historical Perspectives on Gender and Class* (Cambridge: Cambridge University Press, 1995), 227–276; Leonore Davidoff and Catherine Hall, *Family Fortunes: Men and Women of the English Middle Class, 1780–1850* (Chicago: University of Chicago Press, 1987).
32. Ceccatelli Gurrieri and Paolucci, 4; Anna Rossi-Doria, "Le donne sulla scena politica," in *Storia dell'Italia Repubblicana*, vol. 1, *La Costituzione della democrazia* (Torino: Einaudi, 1994), 833, 839.

33. See Canning, *Gender History in Practice,* 81 (on conflicting gender discourses and "webs of cross-references") and 89 (on claiming multiple subject positions).

Chapter 1

1. UDI Archivio Centrale, invitation and card sample, archivio cronologico 1946. This reception is documented in the following works, but only another photograph showing eleven of the women at the reception is extant, so the description is my own, based on what I believe to be likely from the information we have on the event and the women there. Lucia Chaivola Birnbaum, *liberazione della donna. feminism in Italy* (Middletown, CT: Wesleyan UP, 1986), 58; M. Michetti, M. Repetto, L. Viviani, *Udi:laboratorio di politica delle donne. Idee e materiali per una storia,* 2a edizione (Soveria Mannelli: Rubbettino Editore, 1998), 18–19; and Mafai, *L'apprendistato della politica,* 177–78.
2. Gabaccia and Maynes, 18.
3. On "oppositional familism" to describe how "against a state that failed to safeguard family interests, family logic fed an antipolitics, if not an alternative, power," see V. de Grazia, *How Fascism Ruled Women: Italy, 1922–1945* (Berkeley: University of California Press, 1992), 82, 113–15 (quote on 113); and G. De Luna, *Donne in oggetto. L'antifascismo nella società italiana 1922–1939* (Torino: Bollati Boringhieri, 1995), 178–80. De Luna (180–85) further discusses the move for women in the Resistance from family to politics in their own right.
4. Biographical information can be found in the first three editions of the parliament's own publication commonly known as *La Navicella: I Deputati e Senatori del Primo Parlamento Repubblicano* (Rome: Camera dei Deputati, 1949); *I Deputati e Senatori del Secondo Parlamento Repubblicano* (Rome: Camera dei Deputati, 1955); and *I Deputati e Senatori del Terzo Parlamento Repubblicano* (Rome: Camera dei Deputati, 1958). In addition the Camera dei Deputati listed biographies of its members in the *Atti Parlamentari. Attività parlamentare dei deputati. Indice alfabetico.* I have used the first three volumes, one from each legislature. Presidenza del Consiglio dei Ministri, *La donna italiana dalla Resistenza ad oggi,* 30. Selected statistics can also now be found online at http://legislature.camera.it/. In addition, on Teresa Noce I have relied on her many autobiographies, including T. Noce, *Vivere in piedi* (Milano: Gabriele Mazzotta, 1978); and *Rivoluzionaria professionale* (Milano: La Pietra, Bompiani, 1974). On Merlin, likewise on her autobiography, L. Merlin, *La mia vita,* a cura di Elena Marinucci (Firenze: Giunti Barbera, 1989); and on each of the above I have used Boneschi, M. *Di testa loro. Dieci italiane che hanno fatto il Novecento,* 2d ed. (Milano: Mondadori, 2003). The trickle of biographies, autobiographies, and testimonies has grown to a flood: Luisa Lama, *Nilde iotti. Una storia poitica al femminile* (Rome: Donzelli, 2013); Giorgio Grigolli, *Elsa Conci. La sposa della DC* (Rovereto: Edizioni Stella, 2005); Nadia Gallico Spano, *Mabruk*; Giovanni Verna and Cinzia Rossi, *Filomena Delli Castelli. Una donna abruzzese alla Costituente* (Teramo: Edigrafital, 2006); Bianca Bianchi, *Il colore delle nuvole* (Florence: Firenze libri, 1993); Bianca Bianchi, *La storia è memoria* (Florence: Giorni and Gambi editori, 1998); Luciana Viviani, *Rosso antico. Come lottare per il comunismo senza perdere il senso dell'umorismo*

(Florence: Giunti Gruppo Editoriale, 1994); Carla Capponi, *Con Cuore di Donna* (Milan: Il Saggiatore, 2000); Marisa Rodano, *Memoria di una che c'era. Una storia dell'Udi* (Milan: Il Saggiatore, 2010); Marisa Rodano, *del mutare dei tempi. Vol.I l'età dell'inconsapevolezza, il tempo della speranza, 1921–1948. Vol. II. l'ora dell'azione, la stagione del raccolto, 1948–1968* (Rome: MEMORI Scarl, 2008); Bianca Guidetti Serra, *Bianca la rossa* (Turin: Einaudi, 2009); Paola Gaiotti de Biase, *Passare la mano. Memorie di una donna dal Novecento incompiuto* (Rome: Viella, 2010).

5. C. Capponi, *Con Cuore di Donna*, 142.
6. T. Pizzardo, *Senza pensarci due volte* (Bologna: Il Mulino, 1996), 165.
7. Judt, 64.
8. From the text of her award of the Medal, reprinted in *Partigiane della Libertà* (Rome: Sezione centrale stampa e propaganda del PCI, 1973).
9. Archivio Gina Borellini, Folder B.I.1 Materiale biografico 1945–1987, folder 139 fasc. 8, Modena, Via Canaletto 88. The collection of the Centro documentazione donna in Modena is based on her donation of her papers and she continued to work there until her death in 1993.
10. For more on the ways that these sentiments could "coniugarsi felicemente" in the antifascist choice, see P. Gabrielli, *Il club delle virtuose. Udi e Cif nelle Marche dall'antifascismo alla guerra fredda* (Ancona: Il lavoro editoriale, 2000), esp. 35, 48–49, and 54.
11. L. Scaraffia, "Christianity Has Liberated Her," 274.
12. In 1920 GF counted 700 groups with 50,000 members; in 1925, 15,800 groups with 333,000 members; in 1946, it had grown to 888,992 members of GF and 369,015 members of the AC women's section (Udaci); the maximum numbers came in 1956 with more than 1,265,000 GF members and 630,000 in Udaci. Paola Gaiotti de Biase, "Donne e politica nella Repubblica," 99n24.
13. For an exploration of how fashion operated during Fascism to discipline and communicate a national gender order, see Emilia Paulicelli, "Fashion, the Politics of Style, and National Identity in Pre-Fascist and Fascist Italy," *Gender and History* 14, no. 3 (November 2002): 537–59.
14. Olga Prati in I. Ricci, ed., *Senza camelie. Percorsi femminili nella storia* (Ravenna: Longo Editore, 1990), 97.
15. P. Gaiotti de Biase, "Introduzione," in *Il voto alle donne cinquant'anni dopo*, 8.
16. For the concept of "maternage di massa," see A. Bravo and A. M Bruzzone, *In guerra senza armi. Storie di donne. 1940–1945* (Rome: Editori Laterza, 1995), 66–76.
17. However, Anna Bravo has also recognized elsewhere that portraying the Resistance as a narrative of mothers saving sons is a form of memory politics that avoids the question of national guilt, making the Resistance into a "recuperation of Italian masculinity." Anna Bravo, "Guerra e mutamenti nelle strutture di genere," *Italia contemporanea*, no. 195 (June 1994): 367–74; Willson, "Saints and heroines," 195.
18. On the egalitarian character of the Resistance, see also Rossi-Doria, *Diventare cittadine*, 52. A somewhat dissenting view that the Resistance was a masculinizing project in which the femininity of women participants became invisible is expounded in Patrizia Gabrielli, *Tempio di virilità. L'antifascismo, il genere, la storia* (Milan: FrancoAngeli, 2008).

19. M. Ombra, "'Essere dentro la storia'. Scelta politica e appartenenza di genere nell'esperienza di una partigiana," in *Italia contemporanea*, no. 198 (marzo 1995), 94.
20. The work that refounded the study of Resistance history as a period of difficult, complex, and morally and politically ambiguous choices—because it was more than one kind of war against more than one kind of opponent—is Claudio Pavone, *Una Guerra civile. Saggio storico sulla moralità nella Resistenza* (Torino: Bollati Boringhieri, 1991). It is now available in English: Claudio Pavone, *A Civil War: A History of the Italian Resistance*, trans. Peter Levy, ed. Stanislao Pugliese (New York and London: Verso, 2013). An excellent historiographical essay on the relationship between the mythology of the Resistance, the politics of women's history, and the history of women in the Resistance is Perry Willson, "Saints and Heroines: Re-writing the History of Italian Women in the Resistance," in *Opposing Fascism: Community, Authority and Resistance in Europe*, ed. Tim Kirk and Anthony McElligott (Cambridge: Cambridge University Press, 1999), 180–98.
21. Laura Ingrao testimonianza in M. Alloisio et al., eds., *Mille volte no. Dai no di ieri ai no di oggi* (Rome: Editori Riuniti, 1975), 97.
22. The full name was Gruppi di difesa della donna e per l'assistenza ai combattenti della libertà. On the creation and makeup of the GDD, see Merlin, *La mia vita*, 67; throughout A. Gobetti, *Diaro Partigiano*; and M. L. Odorisio et al., *Donna o cosa?: cronistoria dei movimenti femminili in Italia dal Risorgimento a oggi* (Torino: Edizioni Milva, 1986), 153–58; and Jomarie Alano, "Armed with a Yellow Mimosa: Women's Defense and Assistance Groups in Italy, 1943–45," *Journal of Contemporary History* 38, no. 4 (October 2003): 615–31.
23. P. Gabrielli, *Il club delle virtuose*, 59.
24. This is reflected in the most famous fictional narratives of the Resistance, such as Renata Viganò's *L'Agnese va a morire*, Alba De Cespedes' *Dalla parte di lei*, Elsa Morante's *La storia*; all have women protagonists drawn into the Resistance to save a husband or son, or son-figures; and Agnese in particular meets a martyr's end. This is a total contrast with the heroism, even if sometimes cynically muted, shown by the male protagonists of Calvino's *Il sentiero dei nidi di ragno* (*The Path of the Spiders' Nests*) or Beppe Fenoglio's *Il partigiano Johnny*. An interesting interdisplinary take on the memory politics of the Resistance is in Philip Cooke, *The Legacy of the Italian Resistance* (London: Palgrave Macmillan, 2011). For a useful survey of women's writing in the period, see Ann Hallamore Caesar, "The Novel, 1945–1965," in *A History of Women's Writing in Italy*, ed. Letizia Panizza and Sharon Wood (Cambridge: Cambridge University Press, 2000), as well as other included essays.
25. Slaughter, *Women in the Italian Resistance*, 33. Willson points out that if the broader concept of "civil resistance" is used to measure participation, "this gender disparty disappears, and it has been estimated that the women may have numbered as many as two million." Willson, "Saints and Heroines," 180.
26. The first groundbreaking collection of women's testimonies was Bianca Giudetti Serra's *Compagne*; it did reflect a certain diversity of experience but overall emphasized the role of "staffetta" and insisted on the absolute code of moral and sexual purity that reigned in the partisan brigades. Bravo and Bruzzone's *In guerra senza armi* introduced the concept of "maternage di massa" and, as

is evident from the title, emphasized the idea that the base of the Resistance was in unarmed action. Some younger scholars like Ricardo Pierraci and Silvia Salvateci are now striving for analyses that more fully account for gender roles in both men's and women's Resistance experiences and their oral history narrations of them. On the issue of a specificity to the political militancy and resistance of women, see Robin Morgan, *The Demon Lover: On the Sexuality of Terrorism* (New York: W. W. Norton, 1989); Pickering-Iazzi, *Politics of the Visible.*

27. Commissione nazionale per la parità e le pari opportunità tra uomo e donna, *Ragazze vi racconto la nostra storia* (Rome: Istituto Poligrafico e Zecca dello Stato, 2000), 16.
28. Gabrielli, *Il club delle virtuose,* 170.
29. Michetti et al., *Udi: laboratorio di politica delle donne,* 11.
30. In English, and with the most recent and comprehensive bibliography, see Pojmann, *Italian Women and International Cold War Politics.* Pojmann covers the complete Cold War history of the two main associations, UDI and CIF. While she finds that ideological divides remained a powerful constraint on the activities and cooperation between the two groups, her argument that they remained autonomous without ever being separatist feminist organizations is persuasive and insightful about the grassroots level of women's activism in this period. She argues that these constraints shaped the extent of support the associations could provide for parliamentary initiatives by the first forty-five, but also created a kind of productive competition for women's loyalty that had the consequence of more widely spreading the ideals of the women's movement.The outstanding studies in Italian are Gabrielli, Taricone, and Michetti et al. The associations are also dealt with in the context of European unification and the Cold War women's peace movement, respectively, in Beatrice Pisa, ed., *Cittadine d'Europa: Integrazione europea e associazioni femminili italiane* (Milan: FrancoAngeli, 2003); and Anna Scarantino, *Donne per la Pace: Maria Bajocco Remiddi e l'Associazione internazionale madri unite per la pace nell'Italia della guerra fredda* (Milan: FrancoAngeli, 2006).
31. Pojmann, *Italian Women,* 3.
32. Pojmann, *Italian Women,* 138–47; Simona Lunadei, "Donne e governo nella Capitale," 250. Some examples from CIF's archives include Corso per propagandiste "Lo Stato e la funzione dei partiti nell'ordinamento democratico (1957)" which included Lezione 9: "Puntualizzazione dei principali problemi femminili," and Corso per propagandiste "La vita pubblica ed il Cif (1952)" (CIF National Archives, Serie 11: Corsi, Scheda 176 Busta 877 "Corsi Vari"). In a move perhaps learned from the CIF course for activists, PCI leaders Camilla Ravera, Giglia Tedesco, and Teresa Musci established the "Clara Zetkin course on the struggle for women's emancipation" in 1953 and although they had done it without waiting for permission from the central committee, they successfully fought to keep control of this course rather than have it administered by the "party school" office (all of whose directors were men). Lunadei and Motti, "A scuola di politica," 160–61; Michetti et al., *Udi: laboratorio di politica,* 61–70, 83–85, 92–96.
33. 90% of DC women members were also members of AC. The electoral success of the DC in 1958 doubled the number of women members of AC. Gaiotti de Biase, "The Impact of Women's Political and Social Activity in Postwar Italy," 253n26. She quotes the annals of Azione Cattolica from 1946 and 1956. I was unable to see

these documents myself. See also M. Weber, "Italy," in J. Lovenduski and J. Hills, eds., *The Politics of the Second Electorate: Women and Public Participation: Britain, USA, Canada, Australia, France, Spain, West Germany, Italy, Sweden, Finland, Eastern Europe, USSR, Japan* (Boston: Routledge and Kegan Paul, 1981), 189, 193–97.

34. Pojmann, 2.
35. Italy is still not technically a secular state; Catholicism is the official state religion, and this is enshrined in the Constitution. Marisa Rodano recounts her struggle to acquire "a tranquil vision of the limit of politics" in the era when she, a member of the Christian Communist group, struggled to reconcile Catholics and the PCI in *Del mutare dei tempi. Volume primo. L'età dell'inconsapevolezza, il tempo della* speranza (Rome: Edizioni MEMORI, 2008), 80–107.
36. M. Boneschi, *Santa pazienza. La storia delle donne italiane dal dopoguerra a oggi* (Milano: Mondadori, 1998), 353–54.
37. Taricone, *Il Centro italiano femminile*, 168.
38. Tambor, "Red Saints"; "Patrizia Gabrielli, *La pace e la mimosa: L'Unione donne italiane e la costruzione politica della memoria (1944–1955)* (Rome: Donzelli Edirore, 2005); Wendy Pojmann, "Join Us in Rebuilding Italy: Women's Associations 1946–1963," *Journal of Women's History* 20, no. 4 (Winter 2008): 82–104; on the WIDF and the issue of Marxism vs. feminism in the postwar, see Francisca de Haan, "Continuing Cold War Paradigms in Western Historiography of Transnational Women's Organisations: the Case of the Women's International Democratic Federation (WIDF), *Women's History Review* 19, no. 4 (September 2010): 547–73, and Marilyn J. Boxer, "Rethinking the Socialist Construction and International Career of the Concept 'Bourgeois Feminism'," *The American Historical Review* 112, no. 1 (2007): 131–58.
39. Ascoli, "L'Udi tra emancipazione e liberazione," 140. In some provinces, UDI had severed ties with the PCI already in 1956; as Anna Laura Sanfilippo shows for the province of Latina, this was due as much to power struggles over the men's distrust of the respectability of women's activism as it was to differences of political opinion over current events. Anna Laura Sanfilippo, *Pane, amore e politica. Le comuniste in provincia di Latina dopo la Liberazione (1944–1956)* (Rome: Ediesse, 2013).
40. N. Spano and F. Camarlinghi, *La questione femminile nella politica del P.C.I. 1921-1963* (Rome: Edizioni Donne e Politica, 1972), 203.
41. On the transformation of UDI in the 1970s and 1980s as it dealt with neofeminism as a movement, see Chiara Ferrari, "Contested Foundations: Postmodern Feminism and the Case of the Union of Italian Women," *Signs* 33, no. 3 (Spring 2008): 569–94.
42. Archivio Nazionale CIF, Pesaro, M.P. Flich a M. Federici, 18 febbraio 1946, quoted in Gabrielli, *Il club delle virtuose*, 189.
43. Gaiotti de Biase, *Questione femminile e femminismo*, 40.
44. Archivio Capitolino, *Atti del Consiglio comunale*, 16 novembre 1954, cited in Lunadei, 252. Pojmann emphasizes the difficulties CIF had in cooperating with UDI on any campaign that didn't privilege the role of mother and/or of housewife in its claim for women's rights. For example, UDI was a vocal part of the peace and anti-nuclear movement, which was strongly colored by its association with the Soviet Union and its anti-imperialist anti-American rhetoric, so

that CIF could not participate in such demonstrations. Conversely, while CIF found a great deal of success in campaigning for pensions for housewives and arguing for the value of women's domestic labor, UDI hesitated to embrace any rhetoric that did not insist on women's work outside the home as the most emancipatory path. However, as these examples show, in concrete specific legislative and administrative decisions women from both sides of the aisle generally defended women's right to work and their protection against discrimination at work. Pojmann, *Italian Women and Cold War International Politics,* 46–47 and throughout.

45. L. Scaraffia, " 'Christianity Has Liberated Her and Placed Her Alongside Man in the Family': From 1850 to 1988 (mulieris Dignitatem)," in Scaraffia and Zarri, eds., *Women and Faith: Catholic Religious Life in Italy from Late Antiquity to the Present* (Cambridge: Harvard UP, 1999) (original in Italian 1994), 276–77. Tina Anselmi was Minister of Labor and Social Security from 1976 to 1979; Rosy Bindi was Minister of Health from 1996 to 1999.
46. Elisabetta Bini et al., "Genere, consumi, comportamenti"; Casalini, *Famiglie Communiste*; and Capuzzo, ed., *Genere, generazioni e consumi.* "In a large scale opinion survey among leading Europeans from all walks of life, carried out for the Common Council of American Unity (a prominent New York civil rights group), it was discovered that while all looked to America for economic, military, 'and even a degree of moral' leadership, 'serious doubts' were present about the qualifications of the US to exercise this responsibility. American policy was seen as unreliable, American society as too materialistic, dominated by Big Business and 'not capable of coping with the deeper issues involved' in contemporary struggles. The survey found even elementary concepts such as 'democracy' and 'freedom' to be misunderstood in Europe, and a significant degree of opposition present to capitalism itself, as well as to communism." N. 13 Common Council of American Unity, *European Beliefs Regarding the United States 1949* (New York: Common Council for American Unity, 1949), as cited in Ellwood, *Shock of America,* 6–8.
47. Accounts of the speech and of women's reactions to it come from G. Bonacchi and A. Groppi, eds., *Il Dilemma della cittadinanza: Diritti e doveri delle donne* (Rome-Bari: Laterza, 1993), 155; Rossi-Doria, *Diventare cittadine,* 12; and (including the last quote) Mafai, 161.
48. *"La donna è la casa, e la casa è il mondo . . . e la partecipazione della donna alla vita politica si giustifica in quanto ha il compito precipuo di render più efficace la sua stessa missione di sposa e di madre."* Mafai, 111.
49. Pojmann concurs that this was a "politically astute" choice, arguing that "although the women's associations approached their activism from intensely diverse frameworks, they all placed mothers and children at the center of their efforts for mainly political reasons and used them to attract new and more active members to their associations." Pojmann, *Italian Women,* 14, 76.
50. Taricone, *Il Centro italiano femminile,* 17–18.

Chapter 2

1. Ceccatelli Gurrieri and Paolucci, *Il Paradigma dell'emancipazione. Donne e politica nella Toscana degli anni '50* (Firenze: Edizioni Polistampa, 1995), 122.

2. According to Mafai, 149.
3. In the 1946 national election, 89% of female voters turned out (compared to 89.2% of men); by 1953 the female turnout was 94% (93.5% for men). See Willson, 134, who also estimates female PCI membership higher than this, about a third, 139; G. Galeotti, *Storia del voto alle donne in Italia* (Rome: Biblink, 2006), 232, 270; "two and quarter million" members of the PCI in Judt, 88.
4. Weber, 187. See also G. Galli and A. Prandi, *Patterns of Political Participation in Italy* (New Haven, CT: Yale University Press, 1970).
5. Judt, 206–09, 262–63, gives an interesting sketch of how the PCI was unique among European communist parties—in numbers, intellectual legitimacy and openness, and near-monopoly of power in certain regions. See also R. Gualtieri, C. Spagnolo, and E. Taviani, eds., *Togliatti nel suo tempo* (Roma: Carocci, 2007) for essays on how the Italian communist leader worked to shape a new and different kind of party within the Soviet constellation of power.
6. Perhaps the best account of how Italy's electoral system created a "partitocracy" in Italy, where parties (instead of the executive branch, the state bureacracy, or actual grassroots voters) ruled a clientilistic patronage network and dominated all levels of politics is Pietro Scoppola, *La Repubblica dei partiti*. Paola Gaiotti de Biase has noted that the study of women's enfranchisement in 1946 has untied several knots in the previous historiography of the creation of the Italian Republic: "it bolsters Amendola's argument that the signal development of the postwar is the introduction of a mass society, it confirms Scoppola's thesis that the choice of a democracy of consensus was the combined choice of Togliatti and De Gasperi that guaranteed their victory over the Jacobin style democracy of the Socialists and the Action Party, it disproves the idea that there was a mere return to the past by illuminating how much novelty and activity women brought into constructing a civil society, it reinforces the judgment that the parties played the central role in mediating that new civil consensus, and it privileges the linkage between Resistance and constitutionalism." Paola Gaiotti de Biase, "Donne e politica nella Repubblica, dal Dopoguerra agli anni '60," *Democrazia incompiuta*, 91. See also Judt, 256–60, and Ginsborg, *A History of Contemporary Italy*, throughout.
7. In 1948 CIF reported it could claim six million votes; though that number is probably too high. In addition to votes the DC freqently depended on CIF for volunteers for door-to-door campaigning: De Gasperi's leadership of the DC party was sustained by 16,000 CIF campaigners in 1953. See the account in Tambor, "Red Saints"; also C. Dau Novelli, "'Daremo sei milioni di voti'. Il movimento delle donne cattoliche nei primi anni della Repubblica," *Memoria* 21 (1987): 45–55.
8. See Sandro Bellassai's *La morale comunista: Pubblico e privato nella rappresentazione del PCI (1947–1956)* (Rome: Carocci, 2000) for a fuller and very interesting account of these themes. Marisa Rodano also relates her experience of continuing the habit of destroying documents and refusing to commit real names and identifying facts to paper, including the result that none of the love letters between her and her husband survive. She connects this destruction of documentation to the loss of "memory," both historical and personal, that has led many women of the Lost Wave to publish their autobiographies only in the last decade or so. M. Rodano, *Del mutare dei tempi. Volume primo*, 84–88.

9. Pizzardo, 33.
10. Birnbaum, 62–63. An impressive study of women's difficult experiences—riven by negative moral judgments on the part of the male party leaders—navigating political militance between UDI and PCI on the local level is Anna Laura Sanfilippo, *Pane, amore e politica. Le comuniste in provincia di Latina dopo la Liberazione (1944–1956)* (Rome: Ediesse, 2013). Also strong examples of a local approach to analyzing women's experience as politicians is Adriana Castagnoli, "Le donne nelle élites politiche locali. Torino (1945–1990)," and Simona Lunadei, "Donne e governo della Caitale (1946–2001)," *Democrazia incompiuta*, ed. Filippini and Scattigno, 230–44, 245–53.
11. G. Ascoli, *Perche' Lei: Bellisario, Carra', Cederna, Fendi, Fracci, Jotti, Levi-Montalcini, Marzotto, Mina, Orfei, Vitti* (Rome: Editori Laterza, 1985), 118; Boneschi, *Santa pazienza*, 119–20; Mafai, 147–48; Noce, *Rivoluzionaria professionale*, 435–39.
12. De Leo and Taricone, 213.
13. Mariuccia Salvati, "Behind the Cold War: Rethinking the Left, the State, and Civil Society in Italy (1940s–1970s)," *Journal of Modern Italian Studies* 8, no. 4 (2001): 561.
14. Foundational to this idea of the expansion of the realm of the political is Iris Marion Young, *Justice and the Politics of Difference* (Princeton, NJ: Princeton University Press, 1990), 9.
15. Young, 25; Linda Kerber, *Women of the Republic: Intellect and Ideology in Revolutionary America* (Chapel Hill: University of North Carolina Press, 1980), 284–85.
16. Zincone, *Da Sudditi a cittadini*, 210, 227.
17. "*Intendo armonizzare la vita di militante con il resto della vita.*" Lussana, 12.
18. Lussana, 21.
19. Gobetti, *Diario partigiano*, 386.
20. L. Lilli and C. Valentini, *Care compagne: il femminismo nel PCI e nelle organizzazioni di massa* (Rome: Editori Riuniti, 1979), 218.
21. Gaiotti de Biase, "Donne e politica nella Repubblica," 137.
22. "*Hai molti figli, sei grassa e hai i capelli lunghi. Una dirigente delle donne dev'essere così.*" Mafai, 147. A book-length portrait of Communist family identities and ideology in the postwar is Maria Casalini, *Famiglie comuniste. Ideologie e vita quotidiana nell'Italia degli anni Cinquanta* (Bologna: Il Mulino, 2010).
23. Capponi, 182–83.
24. Diaz quoted in Ceccatelli Gurrieri et al., 185; Mafai interview in Scroppo, *Donne, privato politico. Storie di 21 donne del Pci* (Milan: Mazzotta, 1979), 143.
25. The term "bracciante" denotes a landless agricultural day laborer; the closest common term in English is probably field hand. "Una mondina alla resistenza," August 8,1970, Archivio Gina Borellini, Folder B.I.1 Materiale biografico 1945–1987, folder 139 fasc. 7, Modena, Via Canaletto 88. The popular image of the *mondine* was probably most famously cemented by the portrayal in the 1949 film *Riso Amaro.*
26. Leonide Repaci, "La santa rossa," *Noi donne*, May 10, 1953.
27. "Le nostre candidate," *Noi donne*, May 10, 1953.
28. Lunadei and Motti, "A scuola di politica," 142. A useful general comparison and analysis of UDI and CIF sponsored publications is Pieracci, "Progetti, immagini, modelli." For a full treatment of the model of the "Red Saint" see Tambor,

"Red Saints: Gendering Italy's Cold War," *Cold War History* 10, no. 3 (August 2010): 429–56; Willson also addresses the postwar effort to canonize Resistance martyrs; Willson, "Saints and Heroines," 183–85.

29. Gabrielli, *Il club delle virtuose*, 95.
30. Maria Weber, "Italy," in *The Politics of the Second Electorate: Women and Public Participation: Britain, USA, Canada, Australia, France, Spain, West Germany, Italy, Sweden, Finland, Eastern Europe, USSR, Japan*, ed. Joni Lovenduski and Jill Hills (Boston: Routledge and Kegan Paul, 1981), 185; Camera dei Deputati, *Il voto alle donne. Le donne dall'elettorato alla partecipazione politica* (Rome: Camera dei Deputati, 1965), 67.
31. Anne O'Hare McCormick, "Bulldozer and the Woman With a Broom," *New York Times*, March 28, 1945; "Spring Finds Italy Facing a Vital Decision," *New York Times*, March 3, 1948.
32. Laville, *Cold War Women*, 56. On the concept of women's lack of responsibility for fascism making them more acceptable interlocutors for reconstruction programs, see Laville, 71; Heineman, "The Hour of the Woman," 359; Mariano, "Public and Private in Anne O'Hare McCormick's Journalism."
33. This is only 3.6% of the total, but women had been only 6.5% of the candidates for all offices, so over half of all women candidates were actually elected. Of the women elected to their city councils, many also held higher positions: Ada Gobetti was the vice-mayor of Torino, Ada Natali was mayor of Massa Fermana, and Carla Capponi was the tax assessor of Bologna. Spano and Camarlinghi, 129–30.
34. Lister, *Citizenship: Feminist Perspectives*; Rossi-Doria, *Diventare Cittadine*; Koven and Michel, eds., *Mothers of a New World*; Bock and Thane, eds., *Maternity and Gender Policies*; Walby, "Is Citizenship Gendered?"
35. For a broader analysis of the Italian Constitution and how it defined citizenship, a useful volume of essays on the history of the constitution from the conference honoring its 50th anniversary is Maurizio Fioravanti and Sandro Guerrieri, eds., *La Costituzione italiana. Atti del convegno di Roma del 20-21 febbraio 1998* (Rome: Fondazione Istituto Gramsci, Res cogitans, 1998).
36. Noce, *Rivoluzionaria professionale*, 387, 389.
37. Scroppo, 81.
38. Pojmann, 35.
39. Of the major parties, the PCI elected 9 women out of 68 women candidates and 104 total PCI candidates. The PSI ran 16 women candidates out of a total of 114 and 2 women won. The DC ran 208 total candidates and elected 10 women out of 29. The twenty-first woman was from the *uomo qualunque* ("everyman" or "common man") party, a particularly Southern phenomenon against the Allies, the anti-fascist government coalition, and anything that threatened the "common man." It came to be seen as an opportunistic, potentially Fascist, movement, as many ex-bosses who had been refused admittance to the Liberal Party turned to this one. She was the sister of the party founder. Most of the twenty-one represented the veteran age group rather than the Resistance recruits, and many had spent years in jail, in concentration camps, and in exile. Most of these women would also be part of the first forty-five, notably Angela Maria Guidi Cingolani (DC, b. 1896), Teresa Noce (PCI, b. 1900), Adele Bei (PCI, b. 1904), Lina Merlin (PSI, b. 1899),

Maria Federici (DC, b. 1899), Nadia Spano (PCI, b. 1916), Angela Gotelli (DC, b. 1905), Nilde Iotti (PCI, b. 1920), Maria Jervolino (DC, b. 1902), Maria Maddalena Rossi (PCI, b. 1906), and Vittoria Titomanlio (DC, b. 1899).

40. Vittoria, *Storia del PCI,* 62, 63; Gozzini and Martinelli, *Storia del Partito Comunista Italiano.*
41. Barnes, "The Secret Cold War," 412–13; Brogi, *A Question of Self-Esteem,* 68, 79–81; the quote is from Churchill's lament to Eisenhower over the weakness of the French legislature in the same period; see 17.
42. Ventresca, *From Fascism to Democracy;* Mistry, "The Case for Political Warfare"; Lundestad, "Empire by Invitation"; Lundestad, *The United States and Western Europe Since 1943;* De Luna, "Il 18 aprile"; Divine, "The Cold War and the Elections of 1948"; Woolf, *The Rebirth of Italy.*
43. Judt, 218.
44. Anne O'Hare McCormick, "Spring Finds Italy Facing a Vital Decision," *New York Times,* March 6, 1948.
45. These and other examples of 1948's election excesses are reported in Ventresca, *From Fascism to Democracy,* 197–212 and photographic insert. Spano, *Mabruk,* 86.
46. Still it is clear that women in Europe generally still heard a "lingering insurrectionary undertone" in the rhetoric of the Socialist and Communist parties, and trusted the message of reconciliation and stability more from the Christian Democrat parties. Judt, 80.
47. Judt, 37.
48. On the ideological relationship between the Resistance and the Italian Constitution, see Claudia Franceschini, Sandro Guerrieri, and Giancarlo Monina, eds., *Le Idee costituzionali della Resistenza* (Rome: Presidenza del Consigio dei Ministri, Istituto Poligrafico e Zecca dello Stato, 1997).
49. Renata Micheli, "Voto: 50 anni di democrazia," in *Il voto alle donne cinquant'anni dopo, Campidoglio, 6-7 marzo 1995. Atti del convegno,* by the Centro Italiano Femminile with the Ufficio Progetti Donna del Comune di Roma (Rome: Istituto Poligrafico e Zecca dello Stato, 1996), 113–14.
50. That the citizenship created by the Republican constitution represents a "thickening" of democracy and social and political participation is also the conclusion of Sabina Donati, *A Political History of National Citizenship and Identity in Italy, 1861–1950* (Palo Alto: Stanford University Press, 2013), see esp. chap. 8, "The Birth and First Developments of Italy's Democratic Republican Citizenship"; Donati does not, however, offer any detailed gender consideration of the constitution or the constituents.
51. A fifth woman, Ottavia Penna, dropped out but was later replaced by Angela Gotelli, so that some accounts number the women in the Committee of 75 as five.
52. Centro Italiano Femminile, *Memoria di Donne,* 98.
53. Archivio storico della Camera dei Deputati, Archivio dell'Assemblea Costituente, Gruppo di serie 006, Commissione per la Costituzione, Serie 003, Relazioni, studi e ricerche (27-08-1946/ 13-02-1947) busta 74 sottofascicolo 3, M. Federici, "Relazione su Garanzie economico-sociali per l'esistenza della famiglia," 1, 8.

54. A useful discussion of this context of "after fascism" occurred at the conference of that name and is reproduced in the eponymous volume: Maria Mesner and Matthew Paul Berg, eds., *After Fascism: European Case Studies in Politics, Society, and Identity since 1945* (Berlin: Lit Verlag, 2010). A further comparison is to the constitution making and new republic enacting of the Weimar Republic in Germany after World War I. See, for example, Canning, *Gender History in Practice*, 228–33 for a remarkably resonant analysis of the contradictions between trying to inscribe political equality for men and women while also insisting on sexual difference and inequality in articles concerning the family and marriage; as well as the call by feminists to overturn the pre-existing discriminatory civil code where it now appeared unconstitutional.
55. Robert G. Moeller, *Protecting Motherhood. Women and the Family in the Politics of Postwar West Germany* (Berkeley: University of California Press, 1993), 38, 45, 46.
56. Elizabeth D. Heineman, *What Difference Does a Husband Make? Women and Marital Status in Nazi and Postwar Germany* (Berkeley; University of California Press, 1999), 142–43; Moeller, 41.
57. Moeller, 79; Donald P. Kommers and Russell A. Miller, *The Constitutional Jurisprudence of the Federal Republic of Germany*, third edition (Durham, NC and London: Duke University Press, 2012), xi.
58. Moeller, 82.
59. Jane Jenson, "The Liberation and New Rights for French Women," in *Behind the Lines: Gender and the Two World Wars*, ed. Higonnet et al. (New Haven, CT: Yale University Press, 1987), 274; Claire Laubier, ed., *The Condition of Women in France: 1945 to the Present: A Documentary Anthology* (London and New York: Routledge, 1990), 1.
60. Jenson, 274.
61. Laubier, 192.
62. Jenson; Claire Duchen, *Women's Rights and Women's Lives in France 1944–1968* (London and New York: Routledge, 1994), 44, 175–89.
63. While we might expect more from the country that gave us Simone de Beauvoir's *Le Deuxième Sexe*, the initial reactions after its 1949 publication were more likely to be outrage and hostility than political solidarity. De Beauvoir herself explicitly stated in interviews and articles that she did not see her work as political, stating as late as 1972 that women's rights activists had changed nothing in the last twenty years. She found feminism too bourgeois and conformist, and women's rights activists found her too controversial. Her influence on feminism as a movement seems to have strengthened later, for the women of the generation of 1968. Duchen, 186–89; Simone de Beauvoir, "I Am a Feminist," 1972 interview with Alice Schwarzer, anthologized in *Lives and Voices: Sources in European Women's History*, ed. Lisa DiCaprio and Merry Wiesner (Boston: Houghton Mifflin, 2000), 573–77.
64. Marta Boneschi, *Santa pazienza. La storia delle donne italiane dal dopoguerra a oggi* (Milan: Mondadori, 1998), 260.
65. The "de-Fascistization" of the state and its regulations is a problem running underneath the entire history of the First Republic. For example, as late as 1971, 95% of Italy's senior civil servants had begun their careers under the Fascist regime. Judt, 257n12. See also, Pavone, *La continuità dello stato*.

66. Marina Addis Saba, Mimmo de Leo, and Fiorenza Taricone, eds., *Alle origini della Repubblica. Donne e Costituente* (Rome: Consiglio dei ministri, Commissione nazionale per le pari opportunità, Dipartimento per l'informazione e l'editoria, 1996), 32–33; Elisabetta Palici di Suni, "Tra parità e differenza. Una legislazione incerta e ambigua," *Democrazia incompiuta*, 273ff.
67. Maria Federici, "L'Evoluzione Socio-giuridica della donna alla costituente," in *Le donne nel Parlamento della repubblica dalla Consulta alla VII Legislatura*, ed. Anna Miserocchi, Beniamino Altezza, Daniela Chiassi, Mario Mammuccari (Viterbo: Fondazione Cesira Fiori, Union printing, 1989), 122.
68. Giovanna Ceccatelli Gurrieri and Gabriella Paolucci, *Il Paradigma dell'emancipazione. Donne e politica nella Toscana degli anni '50* (Florence: Edizioni Polistampa, 1995), 22.
69. As discussed below in the chapter on the Cocco Law.
70. Teresa Noce, Lina Merlin, Michele Guia, "Relazioni su Garanzie economico-sociali per l'assistenza della famiglia," Archivio dell'Assemblea Costituente, Gruppo di serie 006, Commissione per la Costituzione, Serie 003, Relazioni, studi e ricerche (27-08-1946/ 13-02-1947) busta 74 sottofascicolo 3. See also Federici, 126–27, 129.
71. The phrase is Margherita Repetto-Alaia's in Coppa and Repetto-Alaia, *The Formation of the Italian Republic*, 275.
72. Federici, 128.
73. Discussions of Article 29's impact on women's equality appear in Coppa and Repetto-Alaia, 274; Anna Rossi-Doria, "Il voto alle donne nel 1945," in *Il voto alle donne cinquant'anni dopo*, 64; Boneschi, *Santa pazienza*, 117–18, 260; and Federici, 128.
74. See, for example, Article 2 which refers to the "inalienable duties of social solidarity" and the "social reality within which the personality develops." Gaiotti de Biase, "Impact of Women's Activity," 236.
75. "Voglio chiudere dicendo che, allora, eravamo 21, abbiamo lavorato molto e credo non male, se la Costituzione non è mai stato un ostacolo per tutte le battaglie delle donne. Guardavamo al futuro." *Il voto delle donne cinquant'anni dopo*, 164.
76. Romero, "Gli Stati Uniti in Italia: il Piano Marshall e il Patto atlantico," "L'Europa come strumento di nation-building," "La scelta atlantica e americana," and "Americanization and National Identity"; Ellwood, "Italy, Europe, and the Cold War," and *Rebuilding Europe*; Varsori, "Reflections on the Origins of the Cold War," and "Italy's Policy Toward European Integration." Also Neri Gualdesi, "L'ancoraggio dell'Italia all'Europa"; Formigoni, "La rifondazione della politica estera nella democrazia repubblicana"; Giovagnoli, *Il partito italiano*.
77. Among those studying the Cold War, cultural historians have so far best taken advantage of the literature on women and gender. For the cultural history of Italy's Cold War, especially the transformation of women's lives and the (not uncontested) rise of consumerism, see Cassamagnaghi, *Immagini dall'America*; De Grazia, *Irresistible Empire* (esp. "The Model Mrs. Consumer"); Piccone Stella, *La prima generazione*; D'Attore, *Nemici per la pelle*; Gundle, *Between Hollywood and Moscow*, and "Cultura di massa e modernizzazione: *Vie Nuove* and *Famiglia Cristiana* dalla guerra fredda alla società di consumi," in *Nemici per la pelle*;

Duggan and Wagstaff, *Italy in the Cold War*, particularly the essays of Allum and Caldwell. Some fascinating questions are raised in the American context by AnnMarie Brennan's collection *Cold War Hothouses: Inventing American Culture from Cockpit to Playboy* (Princeton, NJ: Princeton Architectual Press, 2004), especially the essay by Beatriz Preciado, "Pornotopia."

Chapter 3

1. Noce, *Rivoluzionaria professionale*, 396–97, 415–16.
2. The DC was so large and successful at keeping a mass membership in these years because there were many factions within the party. De Gasperi was a master at keeping the more conservative factions suppressed and steering the party toward stability, compromise, and constitutional implementation. Making use of a coalition that brought the Liberals, Republicans, and Social Democrats into government at different moments, he remained prime minister throughout the first legislature's full five years, a feat never repeated by any prime minister since. For an in-depth history of the first legislature, see Ugo de Siervo, Sandro Guerrieri, and Antonio Varsori, eds., *La prima legislatura repubblicana. Continuità e discontinuità nell'azione delle istituzioni*, 2 vols. (Rome: Carocci, 2004).
3. Giulietta Ascoli, "L'Udi tra emancipazione e liberazione," 123.
4. Willson, *Women in Twentieth-Century Italy*, 105, 112–13; Anna Bravo, "Simboli del materno," in Bravo, ed., *Donne e uomini nelle guerre mondiali* (Roma-Bari: Laterza, 1991); A. Buttafuoco, "Motherhood as a Political Strategy: The Role of the Italian Women's Movement in the Creation of the Cassa Nazionale di Maternità," in G. Bock and P. Thane, *Maternity and Gender Policies*; Aurelia, *La mamma*.
5. Aurelia actually argues that this stereotype, or rather the precise term *mammismo* to describe the societal problem of the damaged, over-dependent son such mothers created, was not invented until 1952, and was thus more of a product of postwar history than an influence creating it. Aurelia, *La mamma*, 7.
6. Canning, *Gender History in Practice*, 140. She asserts that "labor legislation disrupts the dichotomy between the two streams [of male and female access to the welfare state]. For it implicitly erases the boundary between them [male workers' rights versus maternal/child welfare rights]." On the eschewing of political citizenship for social citizenship as characteristic of maternalism, see Bock and Thane, *Maternity and Gender Policies*; Koven and Michel, *Mothers of a New World*.
7. The term emanciaptionist motivated a debate which became very important to second-wave feminists: emancipation versus liberation. At this time the distinction was not yet one to war over, but the word emancipationist was already clearly connected to the politics of the PCI. For more on this, see Giulietta Ascoli, "L'Udi tra emancipazione e liberazione," as well as Bono and Kemp, *Italian Feminist Thought*; Hellman, *Journeys among Women*; Piccone Stella, *La prima generazione*, (esp. 113–44, "Crescere negli anni '50," the famous article originally from Memoria in 1982); and Weber, "Italy," 182–207.
8. Camera dei Deputati, *Il voto alle donne*, 76.

9. The book-length memoirs have been my main sources for many personal details and much of the chronology in this chapter. Where there seems to be a possibility for error or mistruth I have attempted to confirm with outside sources, which I cite in the course of the chapter. The memoirs are: Teresa Noce, *Rivoluzionaria professionale* (Milano: La Pietra, Bompiani, 1974); *Vivere in piedi* (Milano: Gabriele Mazzotta, 1978); and *Gioventù senza sole* (Rome: Editori Riuniti, 1978, first publication 1937).
10. Noce, *Rivoluzionaria professionale*, ix.
11. Noce, *Rivoluzionaria professionale*, ix.
12. "Writing the self into history" is from Sidonie Smith, *Subjectivity, Identity, and the Body: Women's Autobiographical Practices in the Twentieth Century* (Indianapolis: Indiana University Press, 1993), 35. For more on women's autobiographical practices, see Bella Brodzki and Celeste Schneck, eds. *Life/Lines: Theorizing Women's Autobiography* (Ithaca, NY: Cornell University Press, 1988); Smith, *Subjectivity*; and Smith, *A Poetics of Women's Autobiography: Marginality and the Fictions of Self-Representation* (Indianapolis: Indiana University Press, 1987).
13. Noce, *Rivoluzionaria professionale*, xii. UDI members preferred the term "friend" because it did not carry the communist connotations of "comrade" and signalled that the association was open to women of all political opinions.
14. Fanti, *Nilde Iotti*, 57.
15. As Anna Clark shows in a different context, stories of sexual conduct can be useful mobilizing tools for politicians and are representations of proper hierarchies of order in the nation. She argues that scandal doesn not always serve to exclude women and may at times help to democratize politics. Anna Clark, *Scandal: The Sexual Politics of the British Constitution* (Princeton, NJ: Princeton University Press, 2004).
16. Boneschi, *Di testa loro*, 167.
17. Scroppo, *Donna, privato e politico*, 46.
18. Fanti, 75.
19. Noce, *Rivoluzionaria*, 361–62.
20. Noce, *Rivoluzionaria*, 382.
21. Simonetta Soldani, "Prima della Repubblica. Le italiane e l'avventura della cittadinanza," in *Democrazia incompiuta*, ed. Filippini and Scattigno, 74; Galoppini, *Il lungo viaggio verso la parità*, chapter 2; Koven and Michel; Bock and Thane; Pedersen, *Family, Dependence, and the Origins of the Welfare State: Britain and France, 1914–1945* (Cambridge: Cambridge University Press, 1993).
22. Noce, *Rivoluzionaria professionale*, 385.
23. Noce, *Rivoluzionaria professionale*, 400.
24. Noce, *Rivoluzionaria professionale*, 387, 389.
25. Teresa Noce, "Relazione su Garanzie economico-sociali per l'assistenza della famiglia," Archivio storico della Camera dei Deputati, Archivio dell'Assemblea Costituente, Gruppo di serie 006, Commissione per la Costituzione, Serie 003, Relazioni, studi e ricerche (27-08-1946/13-02-1947) busta 74 sottofascicolo 3.
26. Noce, *Rivoluzionaria professionale*, 399.
27. De Grazia, *How Fascism Ruled Women*, 59–68, 166–80.
28. Judt, 95. Many industrial leaders felt this situation was actually part of a permanent and postitve national character: Ellwood has written about Angelo Costa,

the head of the industrialists' foundation and an adversary of the ERP, who criticized the concept of productivity saying "it ignored the basic difference between Italy and America: there capital was cheap, labour expensive; at home the situation was the opposite." Meanwhile, American Marshall Plan policy-makers complained that the Italian conservatives, too ready to use force to hold communism down when they should, had been using mass consumption and mass production. Ellwood, 364–65.

29. On both Britain and France and for the coining of the phrases "male-breadwinner logic" versus "parental logic," see Pedersen, *Family, Dependence, and the Origins of the Welfare State*; on France, see Anne Cova, "French Feminism and Maternity: Theories and Policies, 1890–1918, 119–37; and Karen Offen, "Body Politics: Women, Work and the Politics of Motherhood in France, 1920–1950," 138–59, both in Bock and Thane, *Maternity and Gender Policies*. On Britain, see also Jane Lewis, "Models of Equality for Women: The Case of State Support for Children in Twentith-Century Britain," 73–92, also in Bock and Thane. On Germany, see Moeller, *Protecting Motherhood*, 150, 155–65, 217.
30. Noce, *Rivoluzionaria professionale*, 383; Mafai, *L'apprendistato della politica*, 115–16.
31. Lovenduski and Hill, *The Politics of the Second Electorate*, 191–92; Piccone Stella, *La prima generazione*, 98 (table); Meyer, *Sex and Power*, 40.
32. Elisabetta Vessosi admits that there seems to have been a rise in the number of housewives without external paid employment in Italy between 1951 and 1961, but points out that the census figures from those two years present some difficulty of interpretation since many of the women who identified themselves as housewives were ex-agricultural workers or piece rate workers at home; for many of them, the status of houewife was a symbol of higher quality of life, liberty, and independence compared to their previous work status (rather than a symbol of oppression and dependence). Bini, Vessosi, et al., "Genere, consumi, comportamenti negli anni cinquanta," 8–9. See also de Grazia, *Irresistible Empire*, esp. chapters 8 "Supermarketing," and 9 "A Model Mrs. Consumer."
33. Canning makes a strong point about the analogues between these "bodies" in the discourse about welfare laws for working women. Canning, *Gender History in Practice*, 81ff.
34. On the "virtuous circle" of governments, employers and workers that grew the economy and created the welfare state, see Judt, 236–37, 330. Judt further quips, "There are many explanations for the recovery of European fertility after World War Two, but most of them reduce to a combination of optimism plus free milk" (331).
35. Noce, *Rivoluzionaria professionale*, 408.
36. Spano and Camarlinghi, *La questione femminile nella politica del P.C.I.*, 171–72; Gaiotti de Biase, "The Impact of Women's Political and Social Activity in Postwar Italy," 241.
37. Ginsborg, *A History of Contemporary Italy*, 112–15; Noce, *Rivoluzionaria professionale*, 418–20.
38. I am using the term sponsor and author interchangeably to denote both the person who wrote a bill and whose name might or might not appear as author on a draft of a bill, but I reserve the term proponent to translate the term *relatore*

or *relatrice* specifically. Thus, Fanfani, Noce, and Di Vittorio were authors and sponsors of bills that other deputies at various stages had the responsibility of presenting to the committee or the chamber of deputies or the senate with an introductory persuasive speech. Noce, *Rivoluzionaria professionale,* 408–09; Presidenza del Consiglio dei Ministri, *La donna italiana dalla Resistenza ad oggi,* 35.

39. In the Italian parliamentary system, permanent committees may meet as legislative bodies, so that bills of lesser importance or of a more technical nature may be passed without clogging the schedule of the full Chamber or Senate. Since it is assumed members of Parliament will vote with their party groups, the proportion of votes is assumed to be the same as it would be in full assembly. For other more generally important bills, the committees meet as deliberative bodies and approve a text that they recommend to the full assembly to be voted upon. Maria Federici had submitted a third version of the bill, titled *Assistenza ad alcune categorie di gestanti e puerpere e ai loro bambini,* which was sent to the Labor Committee for discussion. The members decided its topic was subsumed within the two larger projects they were debating.
40. The texts of the original progetto di legge from the opposition and CGIL, with Teresa Noce and Di Vittorio listed as sponsors, the disegno di legge Fanfani from the government, and the progetto submitted to the Parliament from the labor committtee are all from the archives of UDI, although they are collected in the archives of the Chamber of Deputies as well. UDI, Maternità, 1948/1, In Parlamento. The final text of the law as passed is published in the *Gazzetta Ufficiale del 3 novembre 1950,* n. 253, as Legge 26 agosto 1950 n. 860, "*Tutela fisica ed economica delle lavoratrici madri.*" I have also made use of the analysis provided of the various contents of the proposals in Spano and Camarlinghi, *La questione femminile,* 172.
41. UDI, Maternità 1948/1, Udi centro, "Campagna per la tutela della maternità, relazione regione per regione," 25 settembre 1948. For a larger discussion of these festivals and other practices of Italy's political subcultures, see Gundle, *From Hollywood to Moscow.*
42. "Tutela delle lavoratrici madri," *Bollettino di attività del Cif,* no. 18, June 1948, special insert; quoted in Pojmann, *Italian Women,* 59–60nn54, 55.
43. Noce, *Rivoluzionaria professionale,* 409.
44. Camera dei Deputati, *Atti Parlamentari. Discussioni.* Legislatura I. Volume XIV (20 giugno-20 luglio 1950) (Rome: Tipografia della Camera dei Deputati, 1950), 20078–79.
45. Camera dei Deputati, *Atti Parlamentari,* 20092–93, 20086.
46. Camera dei Deputati, *Atti Parlamentari,* 20084.
47. Michetti et al., *Udi: laboratorio di politica delle donne,* 55n5.
48. Camera dei Deputati, *Atti Parlamentari,* 20889; Fiorenza Taricone and Mimma de Leo, eds., *Le donne in Italia. Diritti civili e politici* (Napoli: Liguori Editore, 1992); newspaper quote in Giulietta Ascoli, "L'Udi tra emancipazione e liberazione (1943–1964)," 126–27.
49. Ceccatelli Gurrieri and Paolucci, *Il Paradigma dell'emancipazione,* 26.
50. Taricone, *Il Centro italiano femminile,* 157. The law that addressed this problem was *Legge 9 gennaio 1963,* n. 7 "*Divieto di licenziamento delle lavoratrici per causa di matrimonio.*"

51. Gaiotti de Biase, "The Impact of Women's Political and Social Activity in Postwar Italy," 39 note 29.
52. Willson, 121.
53. Taricone, 99–117.
54. Noce, *Rivoluzionaria professionale*, 435–45; Boneschi, *Di testa loro*, 171.
55. Spano and Camarlinghi, 188–89; Selvaggio, *Desiderio e diritto di cittadinanza*, 47. On the continuing defiance of these laws, see Boneschi, *Santa pazienza*, 333.
56. Michetti et al., *Udi: laboratorio di politica delle donne*, 223; Gaoitti de Biase, *Questione femminile e femminismo*, 58.
57. CIF archives, "Relazione della delegata nazionale," September 20, 1969, XII Convegno Nazionale Elettivo del Movimento Femminile della DC su "Democrazia e partecipazione," Maiori (SA), Serie 10: Convegni, Sottoserie B: Convegni Vari, Scheda 48 Busta 1105 Fascicolo I.
58. Comparative figures for maternity legislation compiled from P. Romito, M. J. Saurel-Cubizolles, and V. Escriba-Aguir, "Maternity Rights, Work, and Health in France and Italy," *Journal of the American Medical Women's Association* 57, no. 1 (Winter 2002): 47–48, 54, 56; and Dorothea Alewell and Kerstin Pull, "An International Comparison and Assessment of Maternity Leave Legislation," *Comparative Labor Law & Policy Journal* 22, nos. 2/3 (2001): 297–326.
59. Noce, *Rivoluzionaria professionale*, 47–48.

Chapter 4

1. For a history of government and politics in this period, see Pier Luigi Ballini, Sandro Guerrieri, Antonio Varsori, eds., *Le istituzioni repubblicane dal centrismo al centro-sinistra (1953–1968)* (Rome: Carocci, 2006).
2. Bruno P. F. Wanrooij, "Josephine Butler and Regulated Prostitution in Italy," *Women's History Review* 17, no. 2 (April 2008): 153–71.
3. L. Merlin and C. Barberis, *Lettere dalle case chiuse* (Milano: Edizioni Milva, 1955), 23. A "virtual museum" has been opened online with artifacts from Fascist-era brothels and their inhabitants in Friuli; Davide Scarpa, Museo Delle Case Di Tolleranza Nel Ventennio Fascista, https://www.facebook.com/MUSEO.CASE.DI.TOLLERANZA.
4. As does Tamar Pitch in an otherwise excellent analysis of the changing legal language in Merlin's proposals. T. Pitch, "La sessualità, le norme, lo stato. Il dibattito sulla legge Merlin," *Memoria: rivista di storia delle donne* 17, no. 2 (1986): 35.
5. The phrase "*civilità erotica*" is from Dino Buzzati, "Come fece Erostrato," in G. Fusco, *Quando L'Italia <<tollerava>>* (Roma: Nanni Canesi, 1965), 105. Surveys are in P. Luzzatto Fegiz, *Il volto sconosciuto dell'Italia: dieci anni di sondaggi DOXA* (Milano: Dott. A, Giuffrè, 1956), 621–56; P. Luzzatto Fegiz, *Il volto sconosciuto dell'Italia: Seconda serie 1956–1965* (Milano: Dott. A Giuffrè, 1966), 945–57.
6. Dates of abolition from N. Roberts, *Whores in History: Prostitution in Western Society* (London: HarperCollins, 1992), 271, and Merlin, *La mia vita*, 144. Details on Nazi Germany in C. Koonz, *Mothers in the Fatherland* (New York: St. Martin's Press, 1987), 150, 241, 349–50; on postwar Germany in A. Elman, ed., *Sexual Politics and the European Union* (Providence: Berghahn Books, 1996), 88–89. Marthe Richard's campaign is contextualized in the flux created by the Allied occupation and the struggle for control over prostitution when the

departure of Vichy and Nazi officials created a power vacuum just as American soldiers provoked a surge in demand in Mary Louise Roberts, *What Soldiers Do,* especially chapter 5, "The Silver Foxhole," 133–58. The term "abolition" when coined in the mid-nineteenth century was meant to explicitly link the fight against trafficking in women, or "white slavery," to the anti-slavery movement. B. P. F. Wanrooij, *Storia del pudore. La questione sessuale in Italia 1860–1940* (Venezia: Marsilio Editore, 1990), 34–35.

7. "Èanche noto che il nostro Paese era purtroppo rimasto alla coda di tutti i Paesi civili"; "... restata solo in Europa a detenere questo triste primato"; "Approvata le legge Merlin," *La Stampa,* January 29, 1958: 1.
8. And vice versa: see the discussion of "Latin feminism" in de Grazia, *How Fascism Ruled Women,* 236–38. On why Italian women activists stopped agitating for suffrage and concentrated on social rights and justice, see G. Chianese, *Storia sociale della donna in Italia (1800–1980)* (Napoli: Guida Editori, 1980), 52–54.
9. Important studies of prostitution from a women's history persepective are Mary Gibson, *Prostitution and the State in Italy, 1860–1915* (New Brunswick: Rutgers University Press, 1986); Judith R. Walkowitz, *Prostitution and Victorian Society: Women, Class, and the State* (Cambridge: Cambridge University Press, 1980); Luise White, *The Comforts of Home: Prostitution in Colonial Nairobi* (Chicago: University of Chicago Press, 1990). From a history of sexuality perspective there is Alain Corbin, *Women for Hire: Prostitution and Sexuality in France after 1850* (Cambridge: Harvard University Press, 1990). A groundbreaking work was Judith R. Walkowitz, *City of Dreadful Delight: Narratives of Sexual Danger in Late Victorian London* (Chicago: Universty of Chicago Press, 1992).
10. Boneschi, *Di testa loro,* 109–10.
11. Merlin, *La mia vita,* 21.
12. Boneschi, *Di testa loro,* 113, 122.
13. M. Gibson, *Prostitution and the State in Italy, 1860–1915* (New Brunswick, NJ: Rutgers University Press, 1986), xvii–xviii.
14. Alloisio, *Mille volte no,* 202–03.
15. Boneschi, *Di testa loro,* pp. 136–37.
16. Document number 10.1 "Progetto di volantino presentato al Comitato direttivo del 9.4.1946" in Michetti et al., 45–46.
17. Boneschi, *Di testa loro,* 122–24.
18. Michela Ponzani, *Guerra alle donne. Partigiane, vittime di stupro, 'amanti del nemico', 1940–45* (Turin: Einaudi, 2012). Mary Louise Roberts reports that 86% of American soldiers sentenced to death for rape and sexual murders were black; the most famous execution of a black soldier in Italy was Louis Till for the crime of rape and murder on July 2, 1945; he was the father of Emmet Till, who was himself murdered in the United States in 1955 for talking with a white woman. Roberts, *What Soldiers Do,* 321n2; see also Insa Meinin, *Wehrmacht et prostitution sous l'Occupation* (Paris: Editions Payot, 2006); Sarah Kovner, "Prostitution in Postwar Japan: Sex Workers, Servicemen, and Social Activists, 1945–1956" (Ph.D. diss., Columbia University, 2004); Sarah Kovner, "Base Cultures: Sex Workers and Servicemen in Postwar Japan," Journal of Asian Studies 68, no. 3 (August 2009): 777–804.

19. Rossi-Doria, *Diventare cittadine*, 22. Isabel Hull, *Sexuality, State, and Civil Society in Germany 1700–1815* (Ithaca, NY: Cornell University Press, 1996) argues that the modern state and civil society were actually created by a process whereby middle-class male activists became the "practitioners of civil society" and therefore citizens through their claim to regulate and codify proper sexual behavior. In this process, she argues, masculine sexual drive was elevated as the mark of the independent citizen; the category of citizen became necessarily sexed male. In several studies Sandro Bellassai has explored the making of Italian masculinity as a public and political identity: specifically dealing with the Merlin law, *La legge del desiderio: Il progetto Merlin e l'Italia degli anni Cinquanta* (Rome: Carocci, 2006); in broader historical context, *La mascolinità contemporanea* (Rome: Carocci, 2004); and *L'invenzione della virilità: Politica e immaginario maschile nell'Italia contemporanea* (Rome: Carocci, 2011).
20. P. Baldwin, *Contagion and the State in Europe* (Cambridge: Cambridge University Press, 1999), 381–82. On abolitionist movements in England and internationally inspired by Butler, see J. Walkowitz, *Prostitution and Victorian Society: Women, Class, and the State* (Cambridge: Cambridge University Press, 1980), especially Introduction.
21. Odorisio, *Donna o cosa?*, 45; Chianese, 39–41.
22. "Della abolizione della regolamentazione della prostituzione e della lotta contro lo sfruttamento della prostituzione altrui." Progetto di legge d'iniziativa della sen. Lina Merlin in L. Merlin and C. Barberis, *Lettere dalle case chiuse*, 173–82. All quotations of this document refer to this citation.
23. Senato, I legislatura, Documentazione-Disegni di legge, n. 63-A, p. 12.
24. Merlin, *La mia vita*, 103–04.
25. Piccone Stella, *La prima generazione*, 85.
26. Roberts, *Whores in History*, 246.
27. P. Gabrielli, "Introduzione," in Gabrielli, ed., *Vivere da protagoniste*, 52; Judith R. Walkowitz, "Dangerous Sexualities," in Fraisse and Perrot, eds., *A History of Women in the West*, vol. 4 (Cambridge: Belknap, 1993), 376–77; Alain Corbin, *Women for Hire: Prostitution and Sexuality in France after 1850* (Cambridge: Harvard University Press, 1990), 134; Gibson, 35.
28. Gibson, 144–45, 129–30; Roberts, 201–05, 208–09.
29. Gibson, 102–03.
30. G. Mosse, *Nationalism and Sexuality: Respectability and Abnormal Sexuality in Modern Europe* (New York: Howard Fertig, 1985), 157.
31. P. Beretta Anguissola, *Prostituzione e legge Merlin* (Firenze: Lucio Pugliese, 1987), 55–56.
32. de Grazia, 136–37.
33. Article 554, Title X in *The Italian Penal Code*, ed. and trans. E. Wise (Littleton: Fred B. Rothman, 1978), 185. On Fascism's insistence on the divide between good and "deviant" women, see Wanrooij, 130–31.
34. Corbin, *Women for Hire*, 348–50.
35. See n. 3. Luzzatto Fegiz, *Il volto sconosciuto dell'Italia: dieci anni di sondaggi DOXA*, v-x, 625–26.
36. Luzzatto Fegiz, *Il volto sconosciuto dell'Italia: dieci anni di sondaggi DOXA*, 627.
37. "L'abolizione della prostituzione organizzata," *L'Unità*, January 19, 1958: 1. See also Camera dei Deputati, *Atti parlamentari. II Legislatura. Discussioni*, 24

gennaio 1958, 39327–9, 28 gennaio 1958, 39361–4. The medical profession was repeating arguments made on their behalf for nearly a century at this point: Wanrooij reports physiologist Paolo Mantegazza's 1877 assertion that "gonorrhea is a hundred times better than the dishonor of masturbation." Wanrooij, "Josephine Butler," 158n21.

38. Doctor Giovanni Lionetti, quoted in "Approvata la legge Merlin," *La Stampa*, January 29, 1958: 1.
39. Buzzati in Fusco, 103.
40. Buzzati in Fusco, 105.
41. Fusco, 83.
42. Fusco, 18.
43. E. Gianeri (GEC), "La donna conquista il potere," *L'Europeo*, November 2, 1958, 16 ff.; and E. Gianeri, "Il sesso forte depone le armi," *L'Europeo*, November 9, 1958, 16ff, cited in Sandro Bellassai, "Mascolinità, mutamoento, merce. Crisi dell'identità maschile nell'Italia del boom," *Genere, generazione e consumi. L'Italia degli anni Sessanta*, ed. Paolo Capuzzo (Rome: Carocci, 2003), 119. Guido Crainz also marks 1958 as a tipping-point year when the boom made itself felt in popular awareness; see Crainz, *Storia del miracolo italiano*.
44. Bellassai, "Mascolinità," 131.
45. Taricone, *Il Centro Italiano Femminile*, 194.
46. Luzzatto Fegiz, *Il volto sconosciuto dell'Italia: dieci anni di sondaggi DOXA*, 621–22.
47. Merlin, *La mia vita*, 97.
48. Luzzatto Fegiz, *Il volto sconosciuto dell'Italia: dieci anni di sondaggi DOXA*, 622.
49. Letter of December 12, 1949, in A. Boggiano Pico, *Vent'anni di vita politica (1945–1965)* (Roma: An. Veritas Editrice, 1980), 72–73.
50. M. Bekardinelli, "Boggiano Pico, Antonio," in *Dizionario Biografico degli Italiani*, vol. 11 (Roma: Istituto della Enciclopedia Italiana, 1969), 176–78.
51. Letter of October 24, 1948, in A. Boggiano Pico, *Vent'anni di vita politica (1945–1965)*, 60.
52. Letter of December 12, 1949, in A. Boggiano Pico, *Vent'anni di vita politica (1945–1965)*, 72–73.
53. Pitch, 29.
54. Senato, I legislatura, Discussioni: 12-10-1949, 10809.
55. Letter of December 12, 1949, in A. Boggiano Pico, *Vent'anni di vita politica (1945–1965)*, 73.
56. Document number 15, "L'assistenza è un diritto," in Michetti et al., 89.
57. These words are usually translated as "favor" and "ease" or "facilitate." They are used here in the Italian to reflect that their meanings were later disputed and specified by the courts in order to set a precedent for the arrest of individuals who, for example, give a prostitute a ride in a car to a place where she is planning to practice prostitution.
58. " Disegno di legge proposto dalla I Commissione Permanente del Senato della Repubblica," in Merlin, *Lettere dalle case chiuse*, 195–99. All quotations of this document refer to this citation.
59. Ginsborg, *A History of Contemporary Italy*, 118–20; also G. Fusco, *Quando l'Italia << tollerava>>* (Roma: Nanni Canesi, 1965), 33.

60. Ginsborg, *A History of Contemporary Italy*, 46–48,110–20, 254–83, 350–51; Hellman, 12–14, 38–40.
61. Luzzatto Fegiz, *Il volto sconosciuto dell'Italia: dieci anni di sondaggi DOXA*, 628.
62. Cartoon in Fusco, 34; quotes from Pitch, 40; Paul Hoffmann, "Legal Brothels Closed by Italy: Ban on Licensed Prostitution Ends Long Campaign by 70-year-old Widow," *New York Times*, September 20, 1958; "Italy Ratifies Bill to Close Brothels," *New York Times*, January 29, 1958, 9; Merlin, *Lettere dalle case chiuse.*
63. Merlin, *Lettere dalle case chiuse*, 9.
64. Merlin, *Lettere dalle case chiuse*, 65–66.
65. Merlin, *Lettere dalle case chiuse*, 36–37.
66. Merlin, *Lettere dalle case chiuse*, 45, 25, 135.
67. Michetti et al., 174–77, 183.
68. Luzzi, *Salute e Sanità nell'Italia repubblicana*, 175.
69. *Raccolta ufficiale delle leggi e dei decreti della Repubblica Italiana, 1956*, vol. 11, 4207–4213; also Pheterson, *A Vindication of the Rights of Whores*, 55; Pitch, "La sessualità, le norme, lo Stato. Il dibattito sulla legge Merlin," 35. This law is used in conjunction with Titles V (Crimes Against Public Order) and IX (Crimes Against Public Morality and Decency) of the Penal Code. See Wise, 145–46, 179–80.
70. John Torpey, *The Invention of the Passport: Surveillance, Citizenship and the State* (Cambridge and New York: Cambridge University Press, 2000), 35.
71. "Disegno di legge approvato dalla I Commissione del Senato della Repubblica nella seduta in sede deliberante del 21 gennaio 1955," in Merlin, *Lettere dalle case chiuse*, 199–203.
72. In 1959, a law was passed by other members of the first forty-five which instituted a special female corps, but their numbers were so small and their institutional support so minimal (they received no offices nor clear orders, and their ranks and management were separate from the general police force) that they had no ability to protect prostitutes. Gibson, 231; a member of the force wrote about these difficulties in the police union members' newsletter: Dora Petrolino, "Donna in Polizia: la storia," *Pubblica Sicurezza* (ottobre novembre dicembre 2011): 48–61, http://www.uilpolizia.it/Rivista/numero%202/pag48.html.
73. Silvia Spinoso, *Il lobby delle donne: legge Merlin e C.I.D.D. Un modo diverso di fare la politica* (Rome: Rubbettino, 2005), 57.
74. Spinoso, 149–50.
75. P. Luzzatto Fegiz, *Il volto sconosciuto dell'Italia: Seconda serie*, 945–57.
76. P. Bianchi, *Le signorine di Avignone. Studio di costume sull'Italia di ieri* (Milano: Ferro edizioni, 1967), 24.
77. Buzzati in Fusco, 103.
78. Camera dei Deputati, *Atti parlamentari. II legislatura. Discussioni*, 24 gennaio 1958, 39321–6.
79. P. Hoffman, "Legal Brothels Closed by Italy," *New York Times*, September 20, 1958: 20; Fusco, 103; Merlin, *La mia vita*, 97; Bianchi, 252–53.
80. R. Tatafiore, *Sesso al lavoro* (Milano: Il Saggiatore, 1994), 131–32.
81. Undated draft letter from CIF, UDI letter 27 ottobre 1965 oggetto proposta di legge n. 144A (modificazione della Legge Merlin), CIF National Archives, Serie

16- Ufficio Legislativo Scheda 30 Busta 1045- riforma legge Merlin Fascicolo I Legge Merlin 1957–1965.

82. Spinoso, 73–74; "Berlusconi suggests legal brothels," BBC News, January 6, 2002, http://news.bbc.co.uk/2/hi/europe/1744859.stm; Giovanni Azzolini (mayor of Mogliano, in the Veneto region), "Referendum abrogazione parziale legge merlin—invio modulo raccolta firme," email dated July 24, 2013, author's possession.
83. Merlin, "Non si ritorna indietro," *Concretezza*, 16 febbraio 1964, 11–12.
84. This bill, presented in 1953, went through another exhausting and controversial debate, getting subsumed in a last-minute government bill, and finally becoming the legge gennaio 1963 n. 7, "Divieto di licenziamento delle lavoratrici per causa di matrimonio."
85. Statistics collected from Camera dei Deputati, *Atti parlamentari. Indice generale dell'attività* parlamentare, legislatures I (Senato, vol. 210, 704–05) and III (Camera dei Deputati, *Atti del parlamento italiano. Attivita' parlamentare dei deputati. Indice alfabetico, 1011–14)*; La navicella. I Deputati e Senatori del Secondo Parlamento Repubblicano, 1955, 482; Miserocchi et al., *Le donne del Parlamento*, 138; Presidenza del Consiglio di Ministri, *La donna italiana dalla Resistenza ad oggi*, 35; *Il voto alle donne cinquant'anni dopo*, 379. Speeches in Angelina Merlin, *Discorsi parlamentari* (Rome: Senato della Repubblica, Segretariato Generale Servizio Studi, 1998).
86. Boneschi, *Di testa loro*, 136–37.
87. Pheterson, 54–55, and Gibson, 227–30, both emphasize the essential continuity between pre- and post-Fascist debates and policies regarding regulation. Authors who emphasize that Merlin attempted wholesale change but was thwarted by the DC are Pitch, 29; and E. Nerenberg, "*Love for Sale* or *That's Amore*: Representing Prostitution During and After Italian Fascism," *Annali d'Italianistica* 16 (1998): 213–35.

Chapter 5

1. Taricone, *Il Centro italiano femminile*, 134–35n28. The National Council of Italian Women, which had originally been founded as a suffragist group between 1899 and 1903 as part of the International Council of Women, was led for some time by Teresa Labriola, who would become the first woman lawyer in Italy in 1919, during which time the council cooperated with the Fascist government. It had been reconstituted in 1944 to agitate for women's enfranchisement, after which it continued as an advocacy group, without, however, becoming a mass association like UDI or CIF.
2. All direct quotes in this section from personal correspondence May–August 2003 and July 2006.
3. de Grazia, *How Fascism Ruled Women*, 155.
4. These comments appear in the published proceedings of the CIF conference of 1995, *Il voto alle donne cinquant'anni dopo. Campidoglio, 6-7 marzo 1995. Atti del convegno* (Roma: Istituto Poligrafico e Zecca dello Stato, 1996), 141–43.
5. Judt, 321; see Chapter 2 above.

6. See Ginsborg, *History of Contemporary Italy*, 254–60, and Miserocchi et al., 49.
7. Maria Cocco, in *La condizione della donna in Europa Atti del Convegno internazionale promosso dall'Associazione degli ex parlamentari e elementi di legislazione comparata (22-23 febbraio 1990)* (Roma: Camera dei Deputati, 1991), 185–86.
8. Vittorio Olgiati, "Professional Body and Gender Difference in Court: The Case of the First (Failed) Woman Lawyer in Modern Italy," in *Women in the World's Legal Professions*, ed. Ulrike Schultz and Gisela Shaw (Portland: Hart Publishing, 2003), 429.
9. Emilia Sarogni, *La donna italiana. Il lungo cammino verso i diritti, 1861–1994* (Parma: Pratiche Editrice, 1995), 155; *Atti Assemblea Costituente* (Resoconto stenografico della seduta del 22 maggio 1947), 4171.
10. The salient parts of these discussions are reproduced in *Alle origini della Repubblica. Donne e Costituente.* Consiglio dei ministri. Commissione nazionale per le pari opportunità, ed. M. Addis Saba, M. de Leo (Roma: Dipartimento per l'informazione e l'editoria, 1996), 137–44. Also see discussion below of the November sessions.
11. Miriam Mafai in M. Antonietta Selvaggio, ed., *Desiderio e diritto di cittadinanza*, 46–47; Romano Canosa, *Il Giudice e la donna. Cento anni di sentenze sulla condizione femminile in Italia* (Milano: Mazzotta, 1978), 40–41.
12. *Alle origini della Repubblica. Donne e Costituente*, 137–44.
13. Rossi-Doria, *Diventare cittadine*, 16–17.
14. Lucia Motti, *Le donne* (Rome: Editori Riuniti, 2000).
15. Sarogni, *La donna italiana*, 156.
16. Paul Ginsborg, *Italy and Its Discontents*, 190. Carlo Guarnieri and Patrizia Pederzoli, *The Power of Judges: A Comparative Study of Courts and Democracy* (Oxford and New York: Oxford University Press, 2002), 54–58.
17. "...di immediata attuazione, di netto carattere precettivo..." Corte di Cassassazione, 26 giugno 1958, n. 2283. Canosa, *Il giudice e la donna*, 44, 45, 59–60.
18. Paul Ginsborg discusses these reforms and makes the argument that reform in general was so difficult in Italy because of the way political parties and individual power brokers exploited contradictory regulations and lack of enforcement to strengthen their own clientilistic networks of power. In Ginsbórg, *A History of Contemporary Italy*, 326–345; see also F. D'Onofrio, "Il diffcle avvio dell'adeguamento dell'ammistrazione pubblica alla Costituzione italiana," in G. Rossini, ed., *De Gasperi e l'età del centrismo* (Rome: Cinquelune, 1984). Mariuccia Salvati revisits the question and concludes that the mass political parties as they developed in Italy led to the perseverance of corporatist economic structures and the potential for corruption, as well as a distrust and distance from the national state on the part of individual that continues to persist: Salvati, "Behind the Cold War," esp. 564–65.
19. Camera dei deputati, *Il voto alle donne*, 76.
20. Camera dei Deputati, *Atti Parlamentari, III legislatura. Documenti. Disegni di legge e relazioni.* N. 1882, novembre 17, 1955. Also see Presidenza del Consiglio dei Ministri, *La donna italiana dalla Resistenza ad oggi*, 36–37.
21. Camera dei Deputati, *Atti Parlamentari, III legislatura. Documenti. Disegni di legge e relazioni.* N. 1882, novembre 17, 1955; also Canosa, *Il Giudice e la donna*, 45. Canosa mentions that this law was challenged in Constitutional Court and the

court, on September 29, 1958 (number 56), upheld the legitimacy of the law. Palici di Suni points out that the court thus ruled in 1958 that Article 51 of the Constitution could be used to limit women's access to public service, while in 1995 and again in 2003 it ruled that that same article could not be used to promote women's access (when candidate quotas were ruled unconstitutional). Palici di Suni, 276–78; also Lorenza Carlassare, "Costituzione democratica e rappresentanza," *Democrazia incompiuta*, 280–90.

22. Linda Kerber, *No Constitutional Right to Be Ladies: Women and the Obligations of Citizenship* (New York: Hill and Wang, 1998), 135–36.
23. Michetti et al., *Udi: laboratorio di politica delle donne*, 55–56; Rossi-Doria, *Diventare cittadine*, 17–18; Canosa, *Il giudice e la donna*, 43.
24. Beatrice Pisa, ed., *Cittadine d'Europa: Integrazione europea e associazioni femminili italiane* (Milan: FrancoAngeli, 2003), 13.
25. Taricone, *Il Centro italiano femminile*, 170–74.
26. These documents, including a copy of a "feminine" registration card, are preserved in the CIF national archive. Serie 18- Ufficio Studi Sottoserie B-Varie Scheda 28 Busta 828- Problemi vari allo studio; studi sulla condizione della donna 1955-1983. Fascicolo I Partecipazione delle donne alla amministrazione della giustizia nelle corti di assise e nei tribunali per i minorenni 1955–1957. For the United States, a good overview of exemplary battles women fought to gain admission as jurors is in Kerber, *No Constitutional Right to Be Ladies*, chapter 4, 124–220.
27. Rossi-Doria, *Diventare cittadine*, 18.
28. Taricone, *Il Centro italiano femminile*, 162–63.
29. Rossi-Doria, *Diventare cittadine*, 18–19.
30. *Il voto alle donne cinquant'anni dopo*, 142.
31. Reported by Giuliana Dal Pozzo, "La Magistratura ha detto: l'articolo 37 è legge," *Noi donne*, October 9, 1955, 5–6; cited in Pojmann, *Italian Women*, 123n64.
32. Invitation, April 26, 1957, in "Problematiche di parità uomo donna 1957," Serie 18- Ufficio Studi Sottoserie B-Varie Scheda 28 Busta 828- Problemi vari allo studio; studi sulla condizione della donna 1955-1983 Fascicolo II Problematiche di parità uomo donna 1957.
33. Maria Sofia Lanza, "La donna e la Costituzione: le giuriste italiane difendono la loro 'giusta causa,'" in CIF National Archives, *Cronache*, June 1955.
34. Taricone, *Il Centro italiano femminile*, 155n58.
35. Canosa, *Il Giudice e la donna*, 42.
36. Taricone, *Il Centro italiano femminile*, 205.
37. Legge 17 luglio 1919, n. 1176, *Raccolta ufficiale delle leggi e dei decreti del regno d'Italia*, Anno 1919, vol. III, 2546–8; Corte costituzionale, Sentenza n. 33, 13 maggio 1960. See also Rossi-Doria, *Diventare cittadine*, 15–16; and Boneschi, *Santa Pazienza*, 258.
38. *Il voto alle donne cinquant'anni dopo*, 142.
39. "*Art. 1. La donna può accedere a tutti gli impieghi dello Stato, degli Enti pubblici e parastatali, nei vari ruoli, carriere, e categorie, senza limitazione di mansioni e di svolgimento della carriera. L'arruolamento della donne nelle Forze armate e nei corpi speciali è regolato da leggi particolari.*" Camera dei Deputati, *Atti Parlamentari, III legislatura. Documenti. Disegni di legge e relazioni.* N. 2441, 5 agosto 1960.

40. Camera dei Deputati, *Atti Parlamentari, III legislatura. Documenti. Disegni di legge e relazioni.* N. 2441, 5 agosto 1960.
41. These *proposte* and the *disegno* are described in Ceccatelli Guerrieri and Paolucci, *Il Paradigma dell'emancipazione,* 110; Camera dei Deputati, *Il voto alle donne,* 83; and Presidenza del Consiglio dei Ministri, *La donna dalla Resistenza ad oggi,* 38–39.
42. This and the following discussion of the committee's deliberations are put together from the extant notes and minutes in Maria Cocco et al., "2441-Abrogazione della legge 17 luglio 1919, n. 1176, sulla condizione giuridica della donna (Presentata il 5 agosto 1960)," Serie "Disegni di legge e incarti delle Commissioni," Archivio Storico della Camera dei Deputati; Camera dei Deputati, *Atti parlamentari,* Legislatura III, Prima Commissione Affari Costituzionali. Sede legislativa. Discussione della proposta di legge Maria Cocco ed altri <<Abrogazione della legge 17 luglio 1919, n. 1176, sulla condizione giuridica della donna>> (n. 2441), novembre 27–28, 1962; and secondary accounts in Camera dei Deputati, *Il voto alle donne,* 83; Presidenza del Consiglio dei Ministri, *La donna italiana dalla Resistenza ad oggi,* 38–39; and Sarogni, *La donna italiana,* 156–58.
43. The final law reads: Legge 9 febbraio 1963, n. 66, "Ammissione della donna ai pubblici uffici ed alle professioni." 1. La donna può accedere a tutte le cariche, professioni ed impieghi pubblici, compresa la Magistratura, nei vari ruoli, carriere e categorie, senza limitazione di mansioni e di svolgimento della carriera, salvi i requisiti stabiliti dalla legge. L'arruolamento della donna nelle forze armate e nei corpi speciali è regolato da leggi particolari. 2. La legge 17 luglio 1919, n. 1176, il successivo regolamento approvato con regio decreto 4 gennaio 1920, n. 39 (2), ed ogni altra disposizione incompatibile con la presente legge sono abrogati (emphasis added).
44. Sarogni, *La donna italiana,* 158.
45. Tullia Carettoni, personal conversation, April 8, 2003.
46. See Pojmann, *Italian Women,* chapter 5, "Opening to the Left."
47. Taricone, *Il Centro italiano femminile,* 207; one such comment was made by Senator Antonio Monni and vigorously protested by the previous CIF president in a letter distributed to six senators and the CIF official archive: Valmarana, letter novembre 20, 1956, Serie 18- Ufficio Studi Sottoserie B-Varie Scheda 28 Busta 828- Problemi vari allo studio; studi sulla condizione della donna 1955–1983, Fascicolo I, Partecipazione delle donne alla amministrazione della giustizia nelle corti di assise e nei tribunali per i minorenni1955–1957, CIF.
48. Miriam Mafai in Selvaggi, *Desiderio e diritto di cittadinanza,* 48; statistics on numbers of concorsi participants are published each year in the *Forze di lavoro* chapter of the Annuario statistico, availiable for download at www.istat.it; Maria Grazia Giammarinaro, personal conversation, October 2002.
49. Ulrike Schultz, "Introduction: Women in the World's Legal Professions: Overview and Synthesis," in *Women in the World's Legal Professions,* ed. Schultz and Shaw, xlvi-xlviii. An interesting point of view on the current experience of women magistrates emerges in the memoir by Paolo Di Nicola, *La Giudice: una donna in magistratura* (Rome: 881 Agency, 2013).
50. Elena Marinucci, "It's Only the First Step towards Real Parity," in Bono and Kemp, eds., *Italian Feminist Thought,* 313–14.

51. Sarogni, *La donna italiana*, 158–59.
52. Information from the Ministry of Defense website at http://www.difesa.it/Approfondimenti/Servizio+femminile/, ANADOS website at http://donne-soldato.org. See also Vicki Nielsen, "Women in Uniform," at http://www.nato.int/docu/review/2001/0102-09-htm; Petrolio, "Donna in Polizia."
53. Maria Cocco, personal correspondence, May 26, 2003.

Conclusion

1. Judt, 360.
2. Presidenza del Consiglio dei Ministri, *La donna italiana dalla Resistenza ad oggi*, 30.
3. Nilde Iotti, "Presenza nelle istituzioni," *Il voto alle donne cinquant'anni dopo. Campidoglio, 6-7 marzo 1995. Atti del convegno* (Roma: Istituto Poligrafico e Zecca dello Stato, 1996), 172.
4. Testimony of Nadia Spano in Scroppo, *Donna, privato e politico*, 80.
5. See the chapter "Crescere negli anni '50," the famous article originally from Memoria in 1982 and reprinted in Piccone Stella, *La prima generazione*; and a paper by Sandro Bellassai, "Identità di genere e processi di modernizzazione nell'Italia del'boom," from the conference on Women in Italy, 1945–1960, University of Glasgow, September 20–21, 2002.
6. Gaiotti de Biase, "The Impact of Women's Political and Social Activity," 242.
7. "Donne dell'anno," *Noi Donne*, December 21, 1968, 5; cited in Pojmann, 157.
8. Ellwood, *Shock of America*, 400–01. Ellwood points out that the party patronage system had also helped spread public money around in ways that erased old cleavages and drew new ones.
9. "Amortized" from Luisa Tasca, "The 'Average Housewife' in Post-World War II Italy," *Journal of Women's History* 16, no. 2 (Summer 2004): 92–115; Paolo Capuzzo, *Genere, generazione e consumi. L'Italia degli anni Sessanta* (Rome: Carocci, 2003), especially Sandro Bellassai, "Mascolinità, mutamento, merce. Crisi dell'identità maschile nell'Italia del boom," 105–38; Jane Slaughter, "What's New? Genere e modernità nella cultura aziendale," 139–54; and Maria Chira Liguori, "La parità si acquista ai grandi magazzini? Boom economico e trasformazione del modello femminile," 155–68; Bini, Capussotti, Stefani, and Vezzosi, "Genere, consumi, comportamenti negli anni cinquanta Italia e Stati Uniti a confronto," *Italia Contemporanea* no. 224 (September 2001); Cynthia Enloe, *The Morning After: Sexual Politics at the End of the Cold War* (Berkeley and Los Angeles: University of California Press, 1993); "Empowering Women as Citizen-Consumers," in *The Sex of Things: Gender and Consumption in Historical Perspective*, ed. Victoria de Grazia and Ellen Furlough (Berkeley and Los Angeles: University of California Press, 1996), 275–86; de Grazia, *Irresistible Empire*; Barbara Einhorn, *Cinderella Goes to Market: Citizenship, Gender, and Women's Movements in East Central Europe* (London: Verso, 1993); Hannah Schissler, ed., *The Miracle Years: A Cultural History of West Germany, 1949–1968* (Princeton, NJ: Princeton University Press, 2001).
10. Michetti et al., 97–98.
11. A notable exception has been the scholar Anna Rossi-Doria, who has championed this period as an important moment in feminism in multiple works. Still,

she downplays the significance of the numbers of women elected to parliament in early years. She also suppresses the Lost Wave's impact when she argues that "women's emancipation began silently in the 1950s." Anna Rossi-Doria, "Italian Women Enter Politics," *When the War Was Over*, 97, 99.

12. Ferrari, "Contested Foundations," 584–88. UDI underwent another reorganization culminating in 2003 when it renamed itself Unione Donne in Italia (the Union of Women in Italy, rather than Italian Women) to reflect the presence of immigrants and women of diverse backgrounds. UDI had also spent the few years previous renewing its structures as a national organization and making its national headquarters in Rome into a center for historical archives, education and outreach, and political organizing. See Pojmann, 183.
13. Robert Lumley, *States of Emergency: Cultures of Revolt in Italy from 1968 to 1978* (London: Verso, 1990), 314.
14. Presidenza del Consiglio dei Ministri, *La donna italiana dalla Resistenza ad oggi*, 30.
15. Palici di Suni, 276–77; Carlassare, 280–90. Current statistics on women in world government can be searched online at "Women in Natinal Parliaments," http://www.ipu.org/wmn-e/classif.htm.
16. Rossi-Doria, "Il voto alle donne nel 1945," 64; Rossi-Doria, *Diventare cittadine*, 16; Spano and Camarlinghi, *La questione femminile nella politica del P.C.I.*, 194–98; Comitato di Associazioni Femminili per la parità di retribuzione, "Schema per un progetto di legge in applicazione all'Art. 37 della Costituzione e della Convenzione n. 100 del B.I.T.," 1956, UDI national archives; Canosa, *Il Giudice e la donna*, 59–63; Mafai, *L'apprendistato della politica*, 122; Boneschi, *Santa pazienza*, 102; Fiorenza Taricone, *Il Centro italiano femminile*, 15.
17. Gaiotti de Biase, *Questione femminile e femminismo*, 38–39.
18. I first encountered this characterization of associationism's citizenship model in Gabrielli, *Il club delle virtuose* (see esp. 111). The model is further elaborated in Giovanni Moro, *Manuale di cittadinanza attiva* (Roma: Carocci, 1998) and is basically equivalent to Benjamin Barber's concept of "strong democracy;" see Benjamin Barber, *Strong Democracy: Participatory Politics for a New Age* (Berkeley: University of California Press, 1984).
19. Berkovitch, 3; Lilli and Valentini, *Care compagne*, 24.

INDEX